PRAISE FOR MARTIN BELL AND
WAR AND THE DEATH OF NEWS

'In prose as crisp and hard-hitting as the bullets he's dodged for decades, Bell sounds the alarm for a TV journalism that's under fire as never before. It's typical Bell – unflinching truth-telling, brilliantly argued; a clarion call to everyone who cares about powerful journalism in a world that needs it more than ever.'

Bill Neely, chief global correspondent, NBC News

'Martin Bell was the finest foreign correspondent of his generation. Night after night on the BBC, we watched him find the front lines and report back to us what he and his camera crews discovered that day. His reporting was honest, courageous, compassionate and clear. The same virtues are evident in this fearless memoir of his work over thirty-five years. With wisdom, candour and integrity, he describes the irony and tragedy of the wars, revolutions and riots he covered in violent places all over the world. He is especially critical of those editors at home who kept the public from seeing the ugly truth of what was going on in places like Bosnia, Iraq and Israel. This is his masterwork.'

John Laurence, author of *The Cat from Hué: A Vietnam War Story*

'He was our rock, steady, trustworthy, a man who would look after not just his own crew, but the whole British press corps, if need be.'

John Sweeney, investigative journalist and author

WAR AND THE DEATH OF NEWS

REFLECTIONS OF A GRADE B REPORTER

MARTIN BELL

ONEWORLD

A Oneworld Book

Published by Oneworld Publications, 2017

Copyright © Martin Bell 2017

The moral right of Martin Bell to be identified as the
Author of this work has been asserted by him in accordance
with the Copyright, Designs, and Patents Act 1988

ISBN 978-1-78607-108-8
eISBN 978-1-78607-109-5

Typeset by Hewer Text UK Ltd, Edinburgh
Printed and bound by Clays Ltd, St Ives plc

Oneworld Publications
10 Bloomsbury Street
London WC1B 3SR
England

For Merita

Mr D.E.H. Moriarty, Appointments Department, Rm.607, 5 P.P. PABX 2145

64.G.413 REPORTERS, NEWS DIVISION. Grade B.

Mr M. Bell through H.A.M.R.   5th August, 1964.

Copies: Area News Editor, Norwich; H.A.M.R.; Asst.A.O.N.(S)

Thank you for coming to the Appointment Board in connection with this
vacancy.

I am pleased to be able to tell you that you have been selected to fill
the Grade B post of Reporter, News Division.

Your transfer will be effected by H.A.M.R. in conjunction with Asst.A.O.N.(S)

D. E. H. MORIARTY.

(D.E.H. Moriarty)

BKP.

CONTENTS

INTRODUCTION

On 5 August 1964 I was sent a memo by Mr D.E.H. Moriarty of the BBC's Appointments Department in London: 'I am pleased to be able to tell you that you have been selected to fill the Grade B post of Reporter, News Division.'

I was working at the time in the newsroom of the BBC in Norwich. We specialised in rural planning disputes, horse shows, farm gate interviews, fatstock prices, flood drainage schemes in the Fens and the fortunes of our football teams. If I was lucky I would travel to Portman Road to interview Alf Ramsey, manager of Ipswich Town and later of England. If I was unlucky I would be sub-editing copy about Peterborough United for the regional radio news. For my metropolitan audition, in the basement of Broadcasting House in London, I reported on the state of the East Anglian bean crop: 'It has failed because of a disease called halo blight. This starts out as a circular patch on the leaf of the plant – hence the name – then spreads down to rot the stem. It is bacterial. It is contagious. And it is causing a whole lot of trouble to the frozen foods firms.'

Nevertheless, they gave me the job and I moved from Norwich to London a month later. Being an ambitious young man, I wondered who were the Grade A reporters. I soon found out. They were the likes of Peter Woods, formerly of ITN and the original foot-in-the-door man of TV news. Prime Minister Harold Macmillan complained: 'Whenever I open the door, there's this huge man with a microphone!' They covered the big bank robberies in Wood Green and Lambeth. I covered the small bank robberies. They did the big fires. I did the small fires. They asked questions on the Prime Minister's doorstep. I interviewed junior ministers at the Queen's Building in Heathrow on their return from insignificant overseas missions. They were inside Parliament. I was outside it. They were covering the lying-in-state of Winston Churchill in the Great Hall of Westminster. I was freezing with the crowds on Lambeth Bridge. They were in the Congo for the civil war and the secession of Katanga. I was at Ascot to report on the fashions of Ladies' Day. There was a perennial celebrity there, a Mrs Shilling, who made sure of her press coverage by wearing a hat made entirely of newspaper cuttings. I went on from there in March 1966 to report the theft of the World Cup trophy, which was retrieved by a dog called Pickles. It was because of the trespasses of Peter Woods that Number 10 eventually penned the press behind a barrier on the far side of the street. He was also the father of Justin Webb, a considerable broadcaster himself. I had to replace Justin once in Bosnia, in circumstances more dangerous for me than they were for him. If you have been around long enough, everything connects.

You know where you come from, but have no idea where you're going to until you have got there, by which time it is too late to take the road less travelled. The world changed beyond recognition and TV news changed with it. It became a player, not a peep-show, and a shaper of our impressions of people and politics. Anything could happen and did. I moved on to eighteen wars and more than a hundred countries, and even served for a term in the surrogate war zone of the House of Commons. But it started with the bean harvest, the Ascot hats and the dog called Pickles.

The chapters that follow are based on the news despatches, documents and diaries of the time. They are the memoirs, reflections and conclusions of a Grade B reporter. If only, I sometimes wondered, I could have made it to Grade A.

1. ONCE A SOLDIER

The family was military on my mother's side and literary on my father's. It included a brigadier, a director of music of the Band of the Life Guards, the news editor of the London *Observer* and the founder of *The Times* crossword puzzle.

The two strands connected in the Second World War. My uncle the Brigadier, who was a German-speaker in military intelligence, assured us that the flat lands of Suffolk would be squarely in the path of the German Panzer divisions in the event of an invasion, which he thought likely. We therefore left as evacuees to Grayrigg in Westmorland, remote from the war and beyond the reach of Panzers and Luftwaffe. We sometimes forget what a close run thing that was. My father Adrian Bell, the crossword puzzle king, was also an accomplished author who wrote with a battered old typewriter and an even older quill pen. His first book, *Corduroy*, was a widely read celebration of farming in Suffolk before its mechanisation, which he lamented. Many soldiers carried the paperback Penguin version to the war in their kitbags as a reminder of the England that they thought they were fighting for, although it was already vanishing when he wrote about it and his book was in a sense its epitaph. Whatever else they left behind they kept *Corduroy*, even on the march from Dunkirk to a German prison camp. He kept in the drawer of an oak chest an envelope full of postcards and letters marked *Kriegsgefangenenpost* from British POWs in Germany, and others from Italy and even Singapore. His book about farming in Westmorland, *Sunrise to Sunset*, was translated into German. After his death in 1980, Harry Hespe, a former POW in Changi Jail, wrote to me that he had learned whole passages of *Corduroy* by heart. My father lifted his spirits: 'Nightly his writings transported me in memory from a bug-ridden prison cell to the cool English countryside.'

We returned to Suffolk when the threat of invasion receded slightly. My father, who was not a military man (too young for one war, too old for the other), joined a group called the Land Defence Volunteers, a predecessor of *Dad's Army*. He recalled later that they had practised standing beside barricades of farm wagons brandishing pitchforks and shotguns, preparing to delay the Germans long enough for their families to escape. They were also instructed to look out for German paratroopers. 'To cope with these,' wrote a company commander in Lavenham, 'we defend our villages and have our patrols out just before daylight and after daylight.' Defensive lines were established between concrete blockhouses that are still standing but overgrown. The railway line was to be blocked by iron struts provided by the Royal Engineers.

The officers were the landowners and the other ranks the farm labourers. My father was a bit of both: his Brick Kiln Farm near Beccles was 89 acres of heavy clay and he worked it hard.

Enlisted in the Land Defence Volunteers and armed with his shotgun, he dissociated himself from a group of country writers with pro-German sympathies. These included Henry Williamson, author of *Tarka the Otter*, who was briefly arrested and interned. Like many others, Williamson never recovered from his experiences in the trenches in the Great War of 1914–18. He had witnessed the Christmas truce of 1914 and held an unshakeable belief in Anglo-German friendship. Another was Rolf Gardiner, founder of a group called Kinship in Husbandry and father of the conductor John Eliot Gardiner.

My own part in the war effort, as an eight-year-old, was to look out for spies, to admire the searchlights over the airfields – Suffolk and Norfolk were like a great aircraft carrier for the US Air Force – and (without telling anyone) to search the fields and ditches for unexploded munitions.

German pilots turning back from bombing raids over the Midlands used to lighten their loads by dumping them on the open spaces of East Anglia. The roadside trees had metal notices nailed to them warning us of the danger of butterfly bombs, cluster munitions that would disperse as they fell, scattering bomblets across the fields. Fortunately I never found any. The abolition of cluster bombs and anti-personnel mines was among my later causes as an MP.

One of our neighbours was Field Marshal Sir Claude Auchinleck, former commander of the Eighth Army in North Africa and (after the fall of Tobruk and his dismissal by Churchill) the Indian Army. The Auk, as we called him, was also the man who, together with General Bill Slim, turned around the fortunes of the 'forgotten' Fourteenth Army from defeat to victory in Burma. He was not only among the best of the generals but one of the few who never wrote his memoirs; he quietly retired to live with his sister in Beccles. He and my father and a mysterious 'Count Baxendale' who lived in the same street were drinking companions in the Cambridge Inn, where their host was the one-legged landlord Harry Young. All they had in common was a fondness for each other's company and for Harry's beer. My father was a master of unconsidered trifles: he could pluck an idea from a conversation and turn it into an eight hundred word meditation for his weekly column in the *Eastern Daily Press*. Whenever I eavesdropped, the discussions at the Cambridge were not about the Auk's extraordinary past, but about the river, the weather and traffic congestion in the Waveney Valley. My father was a practical mystic who ploughed his fields, and dreamed his dreams as he did so: when asked about his politics, he said, 'I am on the side of those who cultivate their gardens.' The Auk had a flagpole beside his house in Northgate, and every morning he raised the family flag, which looked remarkably like one of my father's crossword puzzles. When the Field Marshal was in India, one of the units under his command was the 2nd Battalion of the Suffolk Regiment, which he greatly admired. This was the Regiment that I joined in 1957.

It was not done out of enthusiasm for soldiering. These were the years of National Service and I had no choice in the matter. So overnight I became Private 23398941 Bell M of the Suffolk Regiment. I completed the ten weeks of basic training at Gibraltar Barracks in Bury St Edmunds. The massive red brick Keep, which is all that remains of it now, housed the offices of the Officer Commanding and the Adjutant, the Quartermaster's store, the guard room and the coal store. The coal was painted white for a reason. If any of it was pilfered, the Quartermaster Sergeant would know immediately.

I had never been shouted at before, and it seemed that anyone with the badge of authority on his sleeve had the right to shout at me and did so regularly, not only on the parade ground, but wherever he could find me. There would be no escape until demob. The first of many warlords in my life was Jack Gingell, Regimental Sergeant Major of the regiment's 1st Battalion, who served in Palestine, Cyprus and later Bury St Edmunds. He had a voice like a megaphone and the ground shook when he drilled on it. Even the officers were terrified of him. They were a somewhat mixed bunch. The Commanding Officer, Lieutenant Colonel Bertie Bevan, was like Captain Mainwaring minus the social skills. I looked back on army life, without nostalgia, as the proliferation of all things uncivilised. When I was demobbed, the certificate of discharge signed by his successor, Lieutenant Colonel Malcolm Dewar, described my military conduct as 'very good'. The RSM would have taken issue with that. I still have nightmares about him.

From October 1957 to May 1959 I was an OR (other rank) in the Battalion in Cyprus, having spectacularly fallen short of becoming an officer when I failed the intelligence test, not just once but twice. It was clear to the presiding Brigadier in Westbury, and even to me, that I was just not officer material. It was the first of life's fences that I fell at and did me no end of good. I started as a private soldier and rose eventually to the rank of Acting Sergeant, complete with its trappings of silver-topped pace-stick and red sash, in the campaign to defeat the rebels of EOKA.

Cyprus had been acquired by Britain from Turkey as a protectorate in 1878. It later became a colony and slept in the sun until April 1955, when the insurgents of EOKA, the National

Organisation of Cypriot Fighters, staged an armed uprising against their British rulers. The population was eighteen per cent Turkish and we in the Suffolks spent much of our time putting down riots in the Turkish quarter of Nicosia. The counter-insurgency campaign ultimately failed, although when we sailed away from Limassol on the troopship *Dilwara* in May 1959, under the cover of a constitutional agreement, we were congratulated by the Governor and led to believe that we had contributed to a lasting settlement. But it was the best education that I ever had.

The first lesson was about *fieldcraft*, which is the art of staying alive in dangerous places. I had no idea at the time how useful it would be in a career that started in the ditches of Vietnam and ended in the trenches of Bosnia. It makes quite a difference in a war zone to go into it knowing the uses of dead ground, and which kinds of cover will stop a high velocity bullet and which will not. It is the application of common sense to life-threatening situations. Map-reading can come in handy too. So can battlefield first aid. The gifted film-maker Tim Hetherington, creator of *Restrepo*, the documentary masterpiece about Afghanistan that I introduced in the West End in December 2010, died in Libya six months later because he had no one with him who knew how to bind up a wound.

War-zone reporting required fieldcraft *plus*: never enter no man's land, never cease asking minefield questions, always have an escape route open, agree among yourselves what risks to take and not to take – and when you have done the business get the hell out as fast as you can. I knew some who lingered too long and who paid with their lives. Or, in the worst case, others paid for them, as happened most tragically in Afghanistan. Soldiers do not enjoy having to risk their lives by rescuing journalists from scrapes that they have got themselves into.

Having been a soldier was useful too in the Gulf in 1991, when the Army adopted the practice of embedding, which meant going to war with the press alongside them in the order of battle. I already knew such basics as that a soldier in the Parachute Regiment is called a 'Tom' (as in Thomas Atkins). I did not have to ask the difference between direct and indirect fire, a battalion and a brigade, a colonel and a lieutenant colonel, or an armoured personnel carrier and a tank. I was at least semi-trained. My intrepid cameraman at the time, and later in Bosnia, was Nigel Bateson, who had seen active service with the South African Army in Namibia. He too could relate to soldiers, having been one. One of his techniques was to tell them how ugly they were (he was no beauty himself). So we started off on the front foot.

Lesson two was about *people*. I had led too sheltered a life till then. Soldiering in general and the RSM in particular shook me up and brought me face to face with the real world. It taught me too that leadership is not about giving orders: it is about earning trust and respect. I applied this many years later in Sarajevo, where I ran the BBC team like an infantry section, of which I as an ex-corporal was only the nominal leader. There were only four of us, the correspondent myself, the cameraman Nigel, the videotape editor Carl and the interpreter Anamarija who called herself, with reason, our 'wicked witch'. We worked together and were totally dependent on each other, as if it was a matter of life and death, which it sometimes was. I would even say that we loved each other. I loved the mountainous South African as much as the beautiful Croat. The Army teaches togetherness. It does not believe in 'jacking', which means wandering off and doing your own thing. You succeed together or you fail together. The same applies to television. In spite of the pressures, or perhaps because of them, we had the time of our lives. It was not in any of the training manuals like *Staff Duties in the Field*, but the Army taught me about teamwork. You become firm friends with people in wartime who, in peacetime, you would cross the street to avoid. A French radio reporter in Sarajevo, Paul Marchand, had a sign on the back of his battered old soft-skinned car that said: 'Don't shoot, you will waste your bullets – I'm immortal!' Sadly, it did not work for him. He was wounded during the war and took his own life after it.

Lesson three was that *the British Army has an ingrained suspicion of charismatic officers*. Lieutenant Colonel Arthur Campbell of the Suffolk Regiment was not only an outstanding soldier but an established author. Someone who knew him well observed: 'Larger-than-life characters like Arthur do not come along very often.' He had written a lightly fictionalised account of the British campaign in Malaya in the 1950s, *Jungle Green*, which was an instant best-seller. He was then commissioned by Field Marshal Sir John Harding, Governor of Cyprus, to write a book about the Cyprus campaign, which Harding thought he was winning. Campbell did so in six months. By the time he had finished it Harding had been replaced by a diplomat, Sir Hugh Foot, who ordered the total suppression of the book on the grounds that it would impede a settlement. It was called *Flaming Cassock* (an unflattering reference to the Greek Cypriot leader Archbishop Makarios) and lay in limbo under lock and key until I finally obtained it under the Freedom of Information Act in 2014. After an incident that had nothing to do with his soldiering, Arthur Campbell was let go at the rank of full colonel. A similar fate happened more than thirty years later to Lieutenant Colonel Bob Stewart, Commanding Officer of the 1st Battalion the Cheshire Regiment in Bosnia. He spoke his mind too freely and appeared too much on television (my fault entirely). He too left the Army and started anew. He is now the Conservative MP for Beckenham, resting on a comfortable majority. And he does not have to deal with brigadiers and generals, or Balkan warlords, but only with his party's Deputy Chief Whip whom he cheerfully ignores. Officers who make waves make enemies, and are rewarded with early retirement. It is the ticks-in-the-boxes types who rise to the top and end up with frock coats and knighthoods and peerages.

Lesson four was that *hammers don't build houses*: the indiscriminate use of force not only fails to deliver the results expected of it, but actually defeats its own purposes. In Cyprus an army of thirty-five thousand men trained in counter-insurgency, including myself, failed to put down a force of no more than two hundred lightly armed rebels, most of them hiding in caves and mine-shafts, and many of them escapees from British custody. Even our prisons were porous. Some of the most dangerous EOKA fighters had escaped from Kyrenia Castle by knotting sheets together and climbing down them. We soldiers did not fail through lack of effort. We did all that we were ordered to and more; the problem was that the strategy was mistaken and the orders were dumb. We cordoned and searched the villages comprehensively: it was called 'village-bashing'. We benighted the towns with our curfews. We paralysed the transport system with our roadblocks. We imposed collective punishments on whole communities. In July 1958 we held the entire island under lockdown for forty-eight hours for the big push, which was supposed to deliver victory, called Operation Matchbox. We interned more than three thousand Greek Cypriots of military age and some who were younger. All we achieved was to alienate the people we were trying to win over and to recruit for our enemy. Even as a thoughtless young soldier I described it in one of my letters home as 'armed repression'. We were fighting blind because of lack of intelligence (in both senses) and deaf because of our useless high frequency radios. One of our generals concluded when it was over that campaigns of this kind could not be won by 'an assault on the ordinary people'. The motto of the security forces was 'firmness with courtesy'. Governor Harding lamented that battlefield discipline was weak and that it was in the nature of the young national servicemen to overdo the courtesy and fail in firmness. We conscripts believed that our officers – all of them regulars except the subalterns – were failing in courtesy and overdoing the firmness.

I was trained in anti-riot drill too and riots were everyday events in the summer of 1958. My role, which I fortunately never had to put into practice, was to raise my rifle to the shoulder and shoot the rooftop bombers. But charging at crowds and holding up banners saying 'Disperse or we fire' did nothing to win them over. Governor Harding himself noted: 'Shooting at unarmed crowds creates bitterness and anger out of all proportion to the casualties inflicted.' A document from the files of the Colonial Secretary in 1956 noted that we had particular difficulty with groups of schoolgirls. We were expected to admire the example of the wife of the Regimental Sergeant Major of the Royal Inniskillings: 'She was set on, while shopping, by a crowd of girls. She laid about them with her shopping bag which was loaded with tins from the NAAFI. After she had floored five the crowd dispersed. This method is recommended only to individuals in dire straits.'

Lesson five was that *military formations are of uneven quality*. This is true between armies, as anyone who has seen a multinational force in action will testify. It also applies within armies, the British Army being no exception. The Suffolks were a steady and reliable county regiment, which was why we were assigned to the cauldron of the capital. The Scots and Irish, Paras and Marines, were deployed in less inhabited areas where they could live up to their reputations and do less damage. No doubt that they were tougher than we were, but we were not saints either. When our D Company searched Kykko Monastery, where Archbishop Makarios had trained for the priesthood, all did not go exactly as it should have done. After the search was over, the Orthodox Church complained that the Archbishop's grandfather clock was missing. One of the platoon commanders objected that so large an object could not possibly have been stolen; besides, it was standard practice after an operation for the soldiers to be searched by their officers. Then he took the precaution of visiting the company lines, which were the tents where his soldiers lived. He found them putting the clock back together. It was disposed of in the DTLs (deep trench latrines). A set of ornate church vestments met a similar fate.

A contemporary who was a subaltern in the Welch Regiment was aware that a soldier in his platoon had a bit of a past, or what is now called a 'back story'. One day on stand-by duty the man confided in him: 'Sir, I've done two years in Wormwood Scrubs and one in the Army. Give me the Scrubs any time. At least you gets your kip.' The same subaltern, wishing to distinguish the Welch from the Royal Marines, who had a similar cap badge and had preceded them in the town of Rizokarpaso, had the name LLANFAIRPWLLGWYNGYLLGOGERYCHWYRNDRO BWLLLLANTYSILIOGOGOGOCH painted in red on the school to proclaim the difference. It got him into trouble with his Commanding Officer but made the point: all units are not the same.

It applied too to the later emergency in Northern Ireland. The Suffolks' successor regiment, the Royal Anglians, were ordered by the Commander Land Forces to serve a second tour in East Tyrone because he did not want the Paras to go back there. The Paras had a fearsome reputation. They have many fine soldierly qualities, but a flair for winning the hearts and minds of the people is not invariably one of them.

I also developed a longstanding and regrettable prejudice against the Guards. In the summer of 1958, when one of our rifle companies was outnumbered by a crowd of missile-throwing Turks in Nicosia, we called for reinforcements. They duly arrived in the form of the Grenadier Guards, whose initial response was not to join us in engaging the Turks but to hold a drill parade in the courtyard of the Central Police Station. We could not believe it. Many years later in Bosnia, the Coldstream Guards were the only British battalion under the UN mandate that we had difficulty dealing with. They were a breed apart and seemed to regard not only the press, but other regiments and corps and attached arms on whom they depended, with a measure of suspicion. 'The good thing about being in a battalion,' said one, 'is that you can look inward and don't have to worry about the world outside.' The Army is an assembly of tribes, some more exclusive than others. The regimental system is both its strength and its weakness.

Sir Thomas Browne was surely not thinking of the Guards, but the line infantry, when he wrote that he would 'honour those tattered and contemptible regiments that will die at the command of a sergeant'.

Lesson six was *never hesitate to second-guess your orders*. To have questioned them as a soldier would have earned me a spell of jankers (regimental field punishment), or worse in the Military Corrective Training Centre that was the Army's jail in Nicosia. When I ventured to amend a signal because I thought it would make more sense the Adjutant told me: 'The trouble with you, Corporal Bell, is that you think too much!' I did then and still do. But many of the orders I had to obey were daft and counter-productive. When I received similar instructions as a foreign correspondent, I either ignored them, or pretended I had no knowledge of them, or (which was easy under the opaque John Birt regime) that I had not understood a word of them. Some of the most redundant were about health and safety. We were ordered not to take unnecessary risks, but in the real world you don't know whether a risk is necessary or unnecessary until after you have taken it, by which time it is too late. My much missed colleague Brian Barron, with cameraman Eric Thirer, could have scrambled along with certain eminent colleagues aboard American helicopters from the Embassy roof in Saigon in 1975. Instead he disobeyed orders and filed a memorable report on the North Vietnamese tanks breaking into the grounds of the Presidential Palace. The great reporters, from William Howard Russell to James Cameron to Charles Wheeler to Brian Barron himself, shared a certain bloody-mindedness. The former Defence Secretary Denis Healey observed: 'I have rarely found soldiers, sailors and airmen to be as bloody-minded as journalists and politicians.'

The final and most important lesson was that *governments, including democratic governments, cannot be relied upon to be truthful or even competent*. First the failure, then the cover-up: that is how it goes. There cannot be military solutions to political problems: there can only be political solutions to political problems. The death or glory boys invariably get it wrong. In mid-emergency in Cyprus, and against a flood-tide of evidence to the contrary, the Colonial Secretary Alan Lennox-Boyd, who was a raffish character from the right and imperialist wing of his party, declared: 'I cannot believe any responsible statesman, faced with having to find a solution to this intractable problem, could have come to wiser decisions than have Her Majesty's Government.' But the decisions, so far from being wise, were incoherent and disastrous and had the most far-reaching consequences.

The Cyprus Independence Agreements of 1959, negotiated in Zurich and London, were flawed and fragile and ultimately doomed to fail. Nor did the United Kingdom, as one of their guarantors, honour its guarantees when the entire house of cards collapsed with the Turkish invasion in 1974. Long before then, between 1955 and 1959, the people of Cyprus were badly let down both by the British government and by the Army in which I served. Our failure was collective and calamitous. A striking example, drawn from recently declassified documents, was the Geunyeli massacre of 1958. I am proud to have been a soldier, but we surely should have done better than we did. This was the turning point.

2. GEUNYELI

I t was the most notorious and consequential of the attacks by one community on the other. As word of it spread it was known to us soldiers as the Geunyeli massacre. Only to the refined minds of the Colonial Office was it the Geunyeli 'incident'. The Suffolks were not immediately involved in it, since it occurred in the area next to ours and was patrolled by the Royal Horse Guards and Grenadier Guards. But we were on the fringe of it, dealing with a simultaneous (and maybe diversionary) riot by the Turks in Nicosia. Looking back on it now, I see it as the pivotal event in the whole emergency. It was so sensitive politically that the Colonial Office file on it was declassified only in 2013.

Demonstrations in Nicosia and Geunyeli, a large Turkish village just outside it, were set off by an announcement by the Turkish government, on 8 June 1958, that it had reached a full and mature decision to bring about the partition of Cyprus. The two communities had already started separating. North east of the capital groups of young men armed with primitive weapons gathered to defend their own villages and sometimes to attack the other side's. Turks set fire to Greek properties in Nicosia across the so-called 'Mason-Dixon Line'. We had not trained as firefighters but learned to improvise with buckets and hosepipes. 'Suffolks Turn Firemen', said a headline in the local press.

I remember it as a time of maximum 'flaps' and 'panics'. Those were my terms for having to grab a weapon at a moment's notice and rush into town in the middle of the night in full service marching order. The Queen's birthday parade was cancelled for the lack of troops available to take part in it. Too many of us were tied down on static guard duties, with not enough deployed outside Nicosia and able to patrol the flashpoints between Greek and Turkish villages. The overstretch applied particularly to the only truly mobile force on the island, the soldiers of the Royal Horse Guards who had to watch over 800 square miles of the Nicosia rural area. As the intercommunal violence increased they lived for days on end in their armoured vehicles. General Kendrew, the Director of Operations, noted that some of them had been without proper sleep for ninety hours on end and had not seen their base camp for three weeks. This had consequences.

On 12 June a patrol of B Squadron the Royal Horse Guards came upon a group of thirty-five Greeks from Kondemenos hiding in a ditch near the Turkish quarter of the mixed village of Skylloura. General Sir Roger Bower, Commander-in-Chief Middle East Land Forces, said later: 'The cause of the affair was the unlawful and aggressive movement of Greek armed groups.'[1] The men were arrested and escorted eastwards towards the Turkish village of Geunyeli. Somewhere on open ground north of the village they were released and told to find their own way home. Cornet Baring of the Royal Horse Guards immediately set up a roadblock to prevent their pursuit by Turks from Geunyeli 'armed with clubs, sticks, pieces of iron and every possible weapon'. But somewhere along the road to Kondemenos the Greeks were ambushed by other Turks. Eight were killed and five were seriously injured.

The matter was highly charged politically because it was not an attack by one community on the other that the security forces had failed to prevent. It was an attack in which the security forces had played a part, however inadvertent. The practice of dropping people off at remote locations to find their own way home was not to be found in any of the internal security manuals, but had been improvised by the troops on the ground, at battalion and company level, as a method of dealing with suspected trouble-makers. Archbishop Makarios, still in exile the international voice of the Greek Cypriots, accused the British of intentionally leading the Greeks to their deaths. The lawyers for the victims' families said the soldiers had shown 'reckless indifference'.

The day after the murders Governor Foot visited Geunyeli and cabled the Colonial Office: 'feeling runs high and rumours spread so quickly that there is a danger of further disorder breaking out at any time. It may be that we have to face a considerable period of something like civil war between the two communities.' According to the recently declassified Colonial Office and Foreign Office files, he was especially troubled by the accusation that the British had led the Greeks into a death trap. So three days later he announced a judicial inquiry, to be conducted by Sir Paget Bourke, the Chief Justice of Cyprus, 'To investigate and to determine the facts concerning the incidents that occurred at or near the village of Geunyeli on Thursday 12 June 1958 in the course of which certain persons lost their lives and others were injured.'

The Inquiry began on 18 June and ended on 28 June 1958. It was closed to the press and public, but the Governor promised that its conclusions would be published. The understanding was that they would be published *in full*. It heard evidence from the security forces and from civilian witnesses and survivors. According to a cable sent to the Colonial Office during the hearings, the Acting Commanding Officer of the Royal Horse Guards was asked about the practice of 'giving a ride' to suspected law-breakers. 'He said that the system of making people walk home was not a lawful practice but had been done from time to time to teach someone a very small lesson for something done which should not be overlooked but could not be taken to court.'

The Officer Commanding B Squadron, Major Roy Redgrave (nephew of the actor Sir Michael Redgrave and later a major general), said he had received orders from his controller in the Central Police Station, which was beset by rioters (with whom the Suffolks were dealing), not to allow the Greeks into Nicosia but to take them out of town and make them walk home. He said that he had decided that this should take place to the north of Geunyeli and gave his reasons for considering this to be a suitable place. A Corporal of Horse (Sergeant) objected close to the point of mutiny, but was overruled. Major Redgrave said in evidence: 'They had been bad boys – and not for a moment would I have taken them back to the place where I had arrested them.' The Corporal of Horse was mentioned in despatches.

The timing was unfortunate. The Royal Horse Guards were assigned to the area only a day before the murders outside Geunyeli. They were therefore not familiar with it. Major

Redgrave believed that the neighbouring village of Aghurda was Greek. It was actually Turkish. He told the Chief Legal Counsel for the Attorney General, who cross-examined him, that he could not have been expected to know the ethnicity of all the villages in the area. The Army's failure in Cyprus was above all, from start to finish, a failure of intelligence.

As soon as Sir Paget Bourke's report was circulated in Nicosia and London in early July 1958, it sent shudders up colonial spines and a period of intrigue and recrimination set in. The Colonial Secretary Alan Lennox-Boyd objected in the strongest possible terms to its publication: 'The document is undoubtedly a report of which, if published, damaging use could be made by ill-intentioned people.' J.D. Higham, a senior Colonial Office official, wrote on 9 July: 'The initial War Office reaction is one of some distress that publication should be necessary . . . the effect on the morale of the security forces in general and the Royal Horse Guards in particular . . . will be bad . . . The statement that sticks out like a sore thumb is that the course adopted by the security forces was, in the Chief Justice's opinion, unlawful.'[2]

The commotion was caused by the report's paragraph thirty-eight. In it the Chief Justice not only described the practice of 'taking for a ride' as unlawful; he also said: 'The only conclusion I can reach is that the course adopted was unimaginative and ill-considered.'

The Army, who were outraged, demanded that the whole paragraph be deleted on the grounds that it was unfair to them. They were overstretched at the time and unable to deal adequately with both the campaign of violence by EOKA and the simultaneous intercommunal clashes between Greeks and Turks. In a letter to the Governor on 21 October the

Commander-in-Chief Middle East Land Forces objected that to have taken the Greeks back to their village would have been to admit that they had been unjustly arrested, and would have undermined confidence in the security forces at a critical time. Lennox-Boyd was emphatic in his support of the 'walking home method' of dealing with trouble-makers, even though his Permanent Under-Secretary had never heard of it. Neither had two of the most senior police officers on the island. On 5 August the Chief Justice was summoned to a meeting at the Colonial Office and put under the strongest pressure to change his paragraph thirty-eight. According to the minutes of the meeting, 'Sir Paget Bourke said that the remainder of the paragraph formed part of his findings and he could not agree to its deletion.' Governor Foot was on the side of the Chief Justice: he did not wish to dissent from the report because he agreed with it. This drew yet another rebuke from the Colonial Secretary: 'I am at a loss to see how the Governor could possibly agree to this.' A Colonial Office official noted: 'The Governor does not share the liking of the two Secretaries of State for the practice of "taking a ride."'[3] But on 2 August the Governor told the Colonial Office that he too would try to persuade the Chief Justice to 'agree to the deletion of his opinion regarding lawlessness'.[4]

The arguments dragged on through the autumn of 1958. Greek Cypriots complained vociferously about the delay in publication and wondered what it might portend. What it portended was a classic – and ultimately disreputable – British compromise. At some point in October or early November 1958 Sir Paget Bourke, while insisting that the whole of his paragraph thirty-eight should still stand, allowed the contested passages to be omitted from the published report, on the grounds that they were not *findings* but *opinions*. Also omitted (from paragraph thirty-two) was a summary of Major Redgrave's evidence. In this way the contested passages were both part of his report and *not* part of his report. The machinery of colonial government had done its business.

The Royal Horse Guards considered themselves exonerated: 'In the confusion, three contradictory statements being put out by the wireless, the Greeks thought that we had done it on purpose. His Excellency the Governor, therefore, very wisely ordered an Inquiry by the Chief Justice. In his report the Chief Justice said that this wild and monstrous allegation was completely unfounded, and absolved the Regiment of blame.'[5] In his original report, of course, he did nothing of the kind.

After a further delay caused by a United Nations debate, the report was laid before the House of Commons on 9 December 1958. Its altered paragraph thirty-eight included a statement by the Chief Justice that he had been asked by the military to conclude that their actions at Geunyeli had been reasonable. He wrote: 'I am unable to do so. The fact is that a party of Greeks arrested as intending attackers of Turks was put down and compelled, at a time of great tenseness of intercommunal feeling, to walk across Turkish property, away from a Turkish village, but in the general direction of a Turkish hamlet, and out of sight of the security forces remaining on the Kyrenia road.' The transcripts of evidence remained classified.

The Greeks complained of a whitewash – and indeed there *was* a whitewash, though they had no means of knowing the nature and extent of it. The report, which was supposedly a full account of the Chief Justice's findings, did not include his conclusion that 'taking for a ride' was unlawful, or that the actions taken by the security forces in Geunyeli were unimaginative and ill-considered.

The Greeks felt aggrieved and betrayed; and the Turks were up in arms, both literally and figuratively. Six days after the murders sixty-nine prominent Turkish Cypriots signed a petition to the Governor, citing a series of attacks on Turks and claiming that six hundred Greek Cypriot killers were still at large. They concluded: 'Only the Turks can save the Turks of Cyprus. The above-mentioned events are the best proof of the fact that Turks and Greeks can no longer live together in Cyprus.'[6]

Cyprus became independent two years later, and the slide from Independence to partition took fourteen years. The ill-considered steps along the way included an economic blockade of the Turks by the Greeks and the establishment by the Turks of a separate administration with its own municipal services in their quarter of Nicosia. The blockade denied the Turks such 'strategic materials' as petrol and concrete. Their cars were resting on wooden blocks and their refugee shelters were tractor sheds or houses made of mud bricks. They had abandoned a hundred of their outlying villages. The Greek Cypriots offered them some concessions in a programme of 'pacification', but these did not apply to the autonomous Turkish quarter of Nicosia.

Arthur Campbell, formerly of the Suffolk Regiment, returned to the island as a civilian ten years after he left it as a soldier and noted: 'There was nothing in the shops, children went bare-foot and half-naked. There was none of the gaiety and laughter and coffee house chatter so natural to the Cypriot.' A young Turkish Cypriot told him: 'I am taught to hate and not to love. I live with ignorance and not with learning. When will it all end?'

I revisited the island at about the same time, not as a soldier but as a reporter. On 13 January 1968 I interviewed Archbishop Makarios in the Presidential Palace. He called the Turkish move illegal. 'We shall not use force; but we shall not allow the circulation of members of this administration outside the Turkish quarter of Nicosia.' I asked him, was Cyprus moving inevitably towards partition? 'Partition is not possible because the Turks do not live in a prescribed area. They are spread all over the island.'

He was wrong, of course. Partition was only too possible. To the question 'When will it all end?' the answer was in July 1974, after a botched coup against Makarios and the eight-day presidency of the assassin Nicos Sampson. The mainland Turks then invaded and the island has been partitioned and conflicted ever since. None of this had to happen. I am convinced to this day that it would not have happened if we soldiers, instead of chasing the shadows of an elusive enemy in the mountains, had done a better job of quelling the intercommunal disturbances on the plains.

This all occurred at the end of Empire and in the backwash of the Suez misadventure. The decolonisation of Cyprus was complicated by superpower politics, unhelpful interventions by Greece and Turkey and the supposed importance of the British Sovereign Base Areas. Cyprus, we were told by the Tory right, was as British as Gibraltar. But still the affair was not well handled, and we British have much to answer for. The Geunyeli massacre of Greeks by Turks and revenge killings of Turks by Greeks were never forgotten by either side. There was even a grim symmetry: sixty Greeks were killed and fifty-nine Turks. These murders, which we should have prevented, marked the end of the dream of a united, free and independent Cyprus.

3. UNDERTONES OF WAR

I have at home a copy of Edmund Blunden's *Undertones of War*, one of the classic accounts of the Great War from 1914 to 1918. He served longer in the front lines than Wilfred Owen, Siegfried Sassoon and the other war poets except Isaac Rosenberg. He was lucky to survive, as Sassoon did and Owen and Rosenberg did not. He attributed his survival to his relatively small size: he said he made an 'inconspicuous target'. He was a viscerally English character. At the front of his book he quoted Article xxxvii of the Articles of the Church of England: 'It is lawful for Christian men, at the commandment of the Magistrate, to wear weapons, and to serve in the wars.'

Blunden wore weapons and served in the war. He was a friend of my father in postwar Suffolk. On the inside cover of the second edition in 1928 he wrote in a fine hand: 'Adrian Bell having licensed Edmund Blunden wantonly to disfigure this book deserves all that he gets, and may EB say that while no Gainsborough he yet took a prize for drawing at Yalding Boys' School in 1902, which at least is more than some other artists as the late DH Lawrence have done.' On the flyleaf opposite he sketched two detailed maps of the British advance on 13 November 1916 to the River Ancre between Albert and Bapaume. The upper map showed the ruins of Thiepval, the Schwaben Redoubt and Beaumont Hamel on the other side of the river. 'This name Thiepval began to have as familiar and ugly a ring as any place ever mentioned by man.'[1] An arrow in the top right-hand corner pointed to Germany. Blunden wrote: 'I . . . knew that the fear of my infancy, to be among flying bullets, was now realised.'[2]

Blunden was a good soldier and not anti-war in the sense that Sassoon and Owen were. He was awarded the Military Cross for gallantry, which he described as a matter of self-conquest. But by November 1916, the final phase of the Battle of the Somme, he had had enough. He served with the 11th Royal Sussex, which went over the top with four companies and came back with two. 'Yet, still, they were a sound and capable battalion,' he wrote, 'and deserving far better treatment than they were now getting, and a battle, not a massacre.'[3] His Commanding Officer called him 'Rabbit'. His Brigadier, who was clearly a bit of a lunatic suitable for casting in *Blackadder Goes Forth*, issued an order that all officers must take a constitutional walk round the wire in no man's land every night; some died as a result, including a captain in an adjacent battalion well respected in the trenches because he had once played cricket for Surrey. One night in the front line near Festubert, Blunden and his men saw a luminous cloud that took the shape of a cross and then a sword. 'My batman . . . told me he read coming disaster in this sword.'[4] His batman was dead right.

In a review of *Undertones of War* in the *Westminster Gazette* R.H. Mottram wrote: 'Lately, one of our literary Majors asked why we were "ashamed of the war". The question is ill-framed. Here is testimony that we are not ashamed of the freewill sacrifice, unique in the world, that so many humble countrymen of ours offered. We are ashamed of the incompetence and venality that wasted their deaths.'

When Blunden died in 1974 my father wrote: 'His spirit was a lark entangled in that thicket of memory.'

If the ghosts of the British and Empire soldiers who died in the war had marched four abreast past the Cenotaph in Whitehall raised in their honour, it would have taken them three and a half days to complete the posthumous parade.

In the past hundred years there have been two revolutions in armed conflict – one in the way that it is fought and the other in the way that it is perceived. The weaponry changed from rifles and mortars and heavy artillery to drones and loitering munitions and precision-guided missiles. The perceptions changed from war as a great adventure and glorious enterprise to war as an occasional grim necessity to be avoided except as an act of desperation and in the very last resort.

The war poets were not a movement or a group, although Sassoon and Owen knew each other and, while patients at Craiglockhart, a hospital for shell-shocked officers, worked together on the hospital magazine *The Hydra*; and Robert Graves saved Sassoon, his brother officer in the Royal Welch Fusiliers, from a court martial. Blunden was a friend of both Sassoon and Graves and wrote the introduction to Owen's *Collected Poems*: 'Owen was preparing himself . . . to strike at the conscience of England in regard to the continuance of the war.' Owen, who had kept the company of the unburied dead, wrote in a letter home: 'The people of England needn't hope. They must agitate.

But they are not even agitated.' He returned to the front line, perhaps to prove something to himself, and died on a canal crossing a week before the end of the war.

Isaac Rosenberg stood alone. He was a Jewish private soldier who signed on with the Suffolk Regiment in 1915 and was transferred to three other regiments before being killed in the German offensive of March 1918. He too was a witness to the wastefulness of war. 'I never joined the Army for patriotic reasons,' he said. 'Nothing can justify war. I suppose we must all fight to get the trouble over.'[5]

Even the arch-imperialist Rudyard Kipling contributed to the poetry of protest. One of his most haunting and haunted verses was a couplet in *Epitaphs of the War*, after the death of his only son John, a subaltern with the Irish Guards in Loos:

> If any question why we died,
> Tell them, because our fathers lied.

And he wrote an epitaph for the soldiers shot for cowardice or desertion, who were also among the victims of the war:

> I could not look on Death, which being known,
> Men led me to him, blindfold and alone.

It was not immediately after the war but some ten years later that the work of the war poets and other writers, including the dramatist R.C. Sherriff of *Journey's End*, gained the traction that it did. It connected with the grim experiences of the hundreds of thousands of the surviving veterans, some of them amputees and others shell-shocked, all without illusions, injured for life.

Sherriff himself had been badly wounded at Passchendaele. The Horatian myth of *Dulce et decorum est pro patria mori*, engraved on so many war memorials, was no longer sustainable. Wilfred Owen demolished it in his poem of that name. He wrote, he said, 'of war and the pity of war'. This was the literature that entered the bloodstream of the nation and changed its view of warfare, at least until recently when the old soldiers had faded away. The accredited war reporters lied: the poets told the truth. 'If the people had known,' said Lloyd George in 1917, 'the war would be over tomorrow.' But they did not know. The flag-waving and drum-beating newspapers ensured that they did not know. The journalists were rewarded with knighthoods and their employers with peerages: it is not the knights or the peers but the poets whom we honour today.

Wilfred Owen was surely one of the two most influential writers in the English language in the twentieth century: George Orwell was the other. I carried Owen's poems to the war zones – they were few enough to be no burden – but not immediately. The best that can be said of my early reporting, especially from Vietnam in 1967, was that it was energetic rather than adequate, and was informed by no sense of the pity of war whatsoever. On the contrary, I was rather excited by it in a *Boy's Own Paper* sort of way. I was interested in the mechanics rather than the ethics of war-fighting. I showed American infantry creeping through the double canopy rainforest in the central highlands. I showed American artillery pounding suspected Viet Cong positions to unknown effect. I addressed the camera and commentated, in the stilted newsreel style of those times and to the best of my ability, about the difficulties the Americans were facing in defeating a guerrilla army in a long-running and open-ended war. I interviewed generals who deployed helicopters on a scale made famous in *Apocalypse Now*, sixty to a brigade, and assured me that they were winning, although they found their enemy elusive. They preferred to be airborne above the battle than chair-borne behind it. Then the enemy would creep up at night and mortar the hell out of their base camps. But in a war for the hearts and minds of the Vietnamese people, I showed no Vietnamese at all, except a few dead ones, and some of their discarded rations and claymore mines. The same defect was evident in more recent embedded reporting from forward operating bases in Afghanistan: however vivid it was, it showed no Afghans. There was something shallow and *uninsightful* about it. Now as then we skim the surfaces.

Sometime later, in Israel in October 1973, on the long drives from Tel Aviv to the Suez Canal, something got at me and I started to think about the principles of journalism, and whether or not there were any. In the Yom Kippur War we had eighteen days in which to draw breath, look around, sift fact from propaganda and file our reports. It was a tidy war too, fought on two fronts and in three distinct phases: an Arab assault, an Israeli holding operation and an Israeli counter-attack.

I worked out that the mileage-to-footage ratio on the southern front was about a hundred to one. We started early and finished late. We would drive for eleven hours, negotiate at roadblocks and base camps for two hours and actually gather the news for less than two hours (even less, if the tyres were shredded by shrapnel, as they sometimes were). Three hundred miles for a three-minute news report was about average. Sometimes, depending on field security and the fortunes of war, it could be three hundred miles for nothing at all. A notebook of the time contains the following: 'New charge of bias [some Israelis suspected us of pro-Arab sympathies] . . . No condemnation of war and the wastefulness of war . . . Set pieces of the Six-Day War a dangerous fluke . . . Even the IDF [Israeli Defence Force] was guilty of fighting this war like the last one, and paid most heavily . . . This may be the last great tank war . . . The Israelis went so far, in the confusion of war, as to fight a *guerrilla* tank battle . . . Israel was saved by a soldier [Ariel Sharon] in the old gung-ho tradition . . . Splendid pictures, but where was the war? . . . No glamour in war reporting: one of its major ingredients is a feeling of total frustration.'

We shot colour film in those days, which was processed in a production house near Tel Aviv, then edited and transmitted by satellite to London. We were no longer air-freighting news film in coloured onion bags to London or New York. Same-day transmission was possible. TV news had finally come into its own. We were also fiercely competitive, both within networks and between them. The Americans had the advantage of the time difference between Tel Aviv and New York. Dan Bloom of CBS News was an assertive character, formerly the Saigon bureau chief, who specialised in shafting his rivals. He used to pass rolls of unexposed footage through the processing machine, simply to deny its use to his competitors in NBC and ABC. It was not enough that he would win, but also that they must lose. He even festooned the Church of the Holy Nativity in Bethlehem with CBS News signs. The BBC office was a chair beneath a banyan tree. Beside the chair was a broom cupboard with a telephone, which served as the edit room where the strips of news film were glued laboriously together by our Israeli editor Shoshana. On the chair perched our able Australian producer

George James. He negotiated with head office for airtime, pleaded with the Israeli Defence Force for facilities and kept the peace between his three correspondents. The other two were the tough and hard-driven Keith Graves and the smooth and suave Michael Cole, who later became the BBC's royal correspondent and was eminently suited for it, until he innocently fell foul of the *Sun*. Temperamentally I reckoned I was somewhere halfway between them. Michael came up with the first scoop of the war and Keith with the second.

I returned to the banyan tree one day rather pleased with myself. 'Good stuff,' I said, which was the term we used when we thought we had scored a hit. But when the film came out of the 'soup' (processing) the producer expressed disappointment. 'This seems to be just fireworks,' he said. 'Where's the actual fighting?'

'You have to know, George,' I replied, 'that these days the fireworks *are* the fighting. Everything is long distance, rockets and missiles. No more infantry charges. The rifle and bayonet are as obsolete as the bow and arrow. Get real and be happy. Sell it hard and make sure that the bastards run it.' (I had already acquired a field man's dislike of headquarters.) The images were the fireball of a stricken MiG fighter, the arc of missiles, the flash of artillery, the plumes of smoke in the background and the surrendering Egyptian Third Army in the foreground. I noted at the time: 'What can I say in a thousand words that a single image of a file of prisoners will not say more eloquently for me?' The conviction took hold and never left me that, when it came to words, I could say more with less and less with more.

A Jordanian commander on the Syrian front, where the two sides hardly even saw each other after the early tank battles, reproached the Israelis for waging a long-distance war and not having fought face to face, like men. But there was still some line of sight. My cameraman on the Golan Heights, Mike Lewis, a veteran of Arnhem, was wounded by Syrian artillery fire and had to be evacuated. I was lucky and escaped with a scratch. A bright yellow Hertz saloon car was not a wise choice of wheels in a war zone.

Warfare is even more over-the-horizon and remotely controlled now than it was then. A button is pressed on an aircraft carrier and an ISIS fighter dies on the road to Raqqa. Such a change in the nature of armed conflict has had far-reaching consequences, making it easier to resort to and even attractive to watch. The soldiers train on video war games that confuse the reality with the virtual reality. A simulator is cheaper than a Challenger tank or a Warrior armoured vehicle. A battle at night can be a thing of terrible beauty. Tracer fire lights up the sky like a stream of molten hyphens from source to target in a perfect parabola. Cameras show the launch and impact of laser-guided missiles. Drones hover over the battlefield armed with loitering munitions. The devil has all the best fireworks. The casualties are imaginable but usually invisible to the force inflicting them – which of course makes it easier to inflict them.

This connects with another novelty, that for the first time in a century a breed of politicians has come into office who have had, themselves, no experience of armed conflict. This would have surprised their predecessors. Prime Minister Harold Macmillan was badly wounded on the Somme and owed his life to his Sergeant Major who, being a guardsman, had to ask his permission to rescue him. Denis Healey, the well-respected and long-serving Defence Secretary in the 1960s, had been a beach-master under fire at Anzio in 1944. Lord Carrington, who had served with the Guards Armoured Division in Normandy, told me that at one time every member of Margaret Thatcher's Cabinet, except for the lady herself, had served in the armed forces. (And she, we guessed, would have made a formidable machine-gunner.) Willie Whitelaw, her right-hand man and voice of reason, had served in Normandy alongside Carrington. There was thus a measure of personal experience and institutional wisdom among them about what could be achieved, and what could not, by the bomb and the bayonet. And the Falklands War of 1982 was not a reliable precedent. The survivors of the Task Force agree on this, that if the Argentinians had deployed a higher quality of troops to the islands or fused their bombs better, the war could have had a very different outcome.

Tony Blair had no military background. He was quoted by the biographer Tom Bower as having told a senior RAF officer early in his premiership: 'I know we have an army, navy and air force, but I don't know any more.'[6] As a schoolboy at Fettes he had declined to join the Combined Cadet Force, because he did not wish to 'play toy soldiers'. He not only played but deployed real soldiers while in office, and posed with them at annual photo-ops in Iraq and Afghanistan. I was nearly a witness to his last pre-Christmas photo-op in the Basra Air Station, before the British withdrawal, and could see how carefully choreographed it was, with the troops and armoured vehicles arranged in a semi-circle to the cameras' best advantage. I happened to be making a radio documentary at the time, about the work of army chaplains, and Blair's minders, who knew I was not 'on message', made sure that I was held incommunicado, confined to an inner office for the duration. He came and he went and he said his piece and I am sure it was deemed a success. 'Martin Bell's not going to be there, is he?' my military escort was asked by one of the Prime Minister's spin doctors. Politicians who have never heard a shot fired in anger are rather fond of putting on the khaki. The political effect is variable. Posing in the turret of a battle tank worked for Margaret Thatcher in Britain but not for presidential candidate Michael Dukakis in the United States. Politicians should understand that it is not the columnists who will bring them down, but the cartoonists.

Heinz Guderian, the renowned Second World War German tank commander, noted: 'Unfortunately it is not the habit of politicians to appear in conspicuous places when the bullets begin to fly.'

Tony Blair's Cabinet too was as innocent of military experience as Harold Macmillan's and even Margaret Thatcher's had been replete with it. Even those of an age to have been conscripted seemed somehow to have been lucky enough, or clever enough, as I was not, to dodge the draft. As an MP, I looked across at the benches opposite and felt that they were not of the real, but only the make-believe political world. It was at this point that the application of armed force became a policy option to be dusted down and taken off the shelf whenever required. It was used successfully by the Parachute Regiment in a small operation against rebels of the Revolutionary United Front in Sierra Leone. It was used successfully in the bombing of the Serbs in Kosovo and Belgrade, resulting in the overthrow of Slobodan Milosevic. But the run of good fortune did not last: the next adventure in expeditionary warfare was on a much larger scale and neither legal nor successful.

In the afterglow of Kosovo, on 22 April 1999, Tony Blair gave his resonant Chicago speech, in which he outlined his doctrine of 'international community', which meant armed intervention against selected dictatorships. 'We have learned twice before in this century that appeasement does not work. If we let an evil dictator range unchallenged, we shall have to spill infinitely more blood and treasure to stop him later.'

Then he named names: 'Many of our problems have been caused by two dangerous and ruthless men, Saddam Hussein and Slobodan Milosevic,' so the next target was clearly signalled. For the war in Iraq – ill-considered and ill-fated as it was – Tony Blair had the support not only of most MPs but of most of the press as well. The cheerleader in chief was Murdoch's *Times*, which seldom saw a war it didn't like and was known in my household as the *Warmonger's Gazette*. But even the left-of-centre *Observer* joined in. I imagined my grandfather Robert Bell, once its news editor, turning in his grave. He was no super-patriot, but a socialist and republican. As ever, the enthusiasts for war were those who knew least about it. The Kenyans have a proverb: 'He who incites others to go to war is never killed on the battle front.'

History suggests that we British are a belligerent people. How else could we have done what we did? The inhabitants of a small offshore island, we established an empire by force of arms across two-fifths of the surface of the world. Our dead and those of the Empire lie buried in war graves in no fewer than 151 of its countries. Even those that we did not actually invade, like Montenegro, we sometimes bombarded from the sea. Yet we are peaceable people too. We would rather threaten force than apply it. In the closing stages of the stalled British advance in Normandy in 1944

Field Marshal Montgomery observed: 'The trouble with our British lads is that they are not killers by nature. They have got to be so inspired that they will want to kill.' Montgomery was not short of self-esteem. He also remarked: 'God said, in my opinion rightly . . .' (His American ally and adversary General George Patton confided to his diary: 'God damn all British. I would rather be commanded by an Arab.')

Our tendency is always to muddle through. In 1897 the Prime Minister Lord Salisbury said: 'British policy is to drift lazily downstream, occasionally to put out a boathook to avoid a collision.' The boathook at the time was the world's most powerful navy.

The best analysis of where we are now in warfare, and where we have come from, has been provided by General Sir Rupert Smith, the Clausewitz of our time. He is the smartest general I ever knew – and I have known many from a number of armies, and even some who were not so smart. He commanded the 1st British Armoured Division in the first Gulf War in 1991. He commanded the United Nations Protection Force in Bosnia in 1995 and brought a troubled mission to a good conclusion. He had the advantage of never having been to a university, but of having joined the Parachute Regiment as a private soldier, so he could analyse the issues of war and peace by having lived through them, and with an uncluttered mind. His book *The Utility of Force* was mostly written before the war in Iraq in 2003 but published after it. It has been translated into French, Hebrew and Arabic. Every aspiring staff officer has read it from West Point to the Gulf. His central thesis is that war as we have previously known it no longer exists.

He argues: 'Confrontation, conflict and combat undoubtedly exist . . . and states still have armed forces which they use as a symbol of power. Nonetheless, war as cognitively known to most non-combatants, war as a battle in a field between men and machinery, war as a massive deciding event in a dispute in international affairs: such war no longer exists.'[7] Its place has been taken by what he calls 'war amongst the people', in which the application of force on an industrial scale is actually counter-productive: 'Go in amongst the people, and every time we use our strength we fail to achieve our objective. We often reinforce our opponent's ability to achieve his objective, because his strategy is to get us to over-react.'[8]

In a conventional war fought in a desert, soldiering is physically hazardous – take that hill and storm that trench – but it is morally simple. There are no inconvenient civilians in the way. In a war amongst the people and in an *inhabited battlefield* totally different considerations apply. Today's commanders are well versed in the Geneva Conventions and have legal advisers beside them. The British Army's most thriving branches are its Air Corps and its Legal Service.

At the time, I had thought of the 1967 Six-Day War as a 'clean' war, fought in the desert with only battlefield casualties. It was not a clean war at all, but a war amongst the people, in Qalqilia. This was the West Bank town that had the misfortune to lie only 8.5 miles from the sea, at Israel's narrowest point, before the war changed the borders. Israelis had long believed that it was a terrorist haven and had plans for it. It had been a focus of attention in the 'reprisal raids' launched by Israel between 1949 and 1956. Some of these raids were miniwars. Many were led by a young officer named Ariel Sharon. Prime Minister David Ben-Gurion said: 'We have the power to set a high price for our blood, a price that would be too high for the Arab communities, the Arab armies and the Arab governments to bear.'

On 6 June 1967 the town was not caught in the cross-fire. It was targeted. Dozens of its people were killed and 850 of its houses blown up. In his memoirs Moshe Dayan, the Israeli Defence Minister, described the destruction as a punishment. Six months after the conflict was over, when I belatedly got around to learning more about its darker side, I found an elderly survivor, Adel Abdullah, living in a tent in the ruins of what had been his home. 'Look at the damage here,' he said, 'what kind of a civilisation would do this?'

The same applied to three villages in the Latrun Salient, a peninsula of Arab-held territory sticking out into Israel since the war of 1948, having been well defended by the Arab Legion. The Israelis had plans for them too. After the Six-Day War they flattened the villages in the Salient, including the Biblical settlement of Emmaus (later the Palestinian village of Imwas), and turned them into a public park funded by the Canadians. I happened to be in the area at the time, on the old road from Jaffa to Jerusalem, and was told about it at a roadblock. But had we reported the destruction of Emmaus, or attempted to film it, we would first have been arrested and then censored and finally lost our accreditation. These dilemmas are not uncommon in war reporting. It was certainly not my finest hour and I may have made a serious mistake in passing it by, but I wished to go on working.

The Arabs have a saying, that a wise man does not break the cup that he intends to drink from.

4. LESSONS OF VIETNAM

It was called Operation Rolling Thunder. In the course of it, over Vietnam, Cambodia and Laos from 1961 to 1972, the Americans dropped more than twice the tonnage of high explosive bombs than they did on Germany in the whole of the Second World War. And still they lost.

In a guerrilla war the balance of forces tends to matter less than the time frame. A regular army loses by not winning. A guerrilla army wins by not losing. A regular army has countdowns and deadlines. A guerrilla army has time.

From 1961 to 1968 Robert McNamara was the United States Defense Secretary, first under President Kennedy and then under President Johnson. Before that he had been one of the 'whiz kids' who helped rebuild the Ford Motor Company, and in 1960 he became the first of its presidents chosen from outside the Ford family. Kennedy liked 'whiz kids'. According to Special Counsel Ted Sorensen, he regarded McNamara as 'the star of his team'. In 1964 a reporter asked him how he felt about having the Vietnam War named after him. He answered: 'I don't object to it being called McNamara's war. I am pleased to be identified with it and to do whatever I can to win it.'

More than fifty-eight thousand Americans died in that war. Their names are etched on its stone memorial near the State Department in Washington DC. It remains the only war, other than skirmishes, that the United States ever lost. McNamara was its architect. Twenty years after it ended he wrote a four-hundred-page *mea culpa* called *In Retrospect*. 'We were wrong,' he said, 'terribly wrong.' And he listed the causes for the disaster. 'We misjudged . . . the geopolitical intentions of our adversaries . . . and we exaggerated the dangers to the United States of their actions . . . We thus failed to analyze and debate our actions in Southeast Asia . . . with the intensity and thoroughness that characterized the debates of the Executive Committee during the Cuban Missile Crisis.'[1]

On my first assignment to Vietnam, early in 1967, the outcome was by no means obvious. I was far too impressed, as many reporters were (but not all), by weaponry and tonnages and body counts. I attended the 'Five O'Clock Follies', the military briefings and theatre of the absurd, held in Saigon's old Rex Hotel, where the numbers quoted seemed overwhelming. Could the North Vietnamese and Viet Cong *really* have lost two thousand six hundred men killed in action in the week ending 18 March 1967, as we were led to believe at the 'Follies'? Who was counting them, and how? The Americans knew their own casualties exactly, but how could they have known their enemy's with any accuracy, especially when most of these casualties were inflicted out of sight and at long distance? They wished to be seen to be winning the war, and had a professional interest in inflating the figures to suggest a successful outcome. The military intelligence became a conflicted issue in a celebrated court case involving CBS News. McNamara was a number-cruncher, one of the best and brightest of his generation. He had risen from captain to lieutenant colonel in the US Air Force in its Office of Statistics, analysing the bombing of Germany. With an average of five per cent of the aircraft shot down on each mission he discovered that twenty per cent of the pilots turned back, some for technical reasons and others (it was supposed) from a loss of nerve. At that point 'Old Iron Pants' stepped in – Colonel Curtis LeMay, commander of the 305th B17 Flying Fortress Bomb Group. When he received McNamara's report he said: 'I will be in the lead aircraft on every mission. Anyone who does not go over the target will be court-martialled.' The abort rate dropped immediately. LeMay's policy on Vietnam was to threaten to bomb the Viet Cong back to the Stone Age. When he became George Wallace's running mate in the 1968 presidential election, his opponents' slogan was 'Bombs away with Curt LeMay'. When I interviewed him in the course of the campaign he did not come across as a mad bomber at all, but a courteous old gentleman from Ohio.

McNamara knew about bombing and he knew about statistics. If wars could be won by either or both, the Americans could have saved their client state of South Vietnam with ease. I had never seen so much military hardware in my life. It was surely inconceivable, I thought, that the mightiest power on earth could be defeated there.

As the Duke of Wellington observed, 'There is no such thing as a little war for a great nation.'

Here is a typical report on the build-up of the Americans' great logistics base at Cam Ranh Bay. I would like to think that it was ironic, but I fear that it was not.

Cam Ranh Bay grew out of nothing in a year and a half. The authorities have described the pace of growth as testimony to the soundness and greatness of the American way of life. In the storage compounds of Cam Ranh the American way of life is closely guarded and massively provided for. The build-up in Cam Ranh argues the determination of the Americans to stick the war out for as long as they have to. When the tides of war have receded will they leave the debris of their occupation behind them? They say no. They have plans to beat their swords into ploughshares. An oil refinery is being discussed. The local sand could be used in a glass industry. The Americans say they want to leave the base as a tribute to the beleaguered people of South Vietnam.

I could see what it took to be a superpower, and too much of my reporting was about what the Americans were doing to change the face of the country they were defending. The valleys were exalted and the mountains and hills were made low. If wars could be won by bulldozers and Super Sabres, they would have prevailed without difficulty. The bulldozers were to level the runway of the airbase at Tuy Hoa in the centre of South Vietnam, and the Super Sabres were to fly from it. I asked a pilot about their manoeuvrability. 'Manoeuvrable?' he said. 'This bird's so manoeuvrable it can fly up its own backside.' The base was a new one on the coastal plain, with a mushrooming shanty town at its gates – and signs advertising such establishments as The Pittsburgh Bar, The Morning Glory Nightspot and The Moulin Rouge, Refreshments Best in Town. The local air force commander tried to tidy up the base with a beautification campaign, which he called Operation Green Pasture. But the tin city outside the wire was beyond his jurisdiction and more like a suburb of sheds.

I marvelled at the provisioning of the Americans' war effort. It was as if they were a nation of quartermasters. How could an army lose a war if it was able to feed its front-line troops on waffles and maple syrup? And show them NFL football on television in its forward operating bases? The answer which eluded me was that, as it turned out, it could lose quite easily, and maybe *because* of the waffles and maple syrup and television in the FOBs. Its enemy was tougher, more resourceful and fighting for his life on his home soil. Like McNamara, and perhaps even under his influence, I was wrong, I was terribly wrong.

I was twenty-eight at the time, but being young is no excuse for being dumb. It is hard to imagine a dafter question than one that I put to the commander of a wing of F-100 Super Sabres armed with napalm bombs: 'Would you agree that as jobs go yours is fairly destructive?' Fortunately I kept no record of his answer.

In February 1967 I flew to the American airbase at Bien Hoa – even busier than Chicago's O'Hare, it was said – to report on the campaign of defoliation. The Americans were spraying poison, in the form of industrial strength weedkiller, on great tracts of the countryside to destroy the vegetation that gave cover to the Viet Cong and the crops on which they depended. The poison also destroyed the crops of civilians, whether or not they supported the Viet Cong. What began as an agricultural chemical called Weedbegone was developed into Agent Orange, a toxic weapon of war. The programme was called Operation Ranch Hand. It derived from an experiment by the British (of course) in Malaya, who at the time were supposed to be the counter-insurgency experts, although in my personal experience as a soldier in Cyprus we were nothing of the kind. In Vietnam 20 million gallons of defoliant, including 11 million of Agent Orange, were sprayed between 1961 and 1971. The operations room at Bien Hoa had a slogan on the wall for the benefit of its pilots: 'Only you can prevent forests'. The only constraint on the coverage (which should have been a warning sign) was that we were not allowed to interview them. My report on Operation Ranch Hand, delivered in the clipped tones then in vogue and with all the humanity of a programmed robot, conveyed not a hint that I was witnessing a war crime.

I'm sitting on an armour-plated box at the back of a UC-123 transport aircraft. In front of me, a cylindrical tank holding 1000 gallons of defoliating chemicals. Behind me, as if on a crop-spray- ing aircraft back home, the jets spurting out the defoliant over a swathe of jungle below. The aircraft is travelling in a flight of three. Between them, they've taken more hits from ground fire than any others in the Vietnam War. The reason is they are flying as low as they dare – 150 feet or less – as slowly as they dare, and presenting a target which for an enemy gunner must look as big as a barn door. That's what the pilots think anyway. But for every thirty shots fired at them only one makes contact. The defoliant planes have patch marks all over them from previous encounters. Pilot and navigator sit in a specially armour-plated cabin. Fight- ers and rescue helicopters stand by in case of trouble. And of course the areas these aircraft fly over are the ones where the Viet Cong are thickest on the ground, in this case a stretch of forest to the east of the massive Bien Hoa airbase. They run into most gunfire in the east and the north near the Demilitarised Zone.

For fifty minutes or so now the plane will go on spewing out its poisonous cargo: poisonous to vegetation anyway. The Americans insist that the chemicals don't harm anything else. First effects on vegetation will appear in only a week. Maximum defoliation will occur after six to eight months. All plants and trees that took the chemical will by then be dead. But new ones will grow to take their place. The extent of it? The Americans say they have already defoliated an area the size of the state of Maryland. And the rights and wrongs of it? That's not a question that's raised much at 12 Air Commando Squadron. They have a job to do, helping troops on the ground to locate an elusive enemy. They go right ahead and do it. For them it's no more than just a giant weedkilling operation, except that in these weeds there are men lying hidden and waiting to shoot back at them.

The report was a cop-out. Even a novice reporter should have known and done better. Operation Ranch Hand was a campaign of chemical warfare and an indirect attack on the civilian population. Babies have been born in Vietnam, and are still being born, with birth defects as a result of it. There is a high incidence of cancer also in New Brunswick in Canada, where Agent Orange was tested on a military base in 1966 and 1967. Its further use was forbidden by President Ford in an Executive Order in 1976. Robert McNamara, in his penitent old age, could not remember having ordered it, though he conceded that it happened on his watch. In Errol Morris's 2003 documentary *The Fog of War*, he said: 'What kind of a law do we have that says this kind of chemical is legal and which is illegal? There is no such law. Never in the world would I have authorised an illegal act.'

To McNamara's credit, he knew from the start that the war was not primarily a military problem but a battle for the hearts and minds of the people: he entered the phrase into the lexicon of public life. When President Johnson said in the Oval Office (according to a White House recording) 'We're losing at the rate we're going', his public pronouncements were invariably upbeat, and his Defense Secretary dutifully echoed them. McNamara did once observe that 'what was a nasty small war is now a nasty middle-sized war'. But apart from that his consistent message, during and after his many missions to Saigon, was that the war, if not yet won, was always winnable. When he finally expressed his doubts in a memo to Johnson, the President let him go. Till then McNamara had believed what the generals told him. He never appeared to understand, until very much later, that hearts and minds can be intimidated, but not won over, by the application of force.

By his own account he was over-impressed by the military:

I did not then and do not now believe that they consciously misled me. It went against their training and tradition . . . they – as did I – misunderstood the nature of the conflict. They viewed it primarily as a military operation when in fact it was a highly complex nationalistic and internecine conflict . . . I met with COMUSMACV [Commander of the United States Military Assistance Command Vietnam] Gen. Paul D. Harkins. Harkins was tall, handsome, and articulate; he looked and spoke exactly as a general should . . . The differences between me and the [military] chiefs [in late 1966] were not hidden, yet they were also not addressed. Why? Most people wish to avoid confrontation . . . rather than to address it head-on . . . I regret that he

[President Johnson], Dean [Secretary of State Dean Rusk], and I failed to confront these differences among us and with the chiefs directly and debate them candidly and thoroughly.[2]

So it was left to the journalists to swing the debate – and to one journalist in particular. There has never been a bigger shot in TV news than Walter Cronkite, the voice and face of CBS News. At the time of the Tet Offensive in January 1968, a sudden armed uprising by the Viet Cong, he said: 'What the hell is going on? I thought we were winning this war.' He then visited South Vietnam to assess the situation for himself. He was under pressure from the Pentagon on one side, and from the evidence of his own eyes as well as his network's 'young Turks', Morley Safer and John Laurence, on the other. Back in New York on 27 February 1968 Cronkite delivered his verdict. Because of his status as 'the most trusted man in America', it was the most consequential broadcast commentary ever delivered.

It seems to me more certain than ever that this bloody experience of Vietnam is to end in a stalemate. To believe now that we are closer to victory is to believe the optimists who, in the face of the evidence, have been wrong in the past. To say that we are mired in stalemate seems the only realistic, if unsatisfactory, conclusion. On the off chance that military and political analysts are right, in the next few months we must test the enemy's intentions, in case this is indeed his last big gasp before negotiations. But it is increasingly clear to this reporter that the only rational way out will be to negotiate, not as victors, but as honourable people who lived up to their pledge to defend democracy, and did the best they could.

President Lyndon Johnson was reported, when he saw the broadcast, to have turned to his aides and said: 'If I've lost Cronkite, I've lost Middle America.' A little over a month later, on 31 March 1968, he spoke to the nation from the Oval Office: 'I shall not seek, and I will not accept, the nomination of my party for another term as your President.'

Cronkite was offering an opinion, although he retreated into the third person to express it. 'This reporter . . .' is not a device that anyone uses any more. His commentary was a significant departure from the inhibited journalism of an age in which official sources were more widely trusted than they are today. A generation later, in Bosnia and elsewhere, we took his exemplary candour a stage further. It liberated the reporter to make some kind of a fact-based stand for the truth. A BBC colleague called it 'neutrality with attitude'. It started with the BBC's Richard Dimbleby and Walter Cronkite.

Four days after Johnson's broadcast Martin Luther King Jr was killed in Memphis, Tennessee. The black communities – we called them Negroes then – rose up in anger. My first experience of the United States was the burning south side of Chicago . . . then Trenton, New Jersey . . . then Newark, New Jersey . . . then Wilmington, Delaware. The shadow of Vietnam seemed, like the smoke, to hover over everything. It was a revolutionary time. There were infantry in the grounds of the White House and tanks on New Hampshire Avenue. Washington looked like the capital of a banana republic in the throes of an attempted coup. I reported:

> In all these places . . . I was reminded of nowhere else as much as
> of Saigon – the same sense of emergency, the same omnipresence

of American troops, except that in my experience, which pre-dates the Tet Offensive, Saigon was more relaxed . . . One African-American, surveying the scene in a burning part of Wilmington, remarked that the street corner looked like Vietnam. And another said: 'Out there they must think we are the Viet Cong.' It so happens, too, that most of the federal troops called out in Chicago were Vietnam veterans . . . This was not the sense in which they had expected to find the home fires burning.[3]

The shadow of Vietnam also fell over the Democratic Convention in Chicago four months later. Some of the men of the 33rd Infantry Brigade, trained in anti-looting drill, were veterans both of Vietnam and of the city's riots the previous April. In the disturbances on the streets and in Grant Park, the crowds chanted, 'The whole world is watching,' which indeed it was, and I got my second taste of tear gas in two months (the first was in Paris). It was the lethal combination, of the war and the riots, that did for the presidential campaign of Vice President Hubert Humphrey, who won the nomination but lost the election narrowly to Richard Nixon. I remember a placard that declared improbably 'Happiness is Richard Nixon'.

I have a transcript of the background briefing that Nixon gave to reporters, without the presence of cameras, in Key Biscayne, Florida, three weeks before the election. Apart from the run-in of the campaign – what he called 'Operation Extra Effort' – Vietnam was the big issue. Would he bomb more or less? 'Military force is only one string to a multi-string bow for the purposes of bringing about negotiation. If negotiation is to come, it will involve not only military power, not only the power in being, but the possibility of the use of power or taking it away, not using it.'

This was the policy he followed as President, alternating between bombing operations and bombing pauses, to bring Hanoi to the table and extricate the United States from the war. On 30 April 1970 he authorised incursions into Cambodia: 'I would rather be a one-term President and do what I believe is right rather than to be a two-term President at the cost of seeing America become a second-rate power and to see this nation accept the first defeat in its proud 190-year history.' In December 1972, in between the final negotiations with Hanoi, he authorised the notorious 'Christmas bombing' of North Vietnam.

The overwhelming technology underwhelmed – not only the bombing but the surveillance that underpinned it. The Americans set up a programme called TRIM (Trails and Roads Interdiction Multi-sensor), which was operational just after the Tet Offensive and cost $1.7 billion. It was rushed into service during the Battle of Khe Sanh in January 1968. Between 1969 and 1971 they dropped more than twenty thousand seismic intrusion devices (dagger-tipped sensors) that buried themselves in the ground and were intended to detect the sounds of troop movements along the Ho Chi Minh Trail; but they had a high false alarm rate due to bombs, helicopters, storms and wildlife, especially frogs. So even the frogs were on the side of the North Vietnamese. The technology supporting TRIM was known as 'Igloo White' and employed a number of innovations that seem scarcely credible now. These included trained pigeons to carry munitions and blow up North Vietnamese trucks, urine detectors and acoustic sensors that looked like dog excrement. The project was coordinated from outside Vietnam in the Data Correlation Centre, using early IBM computers, in what was at the time the largest building ever constructed in Thailand. The operations ended with the US withdrawal, having accomplished very little.

I returned to Vietnam in 1972, when President Nixon was in office and negotiations had begun. The last American combat troops were handing over their last bases. The stars and stripes were lowered and symbolic keys handed over with assurances of eternal friendship. The war was being 'Vietnamised', which in the long term meant being lost, and I had finally to get round to real reporting, not hide behind the firepower.

This was the only time in my life when, day after day, I would hire a taxi and ask the driver to take me to the war. I had with me the redoubtable Bernard Hesketh (later to be the BBC's heroic cameraman in the Falklands). Every day our journey was shorter but the cost was always the same, $100 plus a generous war-zone gratuity to the driver. Every day the government claimed victories. Every day the victories were closer to the capital, in one case only 14 miles away, where the people were more densely concentrated and the casualties higher. Every day when the traffic ceased, except for the refugees pouring towards us in their ox carts, we would stop the taxi and peer into no man's land, then creep as far forward as we dared. We usually left the sound man Barry Lanchester in the taxi, thus risking only two lives instead of three. It was the time of a land grab, while the Americans and North Vietnamese were negotiating a standstill ceasefire. The government of South Vietnam was distantly consulted but not actually present at the talks, to the dismay of its head of state. President Thieu spoke scathingly of Henry Kissinger, Nixon's chief negotiator, as 'the professor who came here to get his Nobel Peace Prize'. In Thieu's view the only way to end the war was to win it: 'Peace will come when I sign the agreement. Any signature without mine is completely valueless.' Kissinger said that he couldn't believe that a fourth rate power like North Vietnam didn't have a breaking point. The next year he was duly awarded his Nobel Peace Prize.

At this point, late in 1972, the Americans were both withdrawing from the war and escalating it, by a programme called 'Enhance Plus'. This was the despatch of unprecedented quantities of arms and warplanes to South Vietnam, much more than it had the capacity to absorb. It was a smoke-screen to cover a retreat. I observed: 'They are finding their own way out of the war. No dogma or domino theory will commit them any longer to the indefinite defence of such an expensive ally.' In this closing phase of its existence South Vietnam, a country of only seventeen and a half million people, was well on the way to possessing the third largest air force in the world. It could not last and it did not. Kissinger wrote: 'What was success for us – the withdrawal of American forces – was a nightmare for our allies.'[4]

Every day on one of the highways we would be stopped at roadblocks, not for the soldiers to check our identities, but because we were *bao chi* (press) and we were supposed to know how the war was going, which on their side was not well. The idea took hold of a 'stable war', which was one that the South was neither winning nor losing.

It was a war, I reflected, in which the dead buried the living, in the sense that President Thieu was determined to fight on to 'honour the sacrifices of the past'. The argument was that there had been so much blood shed that in order to justify it the shedding of more blood was necessary.

In an earlier war Wilfred Owen wrote ironically in the poem 'Smile, Smile, Smile': 'Peace would do wrong to our undying dead'. Now, Thieu stood among the graves of his fallen soldiers in South Vietnam's National Armed Forces Cemetery and publicly rejected a draft of the ceasefire agreement: was it for this, he asked, a major concession to the Communists in the South, that so many of his brave soldiers had given their lives?

The Third Corps of the Army of South Vietnam was under orders to seize as much territory as possible before the ceasefire. In one of the contested villages the battleground was the cemetery. The graves were used as cover by the South Vietnamese infantry for a tentative advance. But mostly they used artillery, as the Americans had, instead of infantry because it saved the foot soldiers' lives. It was a big bang legacy. The North Vietnamese would infiltrate a village overnight, tear down one flag and raise the other. The people would flee because they knew what was coming. The South Vietnamese would then pound the place to bits and claim a victory. In my report I used the example of Xom Soui, twenty miles north of Saigon.

It has suffered this onslaught twice. As a result its crops are laid waste by bombs and rockets, its banana trees shredded by machine gun fire, and in the whole of a village which held three thousand people only a dozen houses and a buffalo stable are left standing . . . Each time, the village dies a little bit more . . . Xom Soui, on its own small scale, is as much a symbol of this war as An Loc or Quang Tri City: a place so bitterly fought *in* that there is nothing left worth fighting *for*. The red and yellow South Vietnamese flag hangs limply over a ruin.

Flags were important as symbols of possession. In South Vietnam it was a capital offence to be seen with the enemy's red and blue flag. Restrictions were placed on the sale of red and blue cloth. The flying of the flag meant everything. And the places, not the people, were what mattered. A deputy in Saigon's National Assembly warned darkly: 'There will be a time of much killing among those who try to plant their flags on the land.'

An old man stood in the ruins of his village and cursed both sides impartially. While they were about it, he said, they might as well have dropped an atom bomb on the place.

By then, enough years had passed that I had discarded my para-military reporting style and opted, I hope, for something gentler and more appropriate to a war amongst the people. One of my reports was about a mother and her six children sheltering beneath a bullock cart: their only possessions were their pots and pans, a little rice, some clothes, two cows and a buffalo. Another was about a nine-year-old boy who had known nothing but war all his life, and had lost his home and his school, both bombed to bits. For a third I visited the Coconut Monk, who lived with two thousand followers in a 'Peace Pagoda' on an island in the Mekong Delta. It looked like a funfair but was actually a monastery. He was called the Coconut Monk because he used to live in a coconut tree. He exchanged that for his pagoda and a catwalk on which he alone could tread while he meditated and prayed for world peace. The island was described as 'the Peace Region of Vietnam' and was a haven for young men trying to escape from the war. The monk had not washed for twenty-six years; nor had he spoken, except in sign language, for twelve years. He had a table for which magical properties were claimed. He invited world leaders to visit him and to sign a peace treaty on it. If they did not, he prophesied, Saigon would be destroyed in the course of the following year. It was not destroyed but it was, three years later, renamed.

Alongside their military campaign near Qui Nhon, Saigon's South Korean allies ran a civilian campaign called WHAM (winning hearts and minds). It consisted of handing out pens to the children, teaching them taekwondo, rebuilding markets and temples and holding a banquet where villagers feasted on American combat rations and Korean parsnip wine. But the hearts and minds remained un-won. The bloodshed had been futile and the war was by this time unwinnable.

On 12 November 1972, on returning from one of the battles across no man's land, I wrote:

> A memory that sticks in the mind is of waste ground near Highway One – the scene of a particularly bloody encounter between North Vietnamese and government forces. The battlefield is empty of all but the dead, the grave-diggers and a crumpled piece of paper blowing in the wind. It is a verse by a South Vietnamese poet, copied out painstakingly by one of the North Vietnamese, now fallen. The interpreter Viet translates it for me, in the hope he says of an understanding of the point of view of both men, the one who wrote it and the one who carried it.[5]

The verse was written by Trinh Cong Son, an anti-war poet then living in Saigon. My translator noted: 'The composer attacks the stupidity of the war, the blindness of the people who received assistance from abroad (he calls them "beggars"), and he is longing for peace.'

> Live for me, speak for me, breathe for me;
> It has been too long, how can we wait,
> How can you sit there in silence and sleep, my friends?

Live for me, speak for me, breathe for me,
What can you see but bombs, fires and bullets?
Oh my friends, how can you enjoy being beggars?

Can't you hear, can't you hear, the voice of the Vietnamese people
Who are longing for peace after darkness
And a day together, hand in hand?

Whether or not they are together hand in hand, so many years later, they enjoy peace after darkness in the sense of soldiering no more and having no bombs falling on them after the apocalypse. Bomb craters are turned into fishponds, auxiliary fuel tanks into canoes and the Viet Cong tunnels into showpieces for the tourist industry. (Some of the tunnels have been enlarged to fit the over-sized tourists.)

The lesson that Vietnam taught the world, at a terrible cost and over fifteen years of hell-on-earth, is that Rolling Thunder and Igloo White alone do not win wars. Wars are won by ideas with the strength to sustain them.

5. VICTOR'S JUSTICE

Two former foreign correspondents were reminiscing in a courtroom. I was one. The other was Niklas Frank, who had just retired after twenty-two years with *Stern* magazine. He was also the son of Hans Frank, the Nazis' notorious Governor-General of Poland, one of the eleven hanged at Nuremberg. There should have been twelve, but Hermann Göring took his own life with a cyanide pill on the eve of his execution.

Frank's anger against his father never subsided. He addressed his book *In the Shadow of the Reich* to the notorious butcher of Warsaw. He wrote: 'The snapping of your neck spared me from having a totally screwed-up life. You certainly would have poisoned my brain with all your drivel, the fate of the silent majority of my generation, who did not have the good fortune of having their fathers hanged.'[1]

Niklas Frank, who was seven at the time of his father's death, was against the death penalty in principle, but not in his father's case. 'I'm really glad that he got the death penalty,' he told me, 'so at least he experienced the seconds, the hours and the days and nights before death, which he himself brought to millions of people.'

We were in the presence of ghosts, for this was Room 600 of the Justice Building in Nuremberg, where twenty-one prominent Nazis were tried, some in their absence, by the International Military Tribunal between November 1945 and October 1946, when the hangings occurred. The Justice Building, connected by a tunnel to the prison cells next to it, was one of the few buildings left standing after the Allied bombing. And Nuremberg, more than any other, was the city of the Nazis. It was their cradle and their grave. So there was a certain symmetry to the proceedings. The ghosts included Hans Frank, Hermann Göring and the chief American prosecutor Justice Robert H. Jackson.

Justice Jackson was an orator as well as a lawyer. His opening address was one of the great speeches of the twentieth century, in which he looked ahead to the verdict of history and to the charge of victor's justice.

> Some general considerations which may affect the credit of this trial in the eyes of the world must be candidly faced. There is a dramatic disparity between the circumstances of the accusers and of the accused that might discredit our work if we should falter, in even minor matters, in being fair and temperate . . . If these men are the first war leaders of a defeated nation to be prosecuted in the name of the law, they are also the first to be given a chance to plead for their lives in the name of the law.

The charge sheet included the novel charges of crimes against humanity and conspiracy to wage an aggressive war. Justice Jackson described the Tribunal as 'the first trial in history for crimes against the peace of the world'. It was a compromise between the Soviets, who had wanted fifty thousand Nazis to be summarily executed, and the Americans, who wished the accused to have the same rights as defendants in the United States. In the event three of the Nazis were acquitted and one, Albert Speer, escaped the death penalty (the Soviet judge dissented). The Nazis were the victims of their own meticulous record-keeping. The documents, drawn from archives all over Germany and beyond, established the historical record beyond doubt or challenge. It embedded the history in the facts. That was its long-term value and significance. The Nazi myth was exposed for what it was.

My meeting with Niklas Frank took place in February 2002, on the eve of the trial of Slobodan Milosevic, the overthrown dictator of Serbia, in the International Criminal Tribunal for the Former Yugoslavia (ICTY) at The Hague. Milosevic died in its custody. The Tribunal, established by the United Nations in 1993 and sometimes known as 'Madeleine Albright's court' (the then US Secretary of State), was described at the time as the first attempt at international justice since Nuremberg and was modelled on it.

I was making a programme about war crimes for BBC Four called *The Evil That Men Do*. Niklas Frank was one of the witnesses. Another was Robin Theurkauf, a professor at Yale who lectured on war crimes, the International Criminal Court and the issue of whether the captives at Guantanamo should have the status of prisoners of war. What her students did not know, because she did not tell them, was that she had lost her husband in the Twin Towers on 9/11.

Nuremberg inspired other imitations and other trials for crimes against humanity. These were national and political but drew on Nuremberg for their legitimacy and borrowed author-ity. One of the most notorious was in Luanda in June 1976. It was the brief and brutal show trial of thirteen British and American mercenaries captured at the beginning of the Angolan civil war. This followed the overthrow of the fascist regime in Portugal by the country's armed forces in 1974. In the resulting power vacuum Portugal's African colonies were left to be fought for by the armed groups within them, some of which sought help from abroad.

The ten British mercenaries included Costas Georgiou, a former corporal in the Parachute Regiment, dishonourably discharged after robbing a post office, who nonetheless styled himself 'Colonel Callan' and was sought by Scotland Yard for the alleged murder of fourteen other soldiers of fortune whom he had disciplined at the point of a gun. Another former Para, Andrew McKenzie, had been badly wounded in the leg when captured and sat in a wheelchair alongside Callan in the front row of the dock. They had been recruited in England by a former mercenary and offered £150 a week to fight for Holden Roberto's Congo-based FNLA, heavily outgunned and outnumbered by Cuban and Angolan forces. The so-called 'dogs of war' stood as little chance in the courtroom as they had on the battlefield. The outcome was a parody of justice.

The trial started on 11 June 1976 in the Luanda Palace, as grand a courtroom as could be found in the capital. The defend-ants, as in Nuremberg, whispered to each other in the dock with armed guards all around them. It was theatre disguised as justice. Their lawyers, British and American, pleaded in vain that, as in Nuremberg, the charges were retrospective: merely *being a mercenary* was not a crime under national or international law at the time of their capture. They were being tried not for what they did but for who they were.

The lawyers were wasting their breath. The MPLA, the victors in the civil war with Soviet and Cuban support, argued that by putting the prisoners on public trial the government of Angola was doing its duty under national and international law in bringing criminals to justice: 'DOWN WITH IMPERIALISM, LONG LIVE THE OPPRESSED PEOPLES OF THE WHOLE WORLD, FOR PEOPLE'S POWER THE STRUGGLE CONTINUES', as the official introduction to the trial declared. The cover of this document showed a rifle and bayonet splitting open a helmet with dollar bills cascading out of it. The orchestrated chants and demonstrations – 'The struggle continues, victory is certain' – swirled in the streets outside, and could be heard clearly in the courtroom, where a sad and sorry spectacle unfolded.

The accused were pleading for their lives: 'Callan started to swear and shout and accused us of being cowards . . . pulled out a pistol and said, "This is the law here" . . . Next day Callan said we was going after tanks. We crossed the main road and took up positions on a hill. Sammy Copeland said the FAPLA [government forces] were coming . . . Callan saw a rocket launcher which he opened fire on. We was on the run for many, many days and eventually we got captured where we was tortured . . . I didn't come to fight in Angola, sir, we was just conned and tricked.'

The trial was intended to proclaim to the world the legitimacy and authority of the MPLA government – an issue that had divided the Organisation of African Unity at its summit in Addis Ababa a few weeks earlier. So the foreign journalists were made provisionally welcome, on condition of good behaviour.

It was a nerve-testing experience for all of us. We were watching a political show trial that could reach only one conclusion. Angola's penal code stated: 'The People's Revolutionary Court, dealing justice severe but measured . . . will effectively watch over the maintenance and continuation of the revolutionary process in train with the object of the installation of People's Power.' Acquittals were inconceivable. We were witnesses of a judicial execution, guests of the Angolan government, sharing the same hotel as the defence attorneys, and if we questioned the procedures of the court or the justice of the process we were accused of having mercenary sympathies ourselves. We could have been arrested at any time and then deported at best. The pressures were such that two of the journalists had nervous breakdowns. I kept the company of Callan's sister Panayiota, who had flown to Luanda in a vain attempt to plead for his life, and who then became entangled in a strange and singular relationship with the Angolan Army officer assigned to protect her. She was lonely and frightened and I took her on long walks on a breakwater, not for any journalistic reason, but just to try to calm her. We called her 'Blondie'. Luanda was a world away from Camden Town. She had no reason to be there except the ill-fortune of her reckless brother.

She talked to him in his prison cell. 'Everyone makes mistakes, Costas,' she said.

'But not like mine,' he answered, 'mine are big mistakes. I must pay.'

Towards the end of the trial I reported: 'For the past few days in Luanda in quick succession mercenary activity has been denounced, displayed and demonstrated against. It would be hard to imagine anything in terms of British justice more likely to prejudice a fair trial. Yet we're not talking here of British justice. We're talking here of Angolan justice. And we're just about to find out what that is.'

It was swift and summary. On the eighth day of the trial the presiding judge ruled that all the accused were guilty of the crime of 'mercenarism': he called them 'packs of dogs with blood-stained muzzles and strangers with knives between their teeth who had come to carve dark wounds on the face of the country'. Three of them were sentenced to sixteen years in jail, three to twenty-four years and three to thirty. The other four were sentenced to death, including three Britons – Costas Georgiou ('Callan'), Andrew McKenzie and Derek Barker – and one American, Daniel Gearhart. The sentence on Gearhart was especially harsh. He had only just arrived in Angola and had never fired a shot. But he needed the money and had advertised his services as a mercenary in the American magazine *Soldier of Fortune*; and that was what did for him.

A plea for clemency by the British Prime Minister James Callaghan was ignored by President Neto of Angola. On 10 July 1976 the four men were brought before a military police firing squad. McKenzie, still in a wheelchair, stood up to be executed. The bodies were eventually repatriated. I was invited to attend Callan's funeral in Camden Town by his sister, but made an unconvincing excuse, and was then assigned by the BBC to report it. I pretended not to know where it was. I felt troubled and conflicted but knew one thing for sure: show trials without due process were a disgrace to whoever conducted them.

Equally swift and summary were the trials conducted in Kuwait in April 1991 of Palestinians accused of having been collaborators of the Iraqis after their invasion the previous year. It was the first ever session of a Kuwaiti court under martial law.

Four of the accused, who were held in an iron cage at the back of the courtroom, were given prison sentences of between twelve and fifteen years. The 'war crime' of one who drew the maximum sentence was to have worn a Saddam Hussein T-shirt.

But what of a show trial *with* due process? This brings us back to the International Criminal Tribunal for the Former Yugoslavia established at the height of the war in Bosnia in April 1993. It too was modelled on the original of the Nuremberg Tribunal. It too was a prosecutor's court. It too sat in public under the scrutiny of the press. It even offered an opportunity to the accused to play to the international gallery, which some of the leading Serbs, casting themselves as national heroes, did to an extreme degree. Its proceedings were not only broadcast 'as live' (usually with a thirty-minute delay) on television and the internet, but TV monitors were embedded in the desks of judges, counsel and witnesses, for the exhibits included the news reports of the time. In one of the trials fifteen of my reports, edited in haste after a turbulent day, were entered as evidence and had to withstand the scrutiny of the judges and lawyers. First they had to be authenticated.

Judge: Mr Bell, was this one of your reports?

Witness: Yes sir, it was.

Judge: Would you help the court by giving us the proper time frame?

Witness: It was about the battle for Santici, so that would put it in January 1994. [Santici was in central Bosnia.]

The reports were factual and fragmentary, edited under pressure, and subject to the BBC's lamentable 'good taste censorship', but a genuine part of the record. They were real, not reconstructions. Images of snipers' corner in Sarajevo were used repeatedly as evidence in the trials of Bosnian Serb leaders both civilian and military. One sequence showed civilians beside a French armoured personnel carrier that was moving at walking pace to protect them from sniper fire. Another was of the damage caused by rocket-propelled aircraft bombs fired by the Serbs into the city and one of its suburbs. Memories were fading, the history of the war was being reinvented by its surviving participants, and the footage became a sort of historical handrail for the court. It showed how things were at the time. The story that the images told was authentic and could not be altered or Photoshopped for the convenience of one side or another.

It was a contentious issue among the reporters who covered the war, whether or not they should give evidence to the Tribunal. The British usually did. The Americans without exception did not. Jonathan Randal of the *Washington Post* was actually served a subpoena by the court to appear before it. He refused and eventually won the case on appeal. This was seen by the *Post*, and other news organisations that strongly supported him, as a victory for the freedom of the press. The argument of the American media was that to give evidence in a war crimes trial would compromise the journalists' neutrality and safety. I took the opposite view, that we were citizens first and journalists second. Among others who appeared were Ed Vulliamy of the *Guardian*, Aernout van Lynden of Sky News and Jacky Rowland who had been the BBC's correspondent in Belgrade. Ed Vulliamy asked: 'Why should journalists of all people perch loftily above the due process of law?' Since the International Red Cross forbade its delegates to testify, the only neutral civilian observers remaining were the reporters. If we stayed away, there would be no eyewitnesses of war crimes except those victims lucky enough to have survived, and convictions would be based unsafely on hearsay evidence and prejudicial headlines. Who, for instance, would acquit 'the butcher of Bosnia' (a.k.a. Ratko Mladic)? The absence of independent witnesses would make it more likely that the innocent would be convicted and the guilty acquitted. This is an argument for justice that has never been convincingly answered on the other side of the Atlantic. Besides, I still had a newsman's curiosity and wished to see how the Tribunal worked and measure the quality of its justice. There was no better way to do this than by taking part in its proceedings, even though on my first appearance I missed twelve votes on the European Elections Bill in the House of Commons.

I testified five times, including the trials of the Bosnian Serbs' military leader Ratko Mladic and their political leader Radovan Karadzic. Karadzic called me a 'precious witness' and asked me to visit him in his guarded cell before the hearing, which I did unconditionally without having a prosecution lawyer with me. He was affable, relaxed and well briefed. A bullet-proof glass barrier stood between us. It said something of my life till then, I thought, that no one had ever called me precious except an alleged war criminal. As Commander-in-Chief of the Bosnian Serb Army Karadzic had command responsibility for its actions, including the siege of Sarajevo and the Srebrenica massacre.

For all of us it meant recalling, under oath, the events of twenty years earlier and revisiting a past that in many respects we thought we had left behind us. One of the key witnesses in the Karadzic case, a tough professional soldier who had been a mediator between the factions, wept uncontrollably in an ante-room after the five hours of his cross-examination.

In March 2016 Karadzic was found guilty on ten charges of genocide and crimes against humanity, including the Srebrenica massacre, the kidnapping of UN observers and the 'joint criminal enterprise' of the siege of Sarajevo. At the age of seventy he was sentenced to forty years' imprisonment, which meant in effect for life. It was the very reverse of Angola's rush to justice. The trial took five years to complete, including a year and a half for the judges' deliberations. Karadzic conducted his own defence throughout, with the help of an American lawyer Peter Robinson. One of his witnesses was Milorad Dodik, the hardline President of the Bosnian Serbs, who was a strong supporter. Dodik saw Karadzic as a hero and complained about The Hague's 'selective justice'. Karadzic said he was disappointed and astonished by the verdict. He and the International Criminal Tribunal lived in parallel and unconnected worlds.

The Tribunal took its witness protection seriously. I would arrive at Amsterdam's Schiphol Airport to be met by one of its drivers with a code number on a clipboard. I would then be driven to a hotel where I checked in as a number not a name. A court official forbade me to talk to anyone. I would proceed under escort to the court the next morning, unless my presence was challenged, which it sometimes was. The Tribunal, which was housed in the offices of an old insurance company, seemed haunted by ghosts. I was so affected by them that, on a day when I was blocked by the defence, I started writing poetry to lay the ghosts. One of the verses was about the trial of Mladic, who had ordered his gunners to pound Sarajevo 'to the edge of madness'.

The sound of seagulls plays on a loop in the Carlton Beach Hotel,

I am listed there as a number not a name,
And a crowd of ghosts is checked in just the same.
On a screen in the darkened room the scenes from hell
Unfold of the siege and the victims as if tethered,
And the guilt that lurks in the great box files
Of craters, bombs and projectiles
And high rise ruins, miles on miles:
No seagulls there but birds of prey unfeathered,
Hard-eyed and hatred-driven and unforgiving,
Training their rifles and RPGs
On a city of flinching refugees.
Yet once I ran the trench lines among these
And thought, what a wild way to earn a living;
But the courtroom newsreels stand as bedrock fact,
And the edge of madness man in the dock avoids eye contact.

Most of the trials were of Serbs, which played to the paranoia of the Serbs and caused many of them in Belgrade and Banja Luka to see the Tribunal as part of an international conspiracy against them. Where were the trials of the Mujahedin who killed their prisoners? There weren't any. Or of the government forces who cold-bloodedly shot Serbian soldiers in a Yugoslav Army convoy in Sarajevo in May 1992? There weren't any. Or of the Muslims who massacred Serbs in a village near Bratunac in January 1993? There weren't any. Or of the Croats who massacred Serbs in Kupres in April 1992? Again, there weren't any. And if a Serb was acquitted on war crimes charges, like Vojislav Seselj in April 2016, there would be a clamorous outcry in Zagreb and Sarajevo. Even the languages, which were essentially the same, were disputed: the Tribunal was obliged to create the new language of

BCS (Bosnian/Croatian/Serbian) to cover them all. All the documents were translated into BCS.

The most troubling case was that of a non-Serb, General Tihomir Blaskic, who was the first general to come before the court. He was the commander of the HVO, the Bosnian Croat defence force, during the brutal side war in the Lasva Valley between Muslims and Croats from April 1993 to February 1994. The valley, in central Bosnia, was a mainly Croat enclave surrounded by Muslims, not only Bosnian Muslims but men of the 'Mujahed Brigade' who fought in the same cause. These were volunteers who came from Afghanistan, Iran, Yemen, Saudi Arabia and other Islamic countries. The 'Muj' served alongside but not under the command of the Bosnian Army's Third Corps. The HVO were encircled and outnumbered by a factor of four or five to one. They buried their dead at night, when it was safer. Their only access was by helicopters making a corkscrew landing into a chalk pit to evade ground fire, bringing in the ammunition and taking out the wounded. On 16 April a Muslim village in the middle of the enclave, Ahmici, was attacked by Croats. The mosque was blown up and the minaret toppled. More than a hundred people were killed, either burned alive in their homes or shot while trying to escape. The few Croatian houses in the village were left untouched. This was the incident that led to the celebrated outburst by Lieutenant Colonel Bob Stewart, commander of the British UN force in the area, when he was asked by a Croat if he had the permission of the HVO to be there: 'I don't need the permission of the bloody HVO. I am from the United Nations. As far as I am concerned, what happened here is disgraceful. Bad luck, my friend. You know, there are whole families up here that have been massacred, and I'd like to know who's done it.'

Colonel Stewart wore his heart on his sleeve and was more popular with the soldiers below him in the chain of command than those above him. He said afterwards: 'I do not know if you understand the guilt I feel that Ahmici happened almost within sight of my base. It is not as if my mandate would have stopped me, because I am a man and would have done anything I could to save lives.' The Croats justified their ethnic cleansing of Muslims on the grounds that people should not be forced to live where they did not feel safe. One of them said: 'At least when we were fighting the Chetniks [Serbs] we knew where the danger was coming from.'

General Blaskic was charged with crimes against humanity, the ill-treatment of prisoners and command responsibility for the massacre: that even if he did not make it happen he let it happen. I knew Blaskic well and spoke to him regularly. He took me on a tour of his hillside front lines in the snow; for camouflage, he was wearing parachute silk over his HVO uniform. The ground was being contested trench by trench; it was very Bosnian – the men did the fighting and the women at their base camp made the coffee. The two trench lines were 100 yards apart. His men had rushed and taken an enemy trench on the previous day and he was there to congratulate them.

He surrendered himself to the Tribunal in 1996, telling his wife that it could take him three months to clear his name. He underestimated. The Tribunal at the time had only one courtroom and many cases queuing up to use it. His trial lasted for more than two years. The court sat on average for five hours a day. Its schedule was so leisurely that I calculated Blaskic lost six days of his freedom to the judges' coffee breaks alone. When one of the judges died he could have asked for a re-trial but chose not to. I testified on his behalf in February 1999. I believed him innocent, since it was a wild time in the valley and I knew there were Croat fighters there who were not under his command. A Bosnian Croat soldier had told me: 'There are some bad elements in the HVO, but the BiH [government forces] – God help us!' I quoted from notes I had taken at a press conference in nearby Busovaca eleven days after the massacre in Ahmici: 'Blaskic said he was appalled . . . whoever did it [did so] in an organised, systematic way . . . It was an organised group of people operating to a systematic plan and therefore controlled by someone. The culprits must be identified and brought to justice.'

My testimony did Blaskic no good. In March 2000 he was sentenced to forty-five years' imprisonment, the longest term ever imposed by the Tribunal. While he was serving it, new evidence surfaced in Zagreb, following the death of President Tudjman, that there had indeed been an alternative chain of command, and a paramilitary group known as the Jokers with links to the presidency. On appeal, Blaskic's sentence was reduced to nine years, for the ill-treatment of prisoners. He had already served most of it. He was released in August 2004 and returned home as a national hero. I met him later and found him quite without bitterness about his treatment.

But he had been the victim of a grave miscarriage of justice that showed very clearly the limitations of a prosecutor's court. The prosecution lawyers were an integral part of it but the defence lawyers were not. At least one of its judges, who had previously been a defence lawyer, shared my concerns but was not able to express them because he was still serving on one of the last cases. I described the Tribunal at the time as being more interested in convictions than in justice. Since the great majority of those who came before it were Serbs, its scales of justice were tilted (in my view) to balance its judgments by the conviction of as many non-Serbs as possible. Unlike Justice Jackson in Nuremberg, it did not seem sufficiently committed to due process. Its reputation would depend on its fairness, and it had not been fair to Blaskic.

After all that I had been through, in the Balkans and in The Hague, my last speech in the House of Commons, on 3 April 2001, was not about my time in Parliament or any of the issues on which I was elected. It was a defence of the rights of alleged war criminals to a fair trial. We were debating the establishment of the International Criminal Court. I drew on a range of personal experiences.

Inevitably I have been closer to war crimes than most Honourable Members. I know the pile of ash and bone that is left when a family is burned alive in its home, and the son and father have tried in vain to defend their relatives. I know what mass graves look like, and I know the stench of death. I know the tatters of clothes and bloodstains that mark the scene of mass execution . . . I get the impression that the International Criminal Tribunal at The Hague dispenses victor's justice . . . I am afraid that when the new court is established and various high profile cases come before it, as they come before the Tribunal at The Hague, the ICC will then be under pressure to convict . . . We must protect the rights of the accused and, above all, set up a court that will not feed on a diet of convictions.[2]

6. THE SOMETHING MUST BE DONE CLUB

TV news in Britain began on 5 July 1954. Richard Baker, then a twenty-nine-year-old radio announcer, introduced it from Alexandra Palace, out of vision and over a picture of the transmitter tower, with brassy music and the words 'Here is an illustrated summary of the news. It will be followed by the latest film of happenings at home and abroad.' The news stories that followed, with a voiceover by John Snagge of Boat Race fame, were about the Petrov spy case in Australia, early tests on the Comet aircraft, and the end of food rationing. They included the first 'vox pop', a stilted and patronising interview with a housewife about the end of rationing. The pictures in the news summary were black and white still photographs, which were thought to be more authoritative than film. The newsreaders themselves – Richard Baker, Kenneth Kendall and Robert Dougal – did not appear in vision until September 1955. Richard Baker wrote: 'We were not to be seen reading the news because it was feared we might sully the pure stream of truth with inappropriate facial expressions.'[1] It was not an auspicious beginning.

The press critics, always abundant in the BBC's case, declared that television had 'gone back to the days of the magic lantern'. The first news flash, in the same year, announced that Princess Margaret would not be marrying Group Captain Townsend. TV news had arrived, tied and shackled and hopelessly outdated even in its infancy. Winston Churchill, who mastered the microphone but not the camera, dismissed it as a peep-show.

News in the early days was short and cheap. The bulletins were a mere twelve minutes long, plus the weather. The regional camera crews were limited to shooting no more than 400 feet of film, a little under ten minutes, for each story. It retained some antique features, especially in its hectoring newsreel style of commentary. The first boss of TV news was a dour New Zealander, Tahu Hole, who not only had no understanding of television but actively disliked it. The BBC correspondent Gerald Priestland, who was one of his victims, called him a 'monster in every sense'. He was finally eased out of his Kremlinesque fiefdom in 1958 in a job switch with Hugh Greene, soon to become Director General. Alexandra Palace, the hilltop birthplace and museum of the new medium, remained its TV news headquarters until 1970.

The emphasis was on accuracy: I would spend a day writing and fact-checking a sixty-second script, to be read by Robert Dougal, about the United Nations' intervention in the Congo. Everything was checked and double-checked. Unscripted commentary and live interviews were unheard of. We were conscious of the BBC's sacred tradition as the keeper of the flame of impartial news. We took it for granted and never questioned it. We were even-handed to the point of inanity. Not only did we not have opinions, we did not even have *feelings*. Our mantra was 'on the one hand this, on the other hand that, and only time will tell'. Or take it to the extreme, 'Hitler may have established the concentration camps, but he built the autobahns and made the railways run on time.' It was a journalism that was practised without any moral compass at all. It was bound to pass, or at least to evolve, and it did so, under the influence of our brash new competitor ITN. The rivalry was intense. My competitors ranged from true gentlemen like Sandy Gall, Gerald Seymour and Jon Snow at one end of the scale to a complete fabulist at the other who should never have been entrusted with camera and microphone. I preferred to compete against the fabulist.

When we began, as ITN did, we inherited the traditions, and some of the staff, of the cinema newsreels, Pathé and British Movietone. They were the only model we had. The scripts were delivered in the clipped and confident tones of the officers addressing the other ranks. Having failed to join the officer class as a soldier, I imitated it as a reporter, at least for the first few years. The Second World War was not a distant memory. My first boss, the head of home and foreign correspondents, was a former naval commander, Tom Maltby, who shot his cuffs as he instructed us in the basics of news broadcasting. 'I never want to see you lads typing a script,' he said. 'You must dictate it so that it sounds like the spoken, not the written, word when you deliver it.' And of course he was right.

The security services had their own men on the staff, one of them the BBC's representative in Beirut. The BBC office in Paris was directly above that of MI6, disguised as a military charity. On joining, we had to sign on to the Official Secrets Act. At the height of the Cold War, which this was, MI5 believed there were more than a hundred Communists, or Communist sympathisers, in the BBC. One of our most capable sub-editors at Alexandra Palace, who somehow slipped through the net, was a paid-up member of the Communist Party. Security checks on new recruits were conducted by someone known as 'the Christmas tree man', so-called because he would sit in on the interviews and scribble a fir tree next to the name of an unsuitable applicant. It was an age of deference and unquestioning respect for authority. The editors gave the orders and we, the newsroom's foot soldiers, obeyed them.

We were conscious of following in the footsteps of such outstanding reporters as Richard Dimbleby and Frank Gillard. But Dimbleby had been withdrawn from Cairo during the Second World War having fallen out with the censorship. 'It really is disgraceful,' he wrote in his diary, 'to deceive the public . . . and I really believe that's what Cairo is doing.'[2] And Gillard had been sharply critical of his own coverage of the Dieppe Raid. This was the suicide mission in August 1942 in which Allied forces, mostly Canadian, suffered sixty-eight per cent casualties in an abortive attack on the German defences in France. Gillard broadcast a glowing account of it. He was a witness many years later in a programme entitled *What Did You Do in the War, Auntie?* 'I read in BBC literature about my memorable report from Dieppe,' he recalled. 'To me it's memorable in all the wrong ways. It's memorable with shame and disgrace that I was there as the BBC's one and only eyewitness and I couldn't tell the story as I ought to have told it.'

The reporters were then called news observers. In April 1942 A.P. Ryan, Controller of News, wrote a gloomy memo to his Director General: 'We have been criticised by the Board of Governors, by the Minister of Information and by Number 10, for not having a high enough standard of news observers. We must, you will agree, admit that this criticism is justified.' The chain of command went all the way up to Downing Street. Ryan then sent instructions to his news observers about to be mobilised: 'Never seek to "jazz up" a plain story. You are not dramatists. You are broadcast reporters sent out to observe and tell us what you have seen.' In a war for national survival the BBC's news services were as much part of the war effort as government leaflets like *News-facts for Fighting Men*. (Ryan would have been appalled by the later fashion for TV reporters to place themselves at the centre of their stories. It began at ITN in the late 1960s and spread like a contagion to the BBC.)

Great credit is due to Sir Hugh Greene, Tahu Hole's successor, who started a real and original news service, shed the cinema newsreel mannerisms and discarded the straitjacket by redefining the duty of impartiality. When he became the BBC's Director General he said: 'There are some respects in which the BBC is not neutral, unbiased or impartial. That is, where there are clashes for and against the basic moral values – truthfulness, justice, freedom, compassion, tolerance, for example. Nor do I believe that we should be impartial about certain things like racialism or extreme forms of political belief.' He was one of three Directors General to be eased out by a hostile government. The other two were Alasdair Milne in 1987 and Greg Dyke in 2003. The BBC prizes its independence, but its history shows that it is independent of government control only until such time as it is not.

There never was a golden age of news and never will be. But there was a *phase of liberation* between about 1981 and 1995. This was the high noon of ENG – electronic newsgathering. News film was replaced by videotape shot on light hand-held cameras, edited in the field and then transmitted by satellite. It was a change of immeasurable benefit to those of us who worked over the horizon and to a newsroom that we seldom visited. It was also the age of heavy silver boxes, in which the clunking editing machines and fly-away satellite dishes were transported at vast expense and to the profit of the airlines. 1995 was when the mixed blessing of the mobile phone arrived on the front lines. With the technical revolution we became our own news editors, deciding on the spot and usually without reference to higher authority what went into the report and what stayed out. They could broadcast it or spike it, but *they did not have time to change it*. We were free at last, at least for a few years, from editorial interference. Then with the arrival of the mobile phone the centre (literally, the Television Centre) reasserted control.

There was no escape from it. The foreign duty editor, in the morning call, would inform me of 'the feeling of the meeting'.

I didn't care about the feeling of the meeting. We did not do meetings in war zones. We did comradeship. But I had to do some serious thinking about the business of TV news. The technology was already changing its nature and its agenda. It was possible in 1982 in El Salvador (where I was competing against a very young Jon Snow of ITN) to report the clashes between rebels and government forces and – despite a five-hour time difference – to have the footage shown in British homes on the same night. On the way back from Chalatenango we were waylaid by the rebels at gunpoint and ushered into a ditch. We naturally feared for our lives. Both sides had death squads and a Dutch TV crew had just been ambushed and killed by the leftists. Instead, our captors read us a lecture in Spanish on the merits of revolutionary socialism, then let us go. This too appeared on the news on the same day, both in Britain and the United States, through our allies in NBC News. We did it because for the first time ever it was technically possible to do it. Our reports had the edge of immediacy and were full of what was known in the trade as 'bang bang'.

I had never studied journalism but only practised it. (There were no media studies courses available anyway in 1962.) But it was the Bosnian War that really got me thinking about the traditions of even-handedness which we inherited but which did not seem adequate to the realities of a city under siege and the phenomenon that came to be known as ethnic cleansing. So many ceasefire agreements were signed and then broken; on one occasion, at Sarajevo Airport, the signatories took cover from mortar fire under the table on which the agreement had been signed. One of the mediators observed: 'When they start talking peace, that is the time to head for the deepest bunker.' A Serb commander said: 'You can hear the shells are coming, theirs as well as ours. That means that nothing will come out of the peace plans, not with all this weaponry and hardware about.' Another said: 'As far as I am concerned this war will go on as long as I live.'[3] Apart from the Yugoslav Army's Soviet-made tanks the weapons of war were home-made. Sixty per cent of Yugoslavia's arms industry had been based in central Bosnia. Every town and village had an arms depot within easy reach. The means of mass destruction were coinciding, as never before, with the means of mass communication. This presented us with a slew of problems that our predecessors in the radio age had never had to face. We dealt with them for the most part locally, under the pressure of deadlines, without referring them upward. There was very little time for consultations.

In the midst of the new world disorder, the truth about what was happening all around us was somewhere between difficult and impossible to communicate. Or, as Elie Wiesel put it at the opening of the Holocaust Museum in Washington in 1993, at the height of the Bosnian War, 'It is not because I cannot explain that you won't understand: it is because you won't understand that I cannot explain.' He had been to Bosnia and said that he could not sleep at night because of the war. It reminded him of the times that he had lived through and the family that he had lost. He died in 2016.

There is nothing to be ashamed of in shedding tears quietly. Commandant Colm Doyle, an Irish Army officer caught up in Bosnia's holocaust, wrote as he left it in May 1992: 'I packed my bag and before retiring walked out onto my balcony to view the night sky. The sporadic shelling and sounds of machine gun fire were clearly to be heard. I had a sudden urge to weep, but the soldier in me refused to give in to it.'

Our blitzkrieg hotel, the Holiday Inn in Sarajevo, did not weep but it bled. It stood only 200 yards from an active front line. Its four-square outline and bright yellow facade, as if assembled from Lego, made it an easy and irresistible target. It had first been attacked by a crowd seeking vengeance on Radovan Karadzic when the war began and he and his security guards were based there. After he slipped away, its southern side was rendered uninhabitable by Serbian gunfire. If you showed yourself there by day or by night you would be targeted. One of the observation posts opposite, on the Serb side in Grbavica, was in the Philosophy Faculty of the University of Sarajevo, where the commander had been a judge in civilian life and vowed to fight for the survival of his people: a good place to reflect on the meaning of war, I thought. And so I did. When asked to do a longer report on the conflict, for the BBC's *Panorama* at the beginning of 1993, I felt it necessary to do more than list the atrocities of the previous nine months as a sort of video charge sheet. The international negotiators Cyrus Vance (former US Secretary of State) and David Owen (former British Foreign Secretary) were doing their best to offer a plan to end the war, but no one was listening and the plan was shot down in the end both by the Bosnian Serbs and by the Clinton Administration in Washington. David Owen flew into Sarajevo Airport in the first year of the conflict and told the Bosnians: 'Don't, don't, don't live under the dream that the West is going to come in and sort this out. Don't dream dreams.' I took my cue from the UN's political adviser, Victor Andreyev: 'We have reached the point where inaction is costing more than action.' A fire was burning in the southern wing of our common European home, and where was the fire brigade? It was off duty and staying at home.

So I ended the *Panorama* piece with a peroration about the case for intervention, which went up to the limit of what the BBC's neutral 'bystander journalism' (my phrase, not theirs) would allow. It was carefully worded and delivered in front of a burned-out tramcar beside the Miljacka River.

The policy of the outside world till now has been one of drift and inadequate measures taken too late. The hesitation is under-standable. To intervene will almost certainly cost lives, lives from among the force intervening. Not to intervene will cost even more lives, from the hundreds of thousands of civilians in the line of fire. The case for intervention is not to help one side against the other, but the weak against the strong, the unarmed against the armed; to take the side of the everyday victims who, till now, have had no protection. It is, fundamentally, a question of whether we care.

This was followed by the music of Vedran Smaijlovic, the 'Cellist of Sarajevo', playing Albinoni's *Adagio* in the Bar Ragusa, and images from a graveyard that had once been a public park. One of the images was of an infant's coffin carried in the arms of the grieving father. There was nothing more to be said. The closing titles rolled and the programme was over. Whatever else it was, it was not a routine balancing act between the warring factions. When the complaints began, the BBC stood by me.

I had stumbled upon something that I called, for want of a better term, the 'journalism of attachment', a journalism that cares as well as knows, and will not stand neutrally between the victim and the aggressor. It is the reverse of bystander journalism, indifferent and unfeeling. And as the report showed very clearly, the Serbs could be victims too.

It is not only a matter of language: it is a matter of tone as well. You don't report a military offensive in the same voice as you report a flower show or even a political dispute. The words are low key and shorn of embellishment or relish – as well as accurate, for they must be flame-proof and stand up to scrutiny. And you don't use adjectives – the pictures are your adjectives. Nor do you saturate the pictures with too many words. Rather, you caress them with a few. I have been accused of many things, but never in recent years of talking too much, of talking down or of talking posh. A good script is like a poem: it is self-contained and has its own rhythms and cadences.

One of my friends in Bosnia was Captain Mike Stanley (real name Milos Stankovic) of the Parachute Regiment, who was of Serbian origin and knew the country at least as well as we did. 'There you go again,' he said, 'bleeding into your typewriter!' It was a typewriter with a broken carriage return, on which I wrote my book about Bosnia and made the case for a different sort of journalism. Stankovic was discreet and a friend rather than a news source but he knew what was going on. He was the UN Protection Force's liaison officer with the Bosnian Serbs, Karadzic and Mladic. He translated the people as well as the language for the UN. Three years later he was arrested by the Ministry of Defence Police on suspicion of having spied for the Serbs. The suspicion was totally false and he was cleared, but his army career was over. Being an MP by then, I initiated two debates on his behalf in the House of Commons.

At the height of the war, in a well-publicised speech at the Travellers' Club in London, the Foreign Secretary Douglas Hurd spoke scathingly about what he called 'the something must be done club'. 'There is nothing new in such misery,' he said, 'there is nothing new in mass rape, in the shooting of civilians, in war crimes, in ethnic cleansing, in the burning of towns and villages. What is new is that a selection of these tragedies is now visible within hours to people around the world . . . People reject and resent what is going on because they know it more vividly than before.'

He returned to the theme in a speech at Chatham House. 'The air,' he said, 'is full of the eloquence of many Gladstones. Each new tragedy as it is revealed brings its own Midlothian campaign.' Hurd's reputation had been bruised by the war, and he was exercising his right of reply.

The theory I had outlined drew incoming fire from quarters that hardly surprised me. My former colleague John Simpson said: 'Bell is talking nonsense and he knows it.' Actually, I wasn't and didn't. 'Save us from reporters who pass judgement,' wrote the Liberator of Kabul in an outspoken column in the *Sunday Times*. And Mick Hume, formerly of *Living Marxism*, aimed a pamphlet at me, of which Simpson approved, entitled *Whose War Is It Anyway?* Hume wrote: 'It is time that taboo was broken and the unspoken issue of fashionable bias in war reporting was openly debated. Then it might be possible to set about cutting the cancer out . . . It is ultimately a moral crusade for Western governments, through the United Nations and NATO, to take forceful action against those accused of war crimes and genocide.' Simpson later withdrew his support for *Living Marxism*. I admired his courage and his way with words. But he was so far from being at odds with the Foreign Office that he might as well have been an ambassador as a journalist. He came under attack from the Foreign Office just once, in 1999, for his reporting of the bombing of Belgrade. When I fell into politics he wrote: 'He left my World Affairs Unit . . . without a word of goodbye.'[4] *My* World Affairs Unit? I had thought of it as more of a team than a hierarchy.

I believe that over the years my theory has gained traction among journalists and John Simpson's objections have come to look a bit elderly and dilapidated. In the end the UN and NATO did intervene in Bosnia, and took the predicted casualties. The British lost twenty-four men and the French, being in the front line in Sarajevo, lost seventy. But the war dragged on for another two and a half years until the Srebrenica massacre of 1995, and only after that were the decisions taken that brought it to an end.

It could have been ended very much earlier and at a lower cost. And then the world we live in would have been less threatening.

On my intervals away from the war zone, I even stepped aside from journalism and gave speeches – quasi-political speeches – making the case for an effective intervention. The BBC never objected, or maybe it preferred not to know. One of them was delivered in Chichester Cathedral on the first anniversary of the Srebrenica massacre. Another, in the second winter of the war, was in Belfast to an audience familiar with armed conflict on its doorstep.

> The very hopelessness of the situation – the case for turning away from the place – is also of course the case for turning towards it . . . And what risks are we willing to take, for ourselves and our soldiers? . . . The argument for disengagement – or for staying in and doing as little as possible – rests on the assumption that British lives matter more than Bosnian lives. But do they? If you should visit the makeshift hospital in a church in Nova Bila in central Bosnia and see, for instance, a three-year-old girl with a leg blown off by a mortar bomb you might conclude that, morally and practically, it does not matter what nationality she is. She is a three-year-old with her leg blown off. And she needs more help than she's getting.

The great war reporter Martha Gellhorn said she 'couldn't abide all that objectivity shit'. The duty of reporters, in her view, was to include only what they saw and heard, and not to invent or suppress by grafting a veneer of even-handedness onto the raw facts of a war. Kurt Schork of Reuters expressed the message of

Bosnia at the time in three words: 'Arm your children.' Kurt described me as the patron saint of lost causes.

The 'journalism of attachment' is, I believe, quite widely practised. I was not prescribing, but describing, a more engaged and responsible way of reporting the news. One of those who practise it, to great effect, is the BBC's Fergal Keane, whose *Letter to Daniel* in Radio Four's *From Our Own Correspondent* broke new ground in connecting with the audience. Others are Allan Little of the BBC, Robert Fisk of the *Independent*, Jon Snow and Matt Frei of Channel Four News, and Bill Neely, formerly with ITN and now with NBC. Fisk said: 'I think that the duty of a foreign correspondent is to be neutral on the side of those who suffer, whoever they may be.'[5]

Another of our champions is Christiane Amanpour of CNN. She said: 'I learned long ago, in covering the ethnic cleansing and genocide in Bosnia, never to equate victim with aggressor, never to create false moral or factual equivalence, because then you are an accomplice to the most unspeakable crimes and consequences.'[6]

But compassionate journalism comes with dilemmas of its own: one of these is when to stop reporting on the victims and start helping them. In 1980 the Archbishop of El Salvador, Oscar Romero, was assassinated in a chapel by a right-wing death squad. He knew that he might be targeted. He said: 'The shepherd does not want security for himself but for his flock.' His funeral, which was also a political demonstration, was attended by a quarter of a million people, most of them packed into the square outside the cathedral. A few of them were armed. My cameraman Bob Grevemberg and I were just inside the cathedral's railings. A smoke bomb went off. Then shots were fired from buildings overlooking the square. No one knows to this day who fired them. In the panic that followed between thirty and fifty people died, most of them crushed to death. I tried to haul a few people to safety and should have done more: but I also had a duty – or so I felt at the time – to get the story out. The camera had a BBC News sign on it. Someone cried out from the crowd: 'You are the world, you are the world, you have to tell what they are doing to our people.'

The dilemma recurred in Bosnia in April 1992. I had argued for intervention, yet to what extent was I willing to intervene myself? Perhaps not as much as I should have. I had started the day with skirmishes in Sarajevo, which would have been difficult to film without getting killed, then headed east to Zvornik in the Drina Valley. It was the beginning of ethnic cleansing. Twenty thousand Muslims were being driven from their homes by the Serbs. Their escape route was along mountain tracks to the relative safety of Tuzla. There was no one to help them – no aid workers, no UN agencies, no European Community monitors. When we stopped to talk to them they actually applauded us, for we were the only sign they had that anyone knew of their plight. We had the only set of wheels. Could we not at least have taken some of the mothers and babies to safety? Again, we got on with the job.

Twenty years later I received a message from a young man in Canada. He had himself been on that trail of tears, as an infant in a green blanket being carried by his uncle. The uncle was later killed by the Serbs. He was grateful for the video, which was the only record he had of his escape and what had happened to his family. Sometimes bearing witness seemed a waste of breath. At other times it seemed worthwhile. This was one of the worthwhile times. Though my camerawoman Katharina Geissler and

I felt isolated and adrift (the soundman was petrified with fear), the thought occurred to me: if not us, who? And if not now, when? And should we not have done more?

There is a distinction to be drawn between fairness and neutrality. Fairness is the bedrock of good journalism. From South Africa to Belfast to Bosnia I even practised 'positive fairness'. I went out of my way to pay attention, and give airtime, to the supposed 'black hats' – the Afrikaners, the Protestant paramilitaries and the Bosnian Serbs. They alone could hold the keys to solutions, which in every case they did. My contacts included John McKeague of the Ulster Defence Association and Jovan Zametica, a Cambridge academic who was policy adviser to the Bosnian Serbs and provided an insight into their paranoia. Zametica was an Anglo-Serb and a keen yachtsman, so I brought copies of *Yachting Today* to him in Pale, the capital of the Bosnian Serb mini-state, which was unfortunately land-locked. We even helped the Bosnian Serbs' adversarial press office, with supplies of stationery. War reporting needs access; and the trading of favours is an essential part of bargaining for it.

But neutrality? Neutrality is a snare and a delusion. It makes no judgements. It stands aside at an equal distance between good and evil. Take the example of child soldiers, one of the scourges of sub-Saharan Africa. Do we argue neutrally that the warlords who recruit them have the right to defend their territory by training their future soldiers, however unfortunate it is that the future soldiers are just children? Should we be even-handed towards Joseph Kony of the Lord's Resistance Army, the world's most wanted man? Of course not. The enlistment of the young is a war crime. In the Democratic Republic of Congo I visited a centre in Goma run by UNICEF, the United Nations Children's

Fund, for the demobilisation and retraining of child soldiers. One of them admitted he had been excited by the experience. As a twelve-year-old he had killed a man. The Kalashnikov had empowered him. He expressed no regrets; but when the war was over he wished to become a mechanic. Yet all too often in the failed states of Africa the child soldiers, once demobilised, have re-enlisted in order to save their lives. The armed groups become their family and protection.

The first child soldiers I saw, in Angola in 1976, were hardly of an age to shoulder arms. They were in uniform and being drilled by men of the Angolan Army, whose war against the UNITA rebels in the south east had begun with the Portuguese revolution and seemed likely to be long-lasting. My report was long on close-ups and short on verbs: 'Little feet . . . Big boots . . . Big ambitions'. I reflected that the way the war was going they were likely eventually to have to fight in it. Many must have done so. It lasted for another twenty-six years, until the UNITA leader Jonas Savimbi was ambushed and killed in 2002 on the bank of the Luvuei River. He died as he had lived, with a gun in his hand.

7. THE VIOLENT SCREEN

There was censorship in broadcasting long before there was television. One of the most celebrated broadcasts in the entire BBC archive was Richard Dimbleby's report on the liberation of Bergen-Belsen concentration camp by British troops on 15 April 1945.

> Here over an acre of ground lay dead and dying people. You could not see which was which . . . The living lay with their heads against the corpses and around them moved the awful, ghostly procession of emaciated, aimless people, with nothing to do and no hope of life, unable to move out of your way, unable to look at the terrible sights around them . . . Babies had been born here, tiny wizened things that could not live . . . A mother, driven mad, screamed at a British soldier to give her milk for her child, and thrust the tiny mite into his arms, then ran off, crying terribly. He opened the bundle and found the baby had been dead for days. This day at Belsen was the most horrible of my life.

The BBC's initial reaction to Dimbleby's report was to suppress it. It was finally broadcast four days later, on 19 April, after he threatened to resign if it was not. Why the censorship? Surely in part because neither the BBC's editors nor its audiences were ready for such a graphic account. It is natural to shrink from scenes of horror and extreme violence, and nothing like this had ever been broadcast before. Also it was personalised – 'This day at Belsen was the most horrible of my life' – and the BBC's 'news observers' had been ordered to stay in the background.

Even as broadcast the report appeared to have been self-censored. It made little mention of the Jews, who comprised the great majority of the victims of Belsen. Richard Dimbleby's son Jonathan explained: 'It was, I think, because the BBC wanted more sources to support what had happened to the Jews, and worried that if you mentioned one group of people and not others, it might seem biased and wrong.' The BBC retains an inbuilt capacity for doubting its own reporters.

When the war was over and television began, different rules applied to news and documentaries. Scenes from the concentration camps were broadcast uncensored in historical programmes, while scenes of other and later genocides – in Rwanda, Bosnia and elsewhere – were heavily censored to protect the audience from too close a knowledge of them. The past is easier to look at than the present, perhaps because we are not responsible for it.

The first television war is generally taken to have been the Vietnam War, since it was the coverage on the American networks that – in the widely accepted analysis – brought down an administration and changed a policy. But for British viewers it was probably the Nigerian War, which started in July 1967 and ended in January 1970. Nigeria's eastern region, under its military governor Colonel Odumegwu Ojukwu, was seeking to secede from the Federation and establish itself as the independent state of Biafra. Four African countries recognised it but most did not, since the old colonial boundaries were thought to be inviolable and many countries faced similar secessionist threats. The war was fought at the height of the American involvement in Vietnam. But Britain was not militarily involved in Vietnam, despite the persuasions of President Lyndon Johnson: all he wanted, he said, was a token force – a battalion of the Black Watch would be enough. But we were involved, and deeply involved, in Biafra. Despite official denials at the time, we supplied half the heavy weaponry – armoured vehicles, artillery and ammunition – that were the engines of a Federal Nigerian victory. The British also provided aircraft and pilots: the presence of the aircraft was acknowledged but the presence of the pilots was not. I knew about the pilots because I met them on distant airfields. Sometimes in the war zones you settle into the cast of mind that nothing is believable until it is officially denied. The only truth is a lie.

The Nigerian War was extremely difficult to cover, especially on the Federal side, where the denial of access was almost total. We even held a 'press demonstration' one day outside the VIP lounge at Lagos Airport to try to open things up. President Gowon, who had a war to win, quite understandably ignored us. On my first visit to Nigeria in June 1966 I was arrested and deported almost immediately. The conditions were not severe. My 'prison' was the VIP lounge at Kano Airport. (My expenses claim for the ordeal included 'hospitality to armed guards'.) My offence had been to try to report the tribal massacres in northern Nigeria that led to the war in the east. At least 60,000 Ibos (easterners) were killed – I cautiously estimated 1,500 in Kano, 670 in Zaria and the rest across the northern states or in ambushes on the road to Biafra. I did not have time to find out more before the police were on to me. I was lucky. The authorities were so incompetent that they deported me not to another country but to Lagos, which was then the capital. From there I was able to drive to Enugu and interview Ojukwu. He described the killings as 'wanton fratricide' and an attempt to cleanse people of eastern origin from the face of the earth. There were no plans for secession, he told me, and he was doing everything possible to ensure that Nigeria stayed as one.

It did not. The war began ten months later. The TV reports, especially by Alan Hart and Michael Nicholson of ITN, had a seismic impact at home. Biafra then was a bigger story in the United Kingdom than Vietnam. The reports showed babies and children starving to death as a result of Nigeria's economic blockade of secessionist Biafra. They resulted in headlines like 'Land of No Hope' and 'Save Us'. British ministers were denounced in the Commons as baby-killers. MPs rose up in revolt across party lines. The blockade was enforced not only by British-supplied ground troops but by aircraft flown by British and South African mercenaries. These included a DC-3 piloted by a character known to us as 'Boozy Bonzo Bond', who breakfasted on a diet of neat gin and flew by instinct. His aircraft was pressed into service as a warplane: bombs were thrown by hand out of its portside rear door. Hart received a message from his editor: 'Brilliant report – but please control your emotions!' Controlling our emotions was part of the newsreel tradition. The outcome was often a mismatch between style and substance.

So what of the BBC? The BBC, I regret to say, lacked spine and succumbed to government pressure in a way that we thought to be lamentable then and would be unthinkable now. Its man in Biafra, Frederick Forsyth, was disgracefully withdrawn from the conflict on the urging of the British High Commissioner in Lagos, Sir David Hunt. He wasn't exactly marched into a hollow square and court-martialled, but summoned before the editor and reduced in rank from assistant diplomatic correspondent to that of a mere general reporter, like me. We could not pick and choose our assignments in those days, but covered whatever came up on the daily rota. Before we found ourselves on opposite sides in an African war we were once on opposite sides of a train crash in Kentish Town.

Freddie bravely resigned from the BBC. He had never been to Africa before and never reported a war; but, untrained as he was in soldiering, he returned to the conflict to fight for the Biafrans. For his books *The Day of the Jackal* and *The Dogs of War* he drew on his own experiences and the reminiscences of French and Belgian mercenaries alongside him.

We slowly became aware that whether we liked it or not – and our editors did not – we were working in a medium that did not operate in a vacuum, but could have an impact on the events it was reporting and had at least the potential to influence government policy. It was not the intention, but it could be the effect. We were not only onlookers: we were *players*. There were times when the terms for an agreement for the exchange of prisoners would include the presence of a television camera at both the signing and the exchange, so both sides would be seen to deliver on what they had promised. We could surely do more than stand back indifferently and supply snapshots and sound-bites. The executives of both ITN and the BBC began to think seriously about the portrayals of real world and real time violence: what should they show and what should they censor? This applied not only to the images of the starving, but also to a controversial report of the execution by firing squad of a captured Biafran soldier accused of looting. At the critical moment the BBC cameraman raised his hand and asked for delay while he changed his battery. The man was shot, as was the news film, but the incident raised some troubling ethical and editorial questions. The BBC handed them off to its Advisory Group on the Social Effects of Television, set up in response to the vociferous campaign of Mrs Mary Whitehouse against the levels of sex and violence on fictional television.

In March 1972, under the imprimatur of David Attenborough, BBC television's Director of Programmes, the Advisory Group published its *Note of Guidance* on the portrayal of violence in television programmes; it was a classic display of BBC even-handedness.

The viewer is not necessarily helped to understand the realities of government in particular countries by bloody pictures of public executions. All such pictures may achieve is the provision of a spectacle not available in this country. Nevertheless there may be occasions when the scenes of executions do help to make a genuine point which contributes to the viewer's understanding of events. Scenes of the execution of a looter in Nigeria were revealing a state of affairs in that country during the secession of Biafra and on those grounds could be justified.

The dilemmas were similar to those caused today by the televised executions by ISIS of its bowed and shackled captives – with the added element that these events are manifestly staged for propaganda purposes and well-nigh impossible to broadcast.

In the 1960s the debate was moving on from issues of violence and good taste to issues of violence and civil disorder. Were we part of the problem? By showing scenes of rioting did we actually promote and incite it? The argument began with the unrest in Northern Ireland in late 1968 and continued, in different forms, until the Good Friday Agreement. I found myself in the front line of it, and was not a popular figure with either the rioters or the editors.

Some hard-line and ill-intentioned Protestants in Dungannon sent me a message through a third party that they had every intention of sending me home in a box. Trying to report a civil rights meeting in Limavady, County Londonderry, I had to flee for my safety out of a lavatory window in the town hall and hoof it across the fields. In the middle of a riot in the Newtownards Road in east Belfast an elderly lady set upon me with her umbrella and accused me of filming something that wasn't happening. And at a prayer meeting in the centre of Armagh my old antagonist Dr Ian Paisley announced: 'There is one man in this square today who is no friend of the Protestant and Loyalist people of Ulster. That man is Martin Bell of the BBC, or the PBC as I call it – the Papist Broadcasting Corporation.' He urged his followers to do me no harm, but then he turned, pointed slowly and said: 'He's standing over there in a sheepskin jacket.' After they had roughed me up a bit he concluded: 'Now, brethren, let us bow our heads in silent prayer for deliverance from our foes.' I played a part in making him famous, by interviewing him outside jails and court-houses when he was charged with unlawful assembly, yet he saw me as one of his foes. Paisley told the

Radio Times: 'I haven't a good word to say for the BBC. I don't know at what level the twisting is done. All I know is that the coverage is twisted.'[1]

I made up some ground rules: to patrol the streets at all hours, never to report about myself, never to retaliate when physically abused, always to face the front in a riot, to listen and to learn, to seek out the ringleaders, to believe what I saw more than what I was told, and sometimes to keep a distance from the camera crew so that my personal unpopularity should not rub off on them.

If a bomb blew up a pub in west Belfast, was it a Protestant outrage against Catholic lives and property? Or was it a bomb factory where the bomb-makers had blown themselves up? Each side would believe what it wanted to believe, and expect the BBC to reflect its point of view. Any failure to do so would be an indication of bias. 'Tell the truth' was the slogan shouted at us by both sides. It was always the BBC, as the national broadcaster, that attracted the hostility. ITN ran similar reports with nothing like the same degree of grief and harassment.

An enraged householder in Belfast wrote to us, at the end of an especially shattering week, to ask why an explosion in *her* street had not been shown on the news: had the BBC grown callous and unfeeling, or was it conspiring to pretend that all was well?

On one occasion at nine o'clock at night I dashed with a camera crew to the scene of a pub bomb in Belfast. The pub was empty except for the wreckage. The only sign of life was a TV set still flickering in a corner of the bar. It was showing my own report on the day's mayhem and carnage on the BBC's *Nine O'Clock News*. Even then we were not mere bystanders, candleholders shedding light on dark places, but part of the scene we were reporting on, and sometimes ourselves adrift in the encompassing darkness. One of the slogans of the time was 'Buy now while shops last'.

The pressures from the editors were of a different order. In fact they were more than pressures: they were orders. In August 1969 I was preparing a report on the Catholics who had been burned out of their homes off the Falls Road the night before. The images were of desperate people salvaging what they could from the charred ruins. I felt a lurking presence in the edit room behind me. It was that of Waldo Maguire, the BBC's Viceroy (Controller) in Northern Ireland and before that the Editor of TV News, so I knew him well.

'You can't call them Catholics,' he said.

'Why can't I call them Catholics?' I answered. 'They *are* Catholics and everyone knows they are Catholics. Look, Waldo, there's a woman wheeling her things away in a pram with a crucifix on top. She's not a Protestant, is she?'

He stood his ground. 'They can't be Catholics. They will have to be *refugees*.'

He seemed more interested in keeping the peace than in reporting the news. He believed that the BBC had to be ultra-cautious and not say or show anything that might provoke further disorder and reprisals by one community against the other. It was long before the advent of the rolling news channels, which would have made him even more nervous than he was: a satellite news truck would have been a tempting prize to add to the barricades of burning buses. The Controller was quite wrong, of course, but unpersuadable. I had a deadline to meet and no time to argue with him. So the victims became refugees. We

were withholding the truth; the public *knew* we were withholding the truth, because so many of them were out on the streets
and witnesses of it; and all we achieved was to undermine trust
in us as the national broadcaster. The damage was unnecessary
and self-inflicted. In a career with many ups and downs it was
one of the low points. I was thirty at the time, too insecure and
too ambitious to make an issue of it. When I first met him at
Alexandra Palace Waldo Maguire had let me know that there
were four hundred applicants for every post as a BBC news
reporter: it was his way of reminding me that I was by no means
indispensable. Nor did he hold us 'visiting firemen' in very high
regard: he thought that we just did not know enough about the
Province we were reporting from.

In a column in the *Spectator* George Scott said of Mr Maguire:
'His attitude is bound to be that of a man who has to live in
Belfast, year in and year out, and work with Stormont. It is likely
to be that of a man who wishes to play things down.'[2] Gerry Fitt,
the MP for the dispossessed Catholics of the Falls Road, was
incensed by the under-reporting. He said: 'Things are not as bad
as they are shown to be by the press and the other media. They
are ten times *worse* than they are shown to be by the press and the
other media.' The loyalists would have preferred no coverage at
all. A letter in a Belfast newspaper complained: 'As for the BBC
the less said the better. To see Martin Bell interview the self-
styled refugees in the Republic, was that in the best interests of
North or South?' The Unionist MP for North Belfast, Mr
Stratton Mills, complained about my reporting to the BBC's
Director General. For whatever reason, our rivals at ITN never
attracted the same amount of incoming fire as we did. They were
both relieved and envious: relieved because they did not have to

cope with it, and envious because our coverage seemed to matter more.

I was so ultra-loyal to the BBC at the time that, to my discredit, I actually defended the censorship from which I was suffering. I wrote in the *Listener*, a BBC magazine: 'Of course, the Northern Ireland experience *has* wrought changes in broadcasting. It would be strange if it had not . . . There has indeed been a tightening of editorial control: that means in practice that editors edit, which one had always understood was what they were paid to do.'[3]

There is a world of difference between a national broadcaster and a state broadcaster. The national broadcaster speaks for the people. The state broadcaster speaks for the government. There were times in our coverage of the conflict in Northern Ireland when I felt that we were losing our footing between the two.

Merlyn Rees, the former Northern Ireland Secretary, said in a Commons debate: 'I must, however, make it clear that we are firmly against the often expressed populist view that we should pull out quickly and that we should let the two communities fight it out, and that we should watch the result on television.'[4]

As for even-handedness . . . to report the Gordon Highlanders' dawn raid on a nationalist housing estate in Armagh was to get on the wrong side of both the nationalists and the Gordon Highlanders in short order. The nationalists resented us, because we had evidently been tipped off in advance; and the Gordon Highlanders resented us because we then reported allegations of brutality against them, as the young men who had been stopped and searched stripped off their shirts and showed us their bruised backs. My ITN rival at the scene was Martyn Lewis, who later achieved a sort of notoriety by arguing that television should show more 'happy news'. Even he could find no happy news that morning in Armagh. But as usual it was not his report but mine that attracted the flak.

The dilemmas inherent in broadcasting real world violence became more acute as the technology of television advanced and scenes of bloodshed could be broadcast almost as soon as they happened; and, from 1970 onwards, in colour. The bloodshed changed overnight from black to red. The editing was done in the field, but the decision to run a report or to bin it was taken in London. After a while we learned to compromise, and to accommodate the nervousness of our news editors by including extra 'gash' footage and wide shots that could be added to the satellite feed and edited back into the story to replace the more graphic close-ups of our preferred version. An example was the massacre of more than a hundred Muslims in the village of Ahmici in central Bosnia in April 1993. Most of the scenes were too terrible to be shown, and I said so as I knelt in the ashes in one of the cellars of death. Nik Gowing of Channel Four News wrote later of the report, which had a political impact, that 'some called it insensitive'. That was the whole point of it. I was not trying to be sensitive. I was trying to be truthful. But I included just one close-up – of a burned, clenched fist – as a symbol of the rest. It passed the BBC's good taste censorship – only just, but it did. ITN's Paul Davies, working with the same pooled footage from his most gifted cameraman Nigel Thomson, suffered censorship more severe than mine. He was forced into a re-edit.

The BBC's guidelines, typically, managed to be both clear and ambiguous at the same time, depending on how they were interpreted and applied. 'The strongest images of violence should be used with care and need to be clearly editorially justified as necessary to the proper understanding of the story if they are to be acceptable to the audience . . . There are very few circumstances in which it is editorially justified to broadcast the moment of death.' We needed no lectures on the need to proceed with care and, even under the pressure of onrushing deadlines, we did so. But the note contained no guidance at all about what the circumstances were in which it might be justified to show the moment of death. Like the United Nations troops around us, we were left *undirected* in the field, and had to make up our mandate from day to day by trial and error.

Over the years the screw was progressively tightened and never loosened. The process began in the Balkans from 1991 to 1999 – Croatia, Bosnia and then Kosovo – which included massacres from Vukovar to Ahmici and from Srebrenica to Racak. Where the crime scenes were under the camera's eye, in Ahmici and Racak, there were some difficult decisions to be taken. From my vantage point in distant killing fields I sensed a collective shudder in the newsrooms and a progressive weakening of editorial spines. We in the war zones took the risks; our bosses back home played for safety.

I sometimes felt that it was easier to deal with the warlords than the bosses. I was face to face with the warlords, pleading for access at their headquarters, listening to their partisan versions of history and sharing a coffee and slivovitz. The bosses were 900 miles away and on an alien planet in Shepherd's Bush. I was arguing with them over a satellite telephone about footage that I had seen and they had not, and working to guidelines that, as time went by, became ever more unrealistic. When in doubt they would usually aim off for safety, and cut and slash, by a margin that I calculated as at least twenty per cent. It was a prudent move for them career-wise, but it left the truth essentially untold. And we were risking more than our careers.

'Reporters are hope,' said Joseph Pulitzer, 'editors are disappointment.'

In February 1993, in a long-form documentary from Bosnia, I was permitted to show the burial in a mass grave of sixty Serbs massacred by Muslims in a village near Bratunac. The pre-burial scenes were of a Belsen-like quality of horror. No less troubling was an interview, shot in the shadows, about the rape of a six-year-old girl. When the piece was broadcast, Simon Jenkins in *The Times* accused me of indulging in 'the pornography of violence and the pornography of grief in full flood . . . Mr Bell showed both Serb and Muslim atrocities. He showed what he saw and he saw a lot. But he was biased. He wanted to blot out thought . . . His was a bias against understanding.'

My answer to this was that it was necessary to show and hear these images and words, to get people's attention and literally bring home to them the nature of the war, still then in its first year. The true charge against us was not that we did not show too much but that for a number of reasons – personal safety and nervousness being two of them – we did not show enough and were guilty of understatement. As William Howard Russell asked, in a letter to his editor from the Crimea in 1854, 'Am I to tell these things, or hold my tongue?'

Only twelve months after the 1993 broadcast, with the side war between Croats and Muslims at its fiercest, even a limited degree of truth-telling was no longer possible. It was screw-tightening time, and the screwdriver was in the white-knuckled grip of the news editors in London. In January 1994 a British aid driver, Paul Goodall, was murdered by the Mujahedin on a river bank near Zenica. I kept a note of my conversation with the foreign duty editor.

'You're not including any' – she paused as if shocked – '*bodies*, are you?'

'No,' I said, 'the body has been moved.'

'Nothing that will upset people?'

And then she said: 'Is there *blood*? We don't want to see any blood, at least before the 9 p.m. watershed. It's in the guidelines, you know.'

Actually, I didn't know and didn't care – and of course there was blood. When people are shot they bleed. The images from the scene of the murder included close-ups of bloodstains on the snow. We were not allowed to show even those. The good taste censorship was total. The story of Paul Goodall's death was told only in words and wide shots. It should have been done more truthfully.

Then, from a village near Vitez, our redoubtable Croatian cameraman Kresomir brought back footage of a front-line position that had been overrun by Muslims in the early morning mist. The Croats were first tied up with wire and then killed. The position was later retaken. We had images of the victims, which we were not allowed to show. Then, as the word spread through the village, we had images of their grieving wives and mothers and children, which we were not allowed to show either. Too upsetting, we were told. This was a war in which even the grief was off-limits. My protests were, as usual, a waste of breath.

As to the ban on showing the moment of death, there were ways of getting round it. One day in mid-winter Kresomir accompanied an HVO (Bosnian Croat) patrol near no man's land. A single shot was fired and one of the white-camouflaged soldiers fell to the snow. The sniper's bullet killed him. I included the sequence in my report, without drawing attention to what had happened. The BBC turned it around and transmitted it before they realised what it was. It did not increase my popularity in head office but it made a necessary point. Kresomir's life was saved by the flak jacket that I had lent him the day before. A bullet hit him in the lower chest and knocked him over. He was bruised but otherwise unhurt. Adam Holloway of ITN (now Conservative MP for Gravesham) tried to poach him, but he remained loyal and was a vital member of the team. Later I visited the Ghanaians who made his body armour at a factory in the Old Kent Road and thanked them for saving his life.

While the war was still in progress, in September 1995, I even sent a memo to the BBC urging it to be less restrictive in what we could show. It was a memo between hard covers and disguised as a book, called *In Harm's Way* (for obvious reasons). Its key chapter, 'War is a Bad Taste Business', set out the argument for a more truthful portrayal of the realities around us. The readers liked it. The reviewers liked it. Even the Crown Prince of Yugoslavia liked it. But the BBC was so unmoved by it that it made no difference at all and the accursed guidelines were interpreted ever more restrictively.

They actually stifled truth and promoted falsehood. Serbian nationalists had long maintained that the Muslim victims of the Srebrenica massacre in July 1995 had been battlefield casualties killed in action. Then during the trial of Slobodan Milosevic in The Hague in 2005, the prosecution showed video of a Serbian paramilitary unit, the Scorpions, executing prisoners by the side of the road in the village of Trnovo in central Bosnia, and laughing and joking as they did so. No network dared to broadcast it except for B92, a niche opposition station in Belgrade. The mainstream media backed off, and the Srebrenica deniers remained in denial.

As time went by the screw was tightened still further. In August 1996 there was an upsurge in the always latent violence between Greeks and Turks in Cyprus; I returned to the island in which I had first served as a soldier. The flashpoint was outside the abandoned city of Famagusta. A crowd of Greeks laid siege to a flagpole. One of them climbed up it to tear down the Turkish flag. He was shot by the Turks as he did so. The footage of the incident showed a man climbing up a flagpole and then falling down it. That was all. We were not allowed to show it, because it breached the moment-of-death rule. Less than a year later I left journalism for politics with some relief, having lost too many arguments. I thought, at least in Parliament my vote might count for something.

The moment-of-death rule was broken anyway on 9/11, when the networks were broadcasting live as the second aircraft flew into the Twin Towers in New York. It seemed that acts of mass murder could be shown but the deaths of individuals could not.

It takes no courage to censor. No one will know except the correspondent whose report has been shredded. He and his team have risked their lives for nothing and no one else will give a damn. It takes courage *not to censor*, to look reality in the face unflinchingly and to show things as they are. It seems to me retrospectively that such courage has been conspicuously lacking in the half-light of TV news.

Should we really be expected, in the most powerful news medium ever devised, to look away and not to show what we see? Should it really be one of our principles *not to upset people*?

And what is the justification for a disengaged journalism that requires its practitioners to close their hearts to pity? Now there is a phrase with resonance. There was once a national leader who urged his generals to close their hearts to pity, as his armoured divisions rolled across the border on a fraudulent pretext into a neighbouring state. His name was Adolf Hitler.

If this is what we want from our window on the world, that it should also be our filter, then we are in for some nasty surprises from 'black swan' events, catastrophic and unforeseen, like 9/11. There is no need to be unflinching, because there is nothing left to flinch from; no need to be compassionate, because there is nothing left to care about. What remains? Neither violence nor bloodshed nor suffering, not even the mourners who have lost their loved ones, but only a passing show, an acceptable spectacle. Warfare is shocking by nature, but most shocking of all is when, because of these media manipulations, we are so anaesthetised that it no longer jolts and shocks us.

Consider what good taste censorship actually does: it does not just sanitise the nature of warfare, but *falsifies* it. We see the parachute flares lighting up the ruins. We see the supposedly heroic images of soldiers blazing away with their Kalashnikovs, and the outgoing artillery and mortar fire. We see little of what happens at the other end – the pain and grief, the ballistic injuries and the terrible waste of young lives. Warfare as depicted on television resembles an arcade game and is no longer even *upsetting*. It thus becomes, to politicians innocent of it, a policy option and an acceptable way of settling differences. Within ten years of the Bosnian War it did indeed become a policy option, in Iraq in 2003, to tragic effect both short-term and long-term. Journalism was not the cause of the war, despite the cheerleading of the press, but the structural falsehoods of TV news made it easier to resort to.

By that time I had been in the House of Commons and out of it. But I was unable to forget what I saw as the episodes of journalistic *wrong-doing* that I had lived through for much of those thirty years. In 2005 I wrote the introduction to the second edition of *Ballistic Trauma*, a medical handbook for surgeons and their assistants, informed by the realities of war.

> Professionals in the field of ballistic trauma will learn much from each other in this new edition. A more general conclusion they will draw, I hope, is that the present epidemic of global violence is not an acceptable outcome of continuing failures in politics and diplomacy . . . Those who deal with the effects of ballistic trauma surely have the least reason to be indifferent to its causes.
>
> There are certain ways of expressing this in plain English, admittedly nonmedical and nonspecialist. One is religious: that we are all members one of another. The other is political: that politics is too important to be left to the politicians.[5]

Not only are there no atheists in foxholes, there are no news executives either. They do their business and work their shifts, then take the train to Potters Bar and sleep safely in their beds. Across the seventy years of broadcast news, from Belsen to Belfast and from Bosnia to Basra, their instinct has been to protect themselves, to put expediency before principle, to duck for cover, to play for safety and to blunt the edge of truth. They could have done otherwise but chose not to. The choice was always theirs. It still remains so.

8. NEVER WRONG FOR LONG

Unlike influenza, the rolling TV news channels have not always been with us but, like influenza, they will be with us for the foreseeable future and beyond. They are frenzied, excitable, speculative, prone to error and never wrong for long. If they make a mistake, they tend not to correct it but to supplant it with something else, whose truth or falsehood hardly seems to matter. Their fundamental flaw is that they show more than they know.

The constant availability of rolling news is both its strength and its weakness. Its strength, because it is always there when you want it (*if* you want it): just turn on the tap and it gushes out, like water. Its weakness, because it sets up pressures for instant wisdom when the images are available but the facts are not. Even in the age of the internet we need time to find things out and make sense of them. One of my last assignments for the BBC was to report the crash of a TWA aircraft in Long Island in 1996. In the live interview with the newsreader that followed the report, I was of course asked the likely cause. I could have speculated wildly about an accidental missile strike from a nearby Naval Air Station, which would have been plausible enough and easy to do, but NBC's Pentagon correspondent had advised me against it; so I simply said: 'I don't know – and no one else does either.' Through the talk-back I heard a news producer mutter: 'That wasn't really worth it, was it?' (The actual cause was a spark in an empty fuel tank.) For their blend of hype and hysteria and general *unknowingness*, the rolling news channels are Gadarene television, rushing to judgement. But they have to pretend to knowledge. 'I haven't a clue' is a phrase you will never hear uttered in front of their flashing crimson video-walls.

The news channels are especially feverish in their reporting of terrorist attacks on either side of the Atlantic, whether in Boston, Paris, Berlin, Nice or Brussels. They will announce that an arrest has been made, and identify the suspect. Then they will acknowledge the mistake and the identification. It was not that suspect, it was another. Or there may have been no arrest at all. The news satirist Jon Stewart parodied CNN's coverage of the Boston Marathon bombing in 2013: 'Say it first and have Anderson Cooper [a CNN superstar] correct it later.' The network was hit where it hurt, in its self-esteem.

The news channels can be equally erratic in their reporting of elections. The need to be first with the figures overwhelms the need to get them right. So winners lose and losers win on the basis of exit polls and early estimates. This puts me in mind of the Labour MP Bob Marshall-Andrews, who blamed Tony Blair and the war in Iraq for his predicted defeat in his Medway constituency in 2005, only to discover that he had won by just 213 votes, and must therefore withdraw his concession. There was also a BBC correspondent who once miscalled an Israeli election

on the basis of a misleading exit poll. He suffered no ill consequences either, for was he not first with the news?

This is of course an extreme and hostile view from someone
who liked to reflect before he reported. It is only fair to note that
some of the 24/7 practitioners, like Tim Marshall, Alex Crawford
and Adam Boulton of Sky News, are remarkably adept at
making sense of the footage that cascades into them for twenty-four hours a day from satellite trucks and dishes at home and
abroad. Christiane Amanpour of CNN is experienced, brave
and brilliant. With others, you get the sense that the less they
know about something the more convincing they are. My own
daughter Melissa, who worked bilingually for the French news
channel France 24, once fronted a persuasive programme about
the politics of French football: to my certain knowledge, she
knew nothing about football at all.

The prime mover of it all was a medium-scale mogul from
Atlanta, Ted Turner. In 1980 he started the Cable News
Network – CNN, the world's first all-news channel. The established networks derided it as Chicken Noodle News and tried to
exclude it from the White House pooling arrangements, through
which one network's coverage of the President was shared with
the others. They failed and the infant network prospered and
overtook them in the breaking news business. In next to no time
the CNN screen in the corner of the room was part of the furni-
ture of congressional and White House offices. Occasionally they
even turned the sound up. And inevitably it had its successes. By
the time of the launch of the space shuttle *Challenger* from Cape
Canaveral in 1986, shuttle launches had become so routine that
CNN's competitors were no longer broadcasting them live.
CNN was – so when the shuttle exploded on lift-off it had the

story initially to itself. In the first Gulf War, when the air war started in January 1991 with missile attacks on Baghdad, CNN landed another scoop. It was the only network with the capacity to broadcast live from the city. The coverage was long on bangs and flashes and short on information, as is the way with rolling news, but it went round the world to CNN's advantage. It was widely viewed in the Middle East, as the terrestrial networks were not. CNN reporters found that doors were open to them that were closed to others. Soon enough the upstart channel was advertising itself as the 'world news leader'. Christiane Amanpour, who was both a friend and a rival, became a global celebrity.

In the United Kingdom Sky News followed CNN's lead in 1989, challenging the news duopoly of the BBC and ITN. It was an expensive building block, free-to-air in Sky's growing empire of networks. It gave them credibility and its instigator, Rupert Murdoch, kept it as a loss leader for reasons of politics and prestige. As, like its British rivals, it was legally bound to be fair and balanced, he was also reputed to have described it as 'BBC lite'. (His Fox News in the USA operated under no such constraints, and became the megaphone of the American right.) Sky's audiences were modest, no more than sixty thousand initially, which in ratings terms was at the low end of the measurable. But Sky News forced the terrestrial news services, over time, to sharpen their competitive edge. It recruited some excellent journalists. One of these was Aernout van Lynden, a former Dutch marine, who stood his ground in Bosnia when others had fled, and with whom I once shared a ditch while we both had Kalashnikovs pointed at us by the Serbs. Another was the former BBC reporter Michael Sullivan, who had fallen out with the BBC management so badly that he threatened to fly a light aircraft, kamikaze style, into the sixth floor offices of the Television Centre in White City to get his revenge. He found a safer haven at Sky, where he became the network's in-house pedant and language policeman. They needed him. It is a sobering thought that there are students in Poland trying to improve their English by watching the broadcasts of Sky News.

The BBC was slow in responding to Sky's challenge. Its rolling news channel, launched in November 1997 and initially called News 24, was by no means its finest achievement. It managed to be under-resourced and yet at the same time to undermine the BBC's mainstream news programmes by drawing resources away from them. From this point on it was necessary for BBC News, even on a story of medium importance, to deploy two news teams instead of one. The first was to go out and gather the news of the day and report it in the old-fashioned way. The second was to be tethered to the dish and available to respond to questions from the London studio and to fill the airtime for twenty-four hours a day with commentary and speculation. The unfortunate reporters assigned to this task were known as 'dish monkeys'. Jacky Rowland, one of the best of them, described herself as a 'dish bitch'. It was not a job for journalists, but journalists had to do it.

The trick was in *appearing* to be where the news was. In 2001, as the Taliban were being ousted by the Northern Alliance, there was a little corner of Afghanistan across the border from Tajikistan controlled by an enterprising warlord. For a considerable fee, he allowed the networks across the river to broadcast live from a patch of territory that was technically within the borders of Afghanistan, although nothing was actually happening there – and there was no means, except through the internet, of finding out what might be going on elsewhere. On the rolling news planet that was what mattered. The technology made it possible, and it worked both to the advantage of the warlord and of the dish monkey.

As far back as November 1994 I wrote a note to myself: 'I am broadcasting from a field in central Bosnia, with a dish which not only transmits but receives. So video from all over the Balkans flows into it. The danger is to stay rooted to one's communications, packaging not reporting. It is a medium that rewards the glib and the plausible.' A TV news report is known in the business as a 'package'. It is a parcel of images tied up with words, and ideally without loose ends. The sign-off sets the seal on it.

The audience for news-on-demand was seldom more than the readership of a local weekly and the BBC News Channel had a hard time establishing itself. After five years of drift Richard Lambert, the former editor of the *Financial Times*, was commissioned to write a report about it. He was broadly supportive but identified areas that clearly needed improvement. The result was a rebranding, an increased emphasis on 'breaking news' and a closer integration with the mainstream news programmes, which were themselves suffering from dwindling audiences. In 2016, amid much cost-cutting, the News Channel narrowly avoided being merged with BBC World.

The entry into the field of ITV News, formerly ITN, was even less auspicious. Its news channel was launched in August 2000, relaunched in February 2004 and closed in December 2005. The cause of its demise was its numbers: it seldom attracted an audience large enough to make it worth the effort. (This can also happen to terrestrial television. Our original audience for

Newsroom on BBC Two in 1966 was so small that we reckoned it could have fitted into a double-decker bus: it might even have been cheaper to drive the audience to the programme than broadcast the programme to the audience.)

The frenzy of rolling news has had the effect of accelerating the response of governments in the western democracies to the events that are being reported. This is the so-called 'CNN effect'. If it identifies a policy vacuum, the government must fill it with a credible response – not within days but within hours of the first report. 24/7 news is a hungry animal, a beast that has to be fed. James Baker, who was White House Chief of Staff when the rolling news phenomenon began, said of the CNN effect: 'The one thing it does, is to drive policy makers to have a policy position. I would have to articulate it very quickly. You are in real-time mode. You don't have time to reflect.'[1] Television does not make decisions, but it makes the weather in which decisions are made. And rushed decisions can also be mistaken ones. The 24/7 news cycle changes the running order: it tends to give priority to the immediate and trivial over the long-term and important. James Baker observed: 'In Iraq, Bosnia, Somalia, Rwanda, and Chechnya, among others, real-time coverage of conflict by the electronic media served to create *a powerful new imperative for prompt action* that was not present in less frenetic [times].'[2]

An American colleague, back in the presidency of George Bush Senior, recalled that his Chief of Staff, a man of meticulous punctuality, was half an hour late for an appointment with her at the White House. CNN had just aired some vivid footage from Kurdistan, and the Administration was reconsidering its position on the Kurds.

At the height of the Bosnian War Lord Carrington was asked about the CNN effect – in this case the BBC effect – and whether the government's policy had been blown off course by the TV coverage. He replied drily that the question assumed there was a course to be blown off. Brigadier Richard Dannatt (later to be Chief of the General Staff) described it as 'well-intentioned fence-sitting'. British UN commanders on the ground, deployed without briefings on an inadequate mandate, were having to reinterpret it as they went along. One of them in desperation came up with the theory of an *implied mandate*: it was not what the UN said but what it meant that authorised him to be more proactive in the defence of the people he was obliged to protect.

Kofi Annan, who at that time was the UN's Head of Peacekeeping, concluded that where governments had a clear policy television had little effect; but where they did not they had to develop one in short order or risk a disaster in terms of public relations. Hand-wringing over the tragedy unfolding in Bosnia was not a substitute for a policy. We did not set out every morning in Miss Piggy, our indomitable armoured Land Rover, saying to each other, 'Let's seek out some really harrowing pictures of suffering Bosnians to give the Foreign Office a bit of grief and stir the viewers' consciences.' It did not work like that. We simply made a record of what was happening around us – the plight of particular people in particular places. And if the government subsequently took actions that without the TV images it would not have taken, I could see no reason to apologise.

The most often cited example of the CNN effect was the ill-fated American intervention in Somalia between December 1992 and March 1994. The images that got the Americans in were those of Somalis dying in a famine. The images that got them out were of dead Americans, including the body of a Special Forces crewman being dragged through the streets of Mogadishu by gunmen loyal to a warlord, General Aideed. President Clinton then announced the phased withdrawal of US troops. Somalia has been ungoverned ever since.

In 1994, when the tragedies of Bosnia and Rwanda were in full spate, Nik Gowing took time out from being diplomatic editor of Channel Four News to research the CNN effect at the John F. Kennedy School of Government in Harvard. His paper was called 'Real Time Television Coverage of Armed Conflicts and Diplomatic Crises: Does it Pressure or Distort Foreign Policy Decisions?' He concluded that the effect of the 24/7 news cycle was to encourage the making of gestures and taking of half-measures.

> Television coverage in 1991 did not force western governments to adopt policies aimed at preventing armed conflict in the former Yugoslavia which Western intelligence agencies had warned was inevitable. First in Croatia, then in Bosnia in 1992, television encouraged only limited crisis management at the lowest common denominator of agreement by governments who had no decisive political will to pre-empt war . . . Governments worked to apply diplomatic bandages while the warring parties deceived them.

The London Conference on Bosnia in August 1992 was a classic of its kind. It featured ringing declarations, the setting up of working parties and the substitution of words for the actions that could have been taken even then, and were actually taken three years and tens of thousands of lost lives later.

The extreme extension of *showing without knowing* was the live streaming of television images from the changing edge of a war zone. This was initiated by a Kurdish news agency during the Iraqi and Kurdish assault on Mosul in October and November 2016. The K24 live feed was broadcast unmediated by Al Jazeera and Britain's Channel Four News, and widely 'folded in' by CNN and other channels. The images were mostly of distant shell-bursts and plumes of smoke on the city's eastern approaches. All that was lacking was actual *information*. For the first time ever the fog of war was accessible worldwide and at the touch of a button.

To be influential is one thing; to be accurate is another. I can only conclude that the readers of the London *Times* were better informed about the Crimean War than we are today about the wars of the world, reported at a distance in the 24/7 news cycle by the shrill and frenzied purveyors of rolling news. William Howard Russell was an eyewitness. The news channels are distorting mirrors and echo chambers.

As Edward R. Murrow observed, you cannot make good news out of bad practice.

9. THE AGE OF THE EMBED

We were gathered in an army tent in the Saudi Arabian desert, close to the border with Iraqi-occupied Kuwait. The date was 24 February 1991. We were the first 'embeds', reporters and photographers attached to the British 1ˢᵗ Armoured Division: six with 7ᵗʰ Armoured Brigade, six with 4ᵗʰ Armoured Brigade and four at Divisional Headquarters. Colonel John King, head of the MRT (Media Response Team), was setting out the ground rules. We had traded freedom for access. We were as much under military command as if we were soldiers – unarmed, of course, and with nothing to shoot back with but cameras.

Rule One. There would be no 'nuts and bolts', names of units or inventories of equipment, except that we were allowed to name companies and battalions within a formal battlegroup. We could also identify the British 1ˢᵗ Armoured Division (there was only one, after all).

Rule Two. US troops alongside us, Army and Marines, could be identified only as 'an American forces formation'.

Rule Three. Locations could be identified only as 'in Iraqi-held territory'. (This struck us as odd: we could not be in the territory if the Iraqis still held it.)

Rule Four. Prisoners of War: under Article 13 of the 1929 Geneva Convention, concerning the protection of prisoners of war, there would be no close-ups of Iraqi prisoners or interviews with them. There was even a section in the Convention on the courtesies of war: 'All POWs will salute the camp commandant. Soldiers will salute officers of the detaining power. Officers will salute officers of the detaining power.' Fortunately we 'embeds' would not be required to salute anyone, unless of course we were captured by the Iraqis, to whom we would have looked like the soldiers alongside us.

Rule Five. Casualties: Colonel King said: 'My aims and yours are widely divergent here – and I can understand why.' There were no restrictions on the reporting of enemy casualties. No numbers could be given of British casualties. Nor could we use the terms 'light', 'medium' or 'heavy'. Visual images were allowed so long as the soldier could not be identified until his next of kin had been informed. Any characterisation of casualties was forbidden.

Rule Six. General description of operational objectives was allowed, but not of operational plans. We knew the Desert Storm battle plan in detail, all 120 pages of it, but were forbidden to report it.

Rule Seven. Battlefield reverses could be reported 'at any time'. The Army spokesman would give the context. 'But if we get a good kicking we will admit it.'

Rule Eight. The embedded journalists would not be used as part of any deception plan. This was an important concession, since ruses to wrong-foot the enemy are integral to any large scale military operation. The actual deception plan, which involved broadcasting the sounds of fictitious tank movements by loudspeakers close to the border, was itself off-limits to us of course. The Geneva Conventions on the rules of war forbid treachery, like feigning an intent to surrender, but allow battlefield deceptions like the use of decoys, mock operations and planted misinformation.

Rule Nine. (This was added later on the insistence of the Foreign and Commonwealth Office, in deference to Saudi sensitivities.) Since we were in the land of Mecca and Medina, we were to make no reference to the presence of army chaplains among the troops. When I tried to call them 'welfare officers whose services are much in demand', I was instantly slapped down by Lieutenant Colonel Chris Sexton, John King's deputy.

When we crossed the Kuwaiti border four days later, he turned out to be as reasonable a censor as any reporter could wish for.

I could possibly lay claim to being the original 'embed', since my accreditation card – 'Authority to Accompany a British Operational Force' – bore the serial number 001. But that honour should really belong to William Howard Russell of *The Times*, the founding father of what he called the 'luckless tribe' of war reporters. In the Crimea he too was *with* the Army but not *of* it. He too was camped alongside it. He rode out on his horse and saw the battles through his trusty telescope, or he sought out soldiers who would tell him about them. He was a man of great courage – not only battlefield courage, but the courage to tell the truth about an ill-provided Army.

This made him unpopular. Prince Albert called him 'that miserable scribbler'. He had his tent cut down. Lord Raglan advised his officers not to talk to him. A former Secretary of the Army wrote: 'I trust the Army will lynch *The Times* correspondent.' Russell wrote: 'I was honoured by a great deal of abuse for telling the truth . . . There was not a single man in the camp who could put his hand upon his heart and declare that he believed one single casualty had been caused to us by information communicated to the enemy by me or any other newspaper correspondent.' He actually exonerated the generals. 'The officers were not to blame,' he wrote, 'the persons really culpable were those who sent them out without the smallest foresight or consideration.'

In 1868 he tried and failed to become the Conservative MP for Chelsea. A war reporter in Parliament? It seemed a strange career path. But Winston Churchill managed it. And so, much later and less professionally, did I.

Soldiers and journalists are commonly at cross-purposes. Towards the end of the war in Bosnia, in what was called 'the phase of liberation', the BiH (Bosnian) Army clamped down on the press and restricted our movements severely. One of its officers explained: 'When the war began we let the journalists in and were doing very badly. Now that we're keeping you out we're doing great.'

Embedding was a compromise decided on by the British Army under political direction. Both the extremes had been tried by the Americans over the years, total exclusion on one hand and open access on the other. In Grenada in 1983 and Panama in 1989 the press were kept out of the way until the fighting, such as it was, was over. Journalists trying to reach Grenada by boat from Barbados were threatened with being blown out of the water by the US Navy; so much for the land of the free and the freedom of the press. The open access was in Vietnam, from 1965 when the first combat troops arrived, until 1972 when they were withdrawn. It came at a price. Sixty-eight journalists were killed in the course of the war.

The access was obtained through JUSPAO, the Joint United States Public Affairs Office, under the cool and clever leadership of Barry Zorthian, who had himself been a war reporter in Korea. Peter Arnett, then with the Associated Press, complained to him in 1965 about being threatened by an American military policeman during a Buddhist demonstration in Saigon. Zorthian shook his head in mock concern. 'Damn it, Peter, you were threatening him and he was retaliating.' 'What?' said Arnett. 'Yes,' Zorthian explained. 'You were threatening him with a pencil, which is more powerful around here than a .45.'

Zorthian's problem was that he was trying to sell a bad war to people who had easy access to it. JUSPAO's accreditation was issued on request to war reporters, photographers, feature writers and even to novelists. It was valid for three months and authorised them 'to cover the operational, advisory and support activities of the Free World Military Assistance Forces Vietnam'. We talked a lot about the Free World in those days. The theory was that, armed with just this rectangle of coloured cardboard, you could jump on a helicopter on a space-available basis, go anywhere, film anything and tell it as it was to the audience at home, without censorship. Had not President Johnson already assured them that 'America wins the wars she fights'? In practice it was not that easy. Some disturbing episodes of low morale and military indiscipline had already filtered through the system to the public. Facilities on the ground had to be negotiated unit by unit. John Laurence of CBS News, in his epic (848-page) account of the war, *The Cat from Hué*, tells of his first operational story on the US Marines, in Danang in September 1965.

> A Marine officer said we would be allowed to spend a working day with a rifle company on the perimeter, to film activity at the company base, and to interview the officers and men. Nothing more. No patrols. No spending the night. *(No burning villages.)* [Morley Safer of CBS had controversially reported the Marines burning a village earlier in the year.] We had accepted the conditions without protest, happy to be allowed to work on a story.[1]

The story was called 'Waiting for Charlie'. It ran on the CBS Evening News four days later. Both the Marines and the network were happy with it.

Laurence also described the Marines' Combat Information Bureau in Danang, just before the Tet Offensive of 1968. 'More offices had been built for the growing staff of Marine Corps information personnel, the bar and restaurant had been refurbished and expanded, a larger basketball court constructed, and a boat dock built for the colonel's launch.' The colonel wanted to lead troops into battle. Instead he was attending divisional meetings and minding the press.

Not all of them were on-side. There was and always will be the potential for a conflict of interest between the media, whose instinct is to publish and be damned, and the military, whose instinct is to censor and be safe. Laurence wrote: 'Our first loyalty was to the American public to be truthful, then to the Marines we accompanied to be fair, then to CBS News to be competitive and hardworking.' An officer told him: 'Gentlemen, you are *with the program.'* It was taken for granted that, as in the Second World War, the press would be supportive of the war effort.

I did my own version of 'Waiting for Charlie' early in 1967. (Charlie, of course, was Victor Charlie, the Viet Cong.) I waited for Charlie with the South Koreans in the central highlands. I waited for Charlie with the Australians in Vung Tao. And most of all I waited for Charlie with the all-powerful Americans just about everywhere. I reported their military build-up and was probably over-impressed by the sheer scale of the war-fighting hardware on show. No small or medium-sized war had ever been fought in such an industrial way and with such an imbalance of forces. I too was with the programme. Here is an example.

> For the Americans, still getting accustomed to it, the big problem is how to find a foothold in this soggy, hostile country. So what do you do? You put a massive dredger in the middle of the river and pump the sand out shore-wards to build your campsite through a twenty-five-inch pipeline. Having staked your claim, you defend it. Viet Cong territory comes right up to the tree line. So you hide yourself behind your stockade and defend your friends with everything you've got. There are indeed those who have compared the situation with the frontier wars of the last century. The 3rd Brigade actually comes from former frontier country. The GIs add to the confusion by flying the Confederate flag in the Deep South of Vietnam.

With a few exceptions, John Pilger being one of them, we did not offer opinions. We did not need to. In April 1972 Bob Simon of CBS News had to find the words to go with the most graphic pictures of a truck load of refugees blown up by a land mine. He ended his report: 'There's nothing left to say about this war, nothing at all.'

The myth gained currency that it was the press who lost the war for the American military. But it was only a myth. They did it to themselves. All that the press had to do was, literally, go along for the ride and describe them doing it. One of the classic examples was Nicholas Tomalin's report in the *Sunday Times* in June 1966. The headline was 'The General Goes Zapping Charlie Cong'. 'After a light lunch last Wednesday, General James R. Hollingsworth of the US Big Red One Division took off in his personal helicopter and killed more Vietnamese than any of the troops he was commanding.' Tomalin ended the report by quoting the General, who was blazing away at any Vietnamese who moved with his M16 carbine: 'There's no better way to fight than by goin' out to shoot VCs. And there's nothin' I like better than killing Cong, no sir.' (Tomalin was killed on the Golan Heights in 1973 while reporting on the Yom Kippur War.)

Even more powerful than the news reports were the defining images of the war, the frozen-moment snapshots by Don McCullin, Larry Burrows, Horst Faas, Eddie Adams and others: dead and wounded GIs in their besieged fire bases, a Viet Cong suspect executed in the street by a South Vietnamese general, the self-immolation of a monk and a nine-year-old girl fleeing in terror from a napalm attack.

On those terms and under that kind of scrutiny the war was unwinnable. After it, and even occasionally during it, the censorship of the press came back into fashion. If a war could be lost because of the media, then the media had to be controlled. It was a message that reverberated worldwide and found an attentive audience in the British Army Staff College at Camberley. Soldiers are adept at learning the lessons of other countries' wars. They are not always so ready to learn the lessons of their own.

In the Nigerian civil war from 1967 to 1970 (coincident with the war in Vietnam) it became impossible to send a meaningful radio report. I would present a script to the censor, Mr A.K. Disu of the Ministry of Information, and he would laugh out loud as I sat before him and he cheerfully cut it to shreds. Occasionally, when it was sufficiently anodyne, he would stamp it and sign it as 'passed for transmission'. But usually he would just laugh and slash. When that happened, all I was allowed to say on the radio circuit was 'Things are tightening up here: this is the second successive time that the substance of what I have to say has been reduced by circumstances beyond my control.' If even that was disallowed I would send a service message: 'Give my love to Norma', which was BBC code for being silenced by censorship. The BBC's West Africa correspondent Angus McDermid was able to break the news of the overthrow of the first (and only) Prime Minister of Nigeria by phoning his wife and speaking to her in Welsh. The Prime Minister's name was Alhaji Sir Abubakar Tafawa Balewa. The newsreaders were somewhat relieved by the news of his passing.

The Falklands War of 1982 was a reporter's nightmare. Still under the influence of the Vietnam legend that the media lost the war, the Royal Navy had originally intended to sail over the horizon unreported and tell us of its victory afterwards. That was traditionally the way of the senior and silent service. Under pressure from Downing Street the Navy relented and allowed a limited press pool, whose movements were as restricted as their transmission facilities. Brian Hanrahan was the BBC's man of the moment. He noted that while the TV newsroom was full of 'reporters who chewed bullets for breakfast', he was the one who was actually sent – and he was a relative novice, being on attachment from his regular duties in the stills library. He did brilliantly in the most adverse circumstances.

> The flagship imposed radio silence before we were out of the Channel – and the fleet set off hell-bent for the Falklands with journalists tucked under its arm like gagged hostages . . . Communications were impossible. The Navy owned the battlefield, and the only way to get anything in or out was through them. And they weren't going to share their satellite links with us. Television reports had to come back by sea mail – an increasingly lengthy process as we got further south. The longest took three weeks to arrive . . . After this, it would be impossible to consider fighting a war in a democracy without planning proper media coverage.[2]

It was to the government's advantage that the BBC's images of the disaster at Bluff Cove, where the Welsh Guards were bombed in their landing craft, did not reach London until after the Argentinian surrender.

Two of the reporters of the war emerged with their reputations greatly enhanced. One was Brian Hanrahan. The other was Max Hastings of the *Evening Standard*. The Liberator of Port Stanley was feted by his newspaper, but unpopular with his colleagues over an issue of some unfiled news stories. His appeared before theirs did, under the headline 'The First Man into Stanley'. When it was over, one of them threatened him with violence. Another said: 'There is a time and a place to kill Max Hastings, but this is not it.'

The failed media plan of the Falklands was the origin of embedding in the first Gulf War. We had to find a better way of working together. The Ministry of Defence produced a paper which concluded, with typical understatement, that the Falklands War had shown that there was 'scope for updating, improving and modernising our thinking and procedures across a broad spectrum'. From that point on, all operational plans would have a 'media annex'. Since Saddam Hussein's forces had invaded Kuwait in August 1990 and the ground war did not begin until February 1991, there was plenty of time to fine-tune the media annex. On being assigned to our combat units, we were issued with desert camouflage uniforms and even, on the eve of battle, with flak jackets. We were also offered NAPS (nerve agent pre-treatment tablets) with the warning that their side-effects were unknown. We had NBC suits too (against nuclear, biological or chemical warfare) and struggled through many drills with them by day and by night. Sergeant Andy Mason of the Parachute Regiment marched us about like squaddies. We were of course unarmed but we had in a sense surrendered our civilian identities by signing on. We were neither civilians nor soldiers but something unspecified in between. Kate Adie, our desert celebrity, presented the Royal Scots Dragoon Guards with their haggis for Burns Night (the toast, unusually, was drunk in orange juice). John Fullerton of Reuters acted as a watch-keeper for the same regiment. I lectured the Queen's Royal Irish Hussars, on their study day in the desert, about the lessons of Vietnam and other wars. We dug trenches until our hands blistered. Kate was uniquely popular: wearing her camouflaged bush hat (hats/floppy/ridiculous as they were known) she received the Royal Artillery's special award for digging the shallowest shell-scrape in the history of warfare. The Army had mechanical diggers but preferred to put the press to work with spades. And we sent home cheerful stories about the soldiers preparing for war. One of them featured a military policeman, Andy Martorell, who kept a desert rat as a pet in his top pocket while directing the traffic when one formation passed through the lines of another. The guidelines forbade reports about plans and force levels, but encouraged reports about desert rats. We were also a link – the only one but 'blueys' (letters home) – between the soldiers and their families. No mobile phones back then, and no internet either.

At that point an extra restriction was imposed. We were not allowed to show the field hospitals being prepared to take the expected casualties. This, it was thought, would spread alarm and despondency at home. The costs of war became an off-limits topic. Brigadier Patrick Cordingley of 7th Armoured Brigade reminded a group of visiting defence correspondents that when there was a war it was only realistic to expect there would be casualties. The *Evening Standard* headline was 'Bloodbath in the Gulf'. Cordingley was shown the yellow card – nearly relieved of his command – because of it. When Margaret Thatcher was removed from office Kate Adie interviewed him about it somewhere in the desert, and he made some remarks about loyalty that were so indiscreetly pro-Thatcher that he would surely have been shown the red card if they had been broadcast. Kate buried the tape in the sand, thus saving the Brigadier from himself. It was an interesting reversal of roles. Instead of the soldier protecting the journalist, the journalist protected the soldier. I also once saved a brigadier, a media innocent with political ambitions, from shooting himself (metaphorically speaking) in the foot.

The 'embeds' and the 'unilaterals' inevitably fell out with each other. In a C-130 transport aircraft over the Saudi desert, six weeks after the invasion of Kuwait, the irrepressible Robert Fisk of the *Independent* asked me if I had considered the possibility that the Iraqis might actually win the coming war. No, I said, I had not: it was about as likely a result as Walsall 6 Liverpool 0. I read him a lecture about the balance of forces. The Iraqis had promised us 'the mother of all battles'; and Robert, who heartily disliked the military, was our resident prophet of doom. His father had served in the Army but he had not. As a soldier, or even an 'embed', he would have been uncommandable.

'We can't guarantee the price,' said a Pentagon official, 'but we can guarantee the outcome.'

On 28 February the tanks and armoured personnel carriers rolled across the Kuwaiti border, unopposed, in the darkness of dawn. The darkness was caused by smoke from oil wells set on fire by the retreating Iraqis. This was my pooled report of the forced entry, cleared and uncut by the censor.

> It was late afternoon, the entire horizon rimmed with darkness, and the British were gathered in the desert ready to do battle in full armoured formation for the first time in forty-five years. I am not allowed to identify units, but there were regiments here which had charged together at Balaclava – now about to wage, against the Iraqis, the warfare of the 1990s. The tanks and armoured personnel carriers are battened down. Our view is through the letter box window at the back of a Warrior battle taxi. Command and support vehicles behind us. The tanks are out in front and on the flanks. The Iraqis have pulled back – many miles back. The first contact with them comes at night.

The British battlegroup has finally come upon an Iraqi position. The response at one in the morning is ferocious. [Sounds of gunfire]. A twenty-three-minute barrage, using the multi-launch rocket system and two artillery regiments. The desert floor shook with the force of it. A gunner described it as the most intensive bombardment by the Royal Artillery since World War Two. When daylight came some Iraqis, even wounded ones, had struggled out of their positions to give themselves up. British ambulances carried them out. The Army that had been trying to kill them was trying to save their lives. Because it was daylight the yield of prisoners was immediate. They came in great columns, having laid down their weapons and now discarding their helmets. The flags they held were made of parachute silk. Under the terms of the Geneva Conventions we were not allowed to interview them but did not need to, simply to see their relief at having survived. As for the British, the dark skies under which this war is fought are anything but ominous. The war has been conducted according to plan and incredibly cost-free – at least in this battlegroup and up to this point.

The combat report, such as it was, was so far from being live and as it happened it was not broadcast until three days later. It took that long for the satellite dish to catch up with us from Divisional HQ. And if a network announced that it was cutting live to the front, that usually meant the front of the International Airport Hotel in Dhahran, or actually the back, between the hospitality tent and the swimming pool, where the 'stand-up' position was established on a wooden platform. Arthur Kent of NBC News became famous for this. He broadcast live during a missile alert at half-time in the Super Bowl, which assured him of a massive audience. He thus came to be known to colleagues and rivals as the 'Scud Stud'. No one saw the Iraqi missile, but they did see lots of Arthur.

In truth it wasn't that much of a war, lasting just a hundred hours until the leading tanks of the Queen's Royal Irish Hussars and Royal Scots Dragoon Guards reached the Basra Road and paused for resupply. 4th Armoured Brigade lost nine men to the 'friendly fire' of an American A-10 tank-buster that busted the wrong side's tanks. In 7th Armoured Brigade two soldiers were wounded (again, by the Americans) and none killed. We could have been counted out and counted back intact, like Hanrahan's Harriers. For this report and others like it we 'embeds' were chastised by the Australian polemicist John Pilger as 'myth-makers of the Gulf War'. I thought this a touch ungracious of him, since I had once saved his life (and mine) by executing a rapid U-turn from no man's land in Vietnam. One of his mates from the *Sydney Morning Herald* had then disobligingly threatened to rearrange my features in a bar.

But myth-makers we were not. My report was on-the-spot and fragmentary, as with most war journalism. I did not know at the time that the Iraqi soldiers had been abandoned by their officers, or the Irish Hussars would not go further on the Basra Road, because if they had rolled northwards into Iraq the Allied coalition, which included Egyptians and Syrians, would have fallen apart. But the report contained not a word of falsehood. It provided a soldier's eye view of modern warfare. It was accurate in substance and restrained in style, unlike Mr Pilger's shrill and pre-cooked commentaries. It spoke neutrally of the tank regiments as 'the British' rather than 'our troops' or (as the *Sun* did) 'our boys'. (William Howard Russell had written of 'our generals' and 'our dragoons' in the Crimea.) Besides, this was not a gung-ho force. It was fighting alongside, rather than like, the Americans. The commander of 7th Armoured Brigade, Brigadier Cordingley, was a peaceable man and a Christian soldier who took no pleasure in the darker side of what he had to do. When he called in the great bombardment on the second day, on an Iraqi position codenamed Zinc, he said: 'Poor bastards, I can't help feeling sorry for them.'

Soldiers in peacetime are impatient for war, so that they can test themselves and their training. But in wartime they can be equally impatient for peace: they have seen war and had enough of it. The spearhead British troops in Kuwait also held a predictably low opinion of the support troops in the rear echelon. They called them Pontis – persons of no tactical importance. Kate Adie and I were definitely included in the category of Pontis.

In the inquests that inevitably followed the war, I defended the truthfulness of the embedded reporting, while acknowledging its limitations. We were obliged to agree to rules that were not of our making. We were faced with the choice either of going to war as 'embeds' or not at all. Better something than nothing. Of the 'unilaterals' who tried to go it alone very few got through. One who did was Vaughan Smith, founder of the Frontline Club, who posed as a soldier and made it to the British Divisional Headquarters (but he knew the form, for he had once been an officer in the Grenadier Guards). Another was Bob Simon of CBS News, who was captured by the Iraqis inside Kuwait and spent forty days as their prisoner. He called it a 'careless mistake'.

It was after my experience as an 'embed' that I started wearing the white suits. I was determined to cover the next war as an unreconstructed civilian. It was in the summer of 1991 at the start of the war in Croatia. I was wearing a white suit and no body armour as all sorts of sharp metal flew past me, and none of it connected. I ascribed my immunity to the white suit and wore it ever afterwards in hazardous environments, from Bosnia to the House of Commons. Even when I did get hit, it could have been a great deal worse.

I later changed my mind about embedding – or rather, it was changed for me by the coverage of the invasion of Iraq in March 2003. By then I was an analyst with Five News and watched the flood of incoming feeds from the theatre of war. Some of the reporting was admirable. Much of it was appalling. The worst was from television correspondents who were so thrilled to be alongside the military that they took leave of their sense of proportion, and to some extent it seemed to me of their sanity. The technology was by then so sophisticated that it enabled uplinks from the advancing battlegroups. 'This is historical broadcasting,' said one, 'this is historical television.' Actually, it was not historical but hysterical. A reporter and an armoured vehicle are a dangerous combination. One of the 'embeds' was called Walter (as in Walter Mitty) and his network described the campaign as 'Walt's War'. A friend of mine, Sebastian Rich, was working as a cameraman for NBC News, embedded with 2nd Battalion 8th US Marines, and had more experience of warfare than any of the men around him. As they crossed a bridge over the Euphrates they came under sniper fire from a building on the other side. It was Sebastian, not one of the Marines, who called in the air strike. I have encouraged him to write about it: the piece could be called *The Cameraman as Killer*. It would be his second book. His first was titled *People I Have Shot*.

The newspaper reports tended to be less excitable. A mention in despatches was earned by Audrey Gillan of the *Guardian*, who was embedded with D Squadron The Household Cavalry Regiment. After the Royal Marines refused to accept women reporters, credit must go to its commander Major Richard Taylor DSO for welcoming her. The *Guardian* is not exactly required reading in the Army, especially the Cavalry: the officers prefer the *Telegraph* and the other ranks the *Sun* or the *Mirror*. But she fitted in at once. Her nickname was 'Admin' and the soldiers called her their 'little packet of morale'. Her reports were both accurate and moving. The Squadron lost three men in the war, one to a notorious 'friendly fire' incident when it was attacked by American A-10 tank-busters, and two when a Scimitar armoured vehicle overturned in a ditch. Audrey Gillan wrote:

> I watched men desperately try to resuscitate their fallen colleagues and shake at their inability to fight with fate. I saw them weep as they learned of the death of the men they had spoken to just that morning, men they had worked with for years, drank with, played football with. Sometimes, as we took incoming fire, they hugged me but they hugged each other as well.
>
> They spoke to me, sometimes as a journalist, sometimes as a friend, of their fears, of their grief, of their boredom, of their frustration and of their ultimate pride in what they had done in Iraq.[3]

She quoted a trooper wounded in a 'friendly fire' incident: 'I am trained for combat. I can command my vehicle. What I have not been trained to do is look over my shoulder and see if an American is shooting at me.' One of the soldiers asked her: 'If you cop it, can we have your radio?' I would even argue that women are better war reporters than men: they have more endurance and empathy.

I have been on the wrong side of enough roadblocks to know that the most effective form of censorship is a pole across the road. Television lives by its moving pictures and without them it is nothing. Open access is extremely rare. A Lebanese officer explained to me once that his army had nothing to hide and that even the most sensitive border areas were of course open to us and we could visit them whenever we wished; then he added, as if as an afterthought, that there must be *no photography*. The Israelis on the other side of the border were equally restrictive.

In border areas it is standard practice for security forces to arrest the journalists and empty their cameras of the film or videotape. I became expert at hiding shot rolls of tape. On one occasion, between being threatened at a roadblock and interrogated at a police station, I hid them in a hedge and retrieved them later. And in 1989 I reported from Panama: 'The city is more tightly under army control than we can show you without getting arrested.'

In reporting the wars of the twenty-first century there was no other available choice, short of suicide, but embedding. Reporters covering the assault on ISIS-held Mosul in October and November 2016 made their arrangements with Iraqi and Kurdish Peshmerga forces and shared the dangers from roadside bombs and suicide bombers driving improvised armoured vehicles. The fighting was from house to house and street to street. The ISIS fighters had enjoyed two years in which to dig in and prepare their defences. The reporting by Orla Guerin and Ian Pannell of the BBC and John Irvine of ITV News, among others, was vivid and brave, but inevitably – like all embedded journalism – one-sided and fragmentary. If they had tried to report unilaterally, they would have been captured and executed by the city's defenders or blown off the road by its attackers. Access came at a price. Most of the commentary was done from the safety of rooftops in Irbil.

I can offer just two examples of the positive and sensible management of the press in a war zone. One of them, surprisingly, was provided by the Serbs. The Balkan wars began in June 1991 with the unilateral declarations of independence by Slovenia and Croatia. The Yugoslav Army, whose officers were mostly Serb, was mobilised at once. Its units crossed the Croatian border and fought their way through villages and vineyards to Vukovar on the Danube. The town, with some forty thousand inhabitants, had a large Serb minority and a number of Serbian villages to the north of it. The siege of Vukovar lasted for three months. One of the battles was across the cemetery, where the Croats managed to stop the Yugoslav Army's tanks: this was a war in which it was not even safe to be dead. The Yugoslav Army had huge firepower but a shortage of infantry because of the desertions of non-Serbs, so they just flattened the fine old river port with millions of artillery and mortar shells. Not so much as a shrub was left intact. Like the Allies in Dresden in 1945, the Serbs came into possession of a wasteland.

The only way into Vukovar from the Croatian side was a dangerous track through a cornfield. I did not like the look of it. Since you can't report a war if you don't survive it, I decided to head for Belgrade and plead for access from the other side. I was expecting to be refused. Through my friend and interpreter Vladimir Marjanovic I negotiated with Colonel Susnjar, who was head of military intelligence and press liaison. (The connection was an obvious one to the Serbs.) He said that he had studied the British example of limited access and total control of the media in the Falkland Islands, and had decided not to follow it. The armed forces of Yugoslavia, he added, were fighting to save their country and their people from 'terrorists' and had nothing to hide. That night a fax came through with his signature and stamp on it, allowing us to pass through a dozen roadblocks to the front. We were in Vukovar every day for the next week alongside the advancing and pulverising Serbs. They were unfailingly helpful. Nothing was censored. We showed their anti-aircraft guns, aimed laterally, taking out Croatian positions in the Hotel Dunav window by window. We showed the looting of abandoned homes. We showed bands of Chetniks, Serbian irregulars, roaming the streets and chanting bloodthirsty songs. We not only showed the Croatian surrender but enabled it, by lending our fluent interpreter Vladimir to Nicolas Borsinger, the delegate of the International Red Cross (his own interpreter was struggling). We showed Borsinger pleading in vain for access to the hospital with the Yugoslav Army commander Major Veselin Sljivancanin. The footage was later used in evidence at the Major's trial in The Hague. He was sentenced to five years' imprisonment. What we did not show, because it was hidden from us, was the fate of 250 patients and staff of the hospital, including the wounded, who were taken away and executed in cold blood at Ovcara Farm 5 miles away. We had unrivalled access to the war and we showed what we knew, but it was not nearly enough. All war reporting is incomplete, whether embedded or unembedded. War crimes especially – Ovcara and Srebrenica among them – are denied and covered up by those who commit them.

The other example of a positive relationship between the military and the media was provided by the Israelis in the Yom Kippur War of 1973 – what its historian General Chaim Herzog called *The War of Atonement*. The Israeli Defence Force has had an up-and-down relationship over the years with the press, especially the foreign press, but sometimes the domestic press too. But on this occasion the narrative was easier. Israel was not bombarding Gaza or invading Lebanon. It was fighting back from a surprise and coordinated attack by Egypt and Syria for which it was lamentably unprepared and had mobilised too late.

Among the reservists called up were a group of uniformed escort officers assigned to TV news teams. This was a sensible compromise that gave us freedom of movement while leaving the IDF with a measure of operational control. One of my escorts was Chaim Topol, the actor of *Fiddler on the Roof* fame. It was like having wings on our wheels: all roadblocks opened to us. Another was with us in the midst of an artillery barrage near the Suez Canal, fearless and refusing to take cover, at a time when the distance between the two front lines was just beyond the range of an anti-tank rocket. 'Only one thing can happen to you,' he said. 'It happens to all of us sooner or later, and at least you should be honoured to die in a holy land.'

The Israelis' only attempt to deny access was on 22 October 1973, when they were across the Suez Canal and under pressure from the Americans to accept a standstill ceasefire. Unusually they could not find the maps that showed their front-line positions. They had some 'tidying up' to do, in completing the encirclement of the Egyptian Third Army, and so place themselves in a stronger bargaining position with the Egyptians. We left Tel Aviv so early in the morning that the blackout order had not been communicated to the escort officer, who was of a sufficiently senior rank to be able to talk his way through. We got across the Canal on an IDF pontoon bridge, filmed a destroyed SAM missile site on the other side and witnessed the rout of the Third Army. Its men, with their weapons discarded, were struggling up a sand dune and being provided with water by the Israelis. General Bren Adan, one of the front-line commanders, was studying a map on the sand dune and planning his next move. He allowed the Egyptians to be resupplied with rations. It was a scene of Biblical resonance. The escort officer said: 'In Moses' time the Israelis would have been doing the work while the Egyptians stood and watched. It took us four thousand years to turn that around.'

The ceasefire had not held. We saw shells and rockets exploding ahead of us as the Israelis advanced. The escort officer assured us that they were clouds. As the day progressed it became increasingly cloudy. At the end of it he conceded that the shells were shells and the rockets were rockets. The Israelis later changed their 'open access' policy and became more restrictive, but at the time their media management worked for them as well as it did for us. Their communiqués were believable because they were verifiable. The Egyptians' and the Syrians' were not.

Generals are free to choose their styles of communication. General Sir Michael Rose, the UN commander in Bosnia in 1994, was mostly his own spokesman and it worked for him. General Sir Rupert Smith, his successor in 1995, used Lieutenant Colonel Gary Coward as his spokesman and it worked for him too. In March 1995 Coward was being totally frank with us when the ceasefire melted with the snows and he said: 'We are entering a long dark tunnel and I am fucked if I know what lies at the other end.'

The armed forces defend us. The journalists inform us. We do not need to be permanently at loggerheads with each other. It is a lesson that the armies of the western democracies have to learn and relearn, over and over again, that it is actually to their advantage, within the limits of field security, to be open with the media if they are acting lawfully. If they are not, they will have to answer for it elsewhere.

10. THE LANGUAGE OF WAR

Words not only have meanings, they also conceal meanings.

In 1973, having been deported from Lebanon for an evasion of censorship at the start of its civil war, I made my way to Bombay (now Mumbai) to report a famine in the Indian province of Maharashtra – except that I was not allowed to describe it as a famine, under a different kind of censorship, which was linguistic. Famine was a phenomenon of Empire, and those days were long gone. The provincial Chief Minister told me: 'Famine is a frightening word. In the old days when we were under British rule the word famine meant the deaths of millions of people. After Independence the Government of India thought that in future the deaths by starvation of thousands and thousands of people would never arise. So they decided that this word famine should be erased from the Statute Book, and replaced by the word scarcity.'

At the height of the arms race between the United States and the Soviet Union I visited a General Dynamics plant in Florida to report on the birth and baptism of a Tomahawk cruise missile. A US Air Force chaplain, in full robes and uniform, blessed it as a weapon of peace. The language of peace has a weaponry all of its own.

So too with overflying aircraft: not to guarantee the safety of a flight is code for an intention to shoot it down.

In November 1994, when the Americans announced their lifting of the Bosnian arms embargo, the State Department spokesman James P. Rubin did so in language so impenetrable it almost required a code-book: 'We plan to fully implement the legal requirement that no US funds be used to prevent arms from going to the Bosnian Government.' Rubin later married CNN's Christiane Amanpour – a match made in Bosnia if ever there was one.

It was the writer most admired by journalists, George Orwell, who provided us with a masterclass in the uses of euphemism. In his 1946 essay *Politics and the English Language* he made the connection between linguistic and political corruption. 'Defenceless villages are bombarded from the air, the inhabitants driven out into the countryside, the cattle machine-gunned, the huts set on fire with incendiary bullets: this is called *pacification*. Millions of peasants are robbed of their farms and sent trudging along the roads with no more than they can carry: this is called *transfer of population* or *rectification of frontiers*.' He was writing about the French in Indochina. Later, when the Americans took over, the process of forcibly moving civilians into fortified villages was disguised as *revolutionary development*, and included a programme of indoctrination by folk music. Orwell remarked in the same essay: 'In our time, political speech and writing are largely the defence of the indefensible . . . Thus political language has to consist largely of euphemism, question-begging and sheer cloudy vagueness.'

The UN negotiator Herb Okun described Bosnia as the no man's land of the Balkans. In this no man's land, at the fiercest point of its war, I wrote a memo to myself: 'Everyone's lying but it doesn't matter, because no one's listening either.' On a snow-covered track on Mount Igman in November 1992, beautiful but deadly, and beneath trees that were shredded by Serbian gunfire, I was embraced by Yusuf Prazina (a.k.a. Yuka), a warlord who had once been an enforcer for a detective agency. He had been wounded three times when he was fighting for the BiH (Bosnian) Army; he promised to liberate Sarajevo by the beginning of the following year. Then he switched sides. I next came across him with the Croatian HVO and firing a rocket-propelled grenade at his former comrades on a street corner in Mostar. When the war was over his bullet-riddled body was found in a ditch in Belgium. Very few of the freelance warlords actually survived the war. Bosnia's General Rasim Delic said of them: 'We know very well how those, being famous through media, in most cases met their ends somewhere else.'

The targeting of Belgrade by NATO forces in 1999 tended to go awry on Fridays. Being an MP at the time, I rose in the House to make the case for a Friday bombing pause in the interest of saving lives. 'If civilian targets are hit in error, and civilian casualties are inflicted, this must not and cannot be hidden under a smoke-screen of jargon about "collateral damage" and "degrading the enemy's assets".' We degrade the truth when we stoop to using these euphemisms. Likewise 'shaping the battlespace', which means killing people and blowing things up. In the Saudi desert in 1991, before the ground war against the Iraqis began, the briefers fed us the familiar line about degrading Saddam's assets; but the SIGINT (signals intelligence) specialists beside us with their big antennae were picking up cries for help from the Iraqi units, pleading for anything with four wheels to come and take out their dead and wounded.

Acronyms and jargon play a similar part in obscuring the realities to all but the initiated – and perhaps even to them as well. An electronics company in Canada invented something called the Magneto Inductive Remote Activation Munitions System, which destroys an enemy in deep hiding places like mountain caves without laying give-away cables. The project was obviously attractive to Special Forces in Afghanistan and elsewhere. But war-fighting Americans tend to distrust the peaceable Canadians. The production of the weapon was therefore moved to a factory in the United States.

Contrary to legend, laser-guided missiles cannot turn left at the traffic lights on command. Even the 'smart bombs' of modern warfare are not so smart that they can distinguish between military and civilian targets. A bridge over the Danube is both. An oil refinery is both. Even a TV station can be both in the view of the Pentagon. RTS, the government controlled TV station in Belgrade, was bombed by NATO as an assigned target, killing sixteen of its staff, since it was accused of broadcasting lies. But the answer to lies, as I maintained in the House of Commons at the time, is surely not bombs, but truths.

'The surest recipe for killing a lie,' said Charles James Fox in 1772, 'is to multiply the witnesses to truth.'

Soldiers can sometimes use abstract language to hide from themselves the reality of what they are doing. On the eve of battle they can reasonably be fearful of losing their own lives. I once saw a British Army major in a forward position who was shaking with fear and clearly suffering from PTSD even before the first shot was fired: he should have been invalided out there and then. Soldiers can also be reasonably concerned about taking the lives of others: it is not a natural thing to do. 'Thou shalt not kill' is deeply embedded in our consciences. Lieutenant Colonel Tim Collins addressed this in his remarkable eve-of-battle speech to the 1st Battalion of the Royal Irish Regiment about to force their way into Iraq in March 2003.

> We go to liberate, not to conquer. We will not fly our flags in their country. We are entering Iraq to free a people and the only flag which will be flown in that ancient land is their own. Show respect for them . . . It is a big step to take another human life. It is not to be done lightly. I know of men who have taken lives needlessly in other conflicts. I can assure you they live with the mark of Cain upon them.

The killing is probably easier for the navies who do not see their enemy than for the armies – or at least their infantry battalions – who sometimes do, if it comes down to what they call 'gutter fighting', close quarter combat trench by trench, as at Goose Green in the Falklands. There are cultural differences too. At the same time as the speech by Lieutenant Colonel Collins, the Commander of the American Sixth Fleet, Vice Admiral Timothy Keating, was making a different sort of eve-of-battle speech: he told the cheering crew of the USS *Constellation*: 'Make no mistake, when the President says "Go!" it's hammer time! OK? It's hammer time!'

The winners even get to *rename* the wars to their advantage. The Croatian War, which started in June 1991 and ended its first phase in February 1992, was a complex conflict, partly a civil war and partly a war of external aggression. Some of its fiercest battles were fought for the control of Tito's Highway of Brotherhood and Unity. Tanks were parked under its bridges and land mines were laid across it. Serbian paramilitaries crossed a border to seize Croatian territory, just as Croatian main force units crossed a border to fight in Bosnia three years later. The Croats, rearmed and retrained, retrieved their lost lands in 1995 in a well-planned offensive called Operation Storm. Their Defence Minister said: 'We have been waiting for this moment for eight centuries.' The Croats at that point called it the Homeland War, a term first coined by the Zagreb newspaper *Globus*. It was politically convenient, since it took the Serbs out of the equation completely and had the resonance of the German *Heimat* and the Russian Great Patriotic War. The Museum of the Homeland War stands on the mountain above Dubrovnik.

War changes facts on the ground. It redraws borders. It expels civilian populations. It establishes new settlements. It obliterates old ones. It builds forward operating bases and military roads. It lays airfields and minefields. It destroys ancient monuments. It targets high buildings, especially grain silos and church towers. It removes places of worship as though they had never been. This too happened in Croatia. In December 1991, at the height of the 'Homeland War', the bishops of the Roman Catholic Church held a service of prayers for peace in the great cathedral in Petrinja, south of Zagreb. Shortly afterwards the Serbs captured the town and dismantled the cathedral brick by brick and stone by stone, until nothing remained of it but a wooden cross. They did the same in the vineyard village of Erdut, the headquarters of Arkan's paramilitary 'Tigers'.

Arkan had his fighters, who had grown up as Communists, baptised in the splendour of the Cathedral of St Demetrius in Dalj. They were no more devout than most soldiers, but religion *branded* them as Serbs and was important to them as a badge of identity.

The military mind has difficulty grasping the reality of failure. When General Sir Douglas Haig was told of the forty thousand casualties on the first day of the Battle of the Somme in 1916 (the true figure was 57,470) he observed: 'This cannot be considered severe in view of the numbers engaged, and the length of front attacked.' We too excel at reinventing our histories. We turn defeats into victories. Dunkirk, which was a defeat and retreat, was hailed as a deliverance. The Dieppe Raid, which was a costly fiasco, was justified as an exercise in all-arms warfare and a necessary prelude to the invasion of Normandy. But where defeats cannot be turned into victories we are also expert at wiping them from the record.

One of my causes as an MP was a degree of recognition and restitution to the British and Commonwealth troops held as prisoners by the Japanese after the fall of Singapore in 1942. They included two battalions of the Suffolk Regiment and three of the Royal Norfolk Regiment, all from the ill-fated 18th East Anglian Division, which arrived in the colony just as it was falling. The fault was not theirs, but that of the military planners who left the fortress of Singapore without defences on its landward side. So the Japanese just bicycled into it. It was one of the few cases in history when the larger force surrendered to the smaller one. After it was over the soldiers who survived their brutal captivity were ordered to remain silent about it, since it conflicted with the triumphal narrative of VJ Day. One of them sent me a copy of the order, a 'personal message from HQ Allied Forces in South East Asia to all newly-released allied prisoners of war'.

> You are news now and anything you say in public or to press reporters is liable to be published in the press of the whole world. You will have direct or indirect knowledge of the fate of many of your comrades in enemy hands as a result of brutality or neglect. Your story if published in the more lurid and sensational press will cause much unnecessary unhappiness to relatives and friends . . . That is just what will happen to the families of your comrades who died in that way if you start talking to all and sundry about your experiences. It is felt certain that now you know the reasons for this order you will spare the feeling of others.

Where a defeat is less obvious it will be disguised as a victory. The British misadventure in Iraq, just one of several over the years, began with the ill-considered invasion in 2003, and ended with the withdrawal from the last three bases in Basra on 3 September 2007. The only course available by then was not a winning strategy but an extraction strategy. The retreat took place in the small hours of the morning, after a humiliating deal had been done with the hostage-takers of the Mehdi Army. Unsurprisingly, it was not shown on television. The BBC, ITN and Sky News, so often embedded at the Basra Air Station, were somehow not invited to the denouement. The only embedded reporter present was Tom Newton Dunn, defence correspondent of the *Sun*. His report the following day, head-lined 'Our Boys Leave Basra', was a classic that deserves a special place in the annals of embedded reporting. The *Sun* called it 'a touching story of heroism, valour and sacrifice by British troops'.

> 600 men of the 4 Rifles battlegroup moved to the Brits' main base at Basra Airport, paving the way for Iraqi troops to take over the task of maintaining security in the southern city. Since its arrival in May the battlegroup has suffered the worst casualty rate of any unit. Twelve of its number have been killed and seventy-five wounded in a virtually non-stop wave of attacks on the Palace by Mehdi Army insurgents . . . For the first time in many months, a massive British armoured column drove through without a single pot shot taken at them. And after they left, there was no chaos on the streets. People just carried on as normal. With tough new security and police chiefs rooting out corruption with substantial success, it may be a new dawn for the place once known as the Venice of the East. As British officers here love to point out, Basra now has a murder rate half that of Washington DC. It's not perfect yet. But no matter what the rent-a-quotes tell you, it *has* been a good job, a worthwhile one. The rest is down to the Iraqi people – it's their country after all.

The retreat from Basra was called Operation Zenith. (It might more realistically have been called Operation Nadir.) It was executed by Major General Graham Binns, the GOC (General Officer Commanding) who specialised in tactical retreats. When he gave evidence to the Chilcot Inquiry he was notably less gung-ho than the man from the *Sun*: 'Every move outside our base required detailed planning and was high risk. I thought that we were having limited effect in improving the security situation in Basra. Ninety per cent of the violence was directed against us . . . The security situation was such that we spent a lot of time protecting ourselves.'[1]

So much of soldiering is luck, either good or ill. I first met Graham Binns when he was a company commander with the Prince of Wales's Own Regiment of Yorkshire in central Bosnia in 1993. The PWOs were the second battalion in, after the Cheshires. He was an outstanding soldier, and therefore deployed to the hazardous UN outpost in a disused factory in Gornji Vakuf, where he was caught in the side war between Croats and Muslims. It was like camping in a shooting gallery. He assured me repeatedly that he and his men would stand their ground. But they were a relatively small force without heavy weapons. The bombardments intensified. I next came upon them having circled their wagons in the relative safety of a mountain glade on the main supply route. As in Iraq, force protection was paramount.

Fourteen years later Graham Binns, as a two-star general, was doing the same thing at dead of night and on a larger scale. The buglers sounded the advance and the troops withdrew from their last three redoubts in the city. The militiamen let them pass under the terms of the secret agreement. But you do not get to the top in the British Army by calling a retreat a retreat. It is a relocation, a transition or a draw down. Major General Binns said that on taking up his post he thought there would be a 'hardening of the intent to draw down', as indeed there was. He had no choice in the matter. The British by then had begun their major deployment to Helmand Province in Afghanistan. The Army lacked the resources (and to some extent the will) to conduct two major and simultaneous high intensity operations.

Soldiers do not like to serve in unpopular wars. Along with

other military witnesses Major General Binns also testified to the overwhelming defect of Operation Telic, which was the code-name for the invasion of Iraq, that there was no plan for Day Two. Major General Tim Cross, in his evidence to Chilcot, described the operation in March 2003 as a 'catastrophic success'.

The Army's internal report on the Iraq War, declassified in October 2016, identified shortcomings in command structures, equipment, force levels, reconnaissance, targeting, communications and intelligence-gathering. Its author, Brigadier Ben Barry, described the outcome with typical euphemism as 'sub-optimal'. 'We were not as effective,' he said, 'as we should have been.' After the withdrawal from Basra, the report concluded, the Army suffered reputational damage in the eyes of both Americans and Iraqis. The lack of public support was especially disabling: 'Many in Defence and the Army seemed to struggle to find enthusiasm for the campaign.' Fighting its most unpopular war in a century, the British Army did not break but it cracked.

The campaigns in Iraq and Afghanistan were described by the Royal United Services Institute, which is as authoritative a military think-tank as we have, as strategic failures, despite their massive costs in blood and treasure. But in the commentaries of the time, not only in the *Sun*, for the BBC played its part as well in reports with an optimistic gloss on them, they were presented as brave successes. President Obama called them both 'dumb wars'.

In the twentieth century Britain found itself on the winning side in three wars – the First World War, the Second World War and the Cold War. According to RUSI, the record in the twenty-first century, not yet two decades old, was played two lost two.

11. 'TRUST ME . . . I'M A JOURNALIST'

I have in my files a tattered old notebook from the 1967 Six-Day War in Israel. On the cover there is a Jerusalem telephone number and a single name: Elkins.

Michael (Meyer) Elkins was an unlikely figure in the pantheon of British broadcasters. He was an Israeli Jew and Zionist who spoke his scripts with a gravelly New York accent. John le Carré called it the toughest, most beguiling voice he had ever heard on the radio. Elkins was close to Golda Meir, who became Prime Minister of Israel, and to the Mayor of Jerusalem Teddy Kollek. He worked both for the BBC (which upset its Arabists) and for CBS News. When the war broke out another Israeli politician, probably Yigal Allon, gave him the story of the lightning Israeli victory. The censorship blocked it, but he was told that when the censorship was lifted he would be the first to know. When the story got out CBS sent him a message: 'You alone with Israeli victory. You'd better be right.' They did not broadcast his scoop, but the BBC did. When the war was over he visited CBS News in New York and told them: 'Get lost. I resign.' He continued filing for the BBC until his retirement in 1983. He said: 'If anyone can discover a pattern of bias, let him say so.'

The war reporter has sometimes to fight on two fronts: one is the conflict itself, the other is a campaign to discredit his or her account of it. The report by George Steer of *The Times* on the bombing of Guernica by the Germans in the Spanish Civil War stands out as one of the great examples of diligent war journalism. He was not there at the time but arrived soon afterwards, having been strafed by German aircraft on the way. He pieced together what had happened. He spoke to survivors. He saw and measured the craters. He knew the types of aircraft that were used, Junkers 52 (heavy bombers), Heinkel 111 (medium fast bombers) and Heinkel 51 (chasers), and the types of bombs being dropped. He recorded their markings. Yet his own editor needed reassurance, for *The Times* had Nationalist sympathies, and its correspondent on Franco's side maintained that the Republicans had done it to themselves for propaganda reasons. Steer cabled his editor: 'THAT THEY BOMBED AND DESTROYED GERNIKA [*sic*] IS CONSIDERED JUDGEMENT YOUR CORRESPONDENT . . . PLEASE PUBLISH WHOLE MESSAGE WHICH IS UNDERSTATEMENT OF TRUTH STEER.'[1]

In March 1974 a Turkish Airlines DC-10 crashed over France on a flight from Paris to London. The cargo door had not been fully closed and decompression brought it down, killing 245 people. Fleet Street's finest were rushed to the scene against the tightest of deadlines. One of the British broadsheets carried a report from a veteran correspondent including vivid accounts from French eyewitnesses of the aircraft hitting the ground in a ball of fire. The interviews were entirely fabricated. There was not a shred of truth in any of them. When the accident investigators came looking for him, he went understandably AWOL.

A good reason for becoming a journalist is that, distrusting others, you can find things out for yourself.

In the age of the internet plagiarism can easily be discovered, as one of the *Independent*'s high-flying columnists found out the hard way. Outright and brazen falsehood is harder to detect; but a foreign correspondent who shares the same press bus as his rivals, and reports incidents that somehow eluded them, and does so repeatedly from one crisis to another, will inevitably face the suspicion that he made it all up. It is not unknown for a reporter widely admired by those who read him to be regarded by those who know him as a bit of a crook. In journalism, the road to stardom can be paved with good inventions.

'I'm with you on a free press,' says a character in Tom Stoppard's *Night and Day*, 'it's the newspapers I can't stand.'

Under the BBC's original ground rules, a news story could not be reported unless it was confirmed by two sources, usually news agencies: to which, if I had seen it for myself, the answer was that one source was my left eye and the other was my right eye. Sometimes we would feed stories to the agencies to provide ourselves with the necessary second source.

Trust has not just to be earned but accumulated. It is a matter of consistently getting things right, or at least not getting them wrong, and of never shading the truth for the sake of a tidier story. It is also sometimes a matter of challenging the Department of Preconceived Notions, not among the audience but among the ruling class of news editors.

After the fall of the Berlin Wall and my move from Washington to Berlin, a rival from ITN filed a report about the liberation of

East Germany from the grip of the secret police, the Stasi, with its network of eighty-five thousand agents and a hundred and five thousand paid informers. He received an instant call back from one of his editors: 'If this story is about Communists, I want to see more *red* in it!'

I had the good fortune to be the BBC's Washington correspondent during the eight years of Ronald Reagan's presidency, from 1981 to 1989. My difficulty was to persuade the upper echelons of BBC News that an actor who had once co-starred with a chimpanzee could also be an effective President of the United States of America. At the high point of his presidency, before it was undermined by old age and the Iran Contra affair, I likened him to a constitutional monarch. He reigned rather than ruled. He carried off the decorative function brilliantly – and movingly too, when the flag-draped coffins of the Marines came back from Beirut or the space shuttle *Challenger* exploded on lift-off from Cape Canaveral. He had a speech-writer, Peggy Noonan, who knew his cadences and thought inside his mind. He had actor's timing and delivery. 'You can make your own breaks,' he said, 'if you know what to say when the red light goes on.' His biographer Lou Cannon described him as a man both shrewd and oblivious, playing the role of a lifetime. As an actor he was often cast as a war hero, but now he was a real commander-in-chief and never happier than in the company of his soldiers, sailors and marines. One of his objectives was a six hundred-ship navy. By the twilight of his presidency he was close to achieving it.

Aside from primaries he never lost an election. He served two terms as Governor of California and another two terms as US President. On his re-election in 1984 he carried forty-nine out of the fifty states – all except Walter Mondale's Minnesota. I wrote in my notebook: 'No one ever got rich around here by betting against the fortunes of Ronald Reagan.' He delegated the details of government to able figures like Chief of Staff James Baker and Treasury Secretary Donald Regan. While rearming America from the seas to the stars, he signed a strategic arms limitation treaty with the Soviet Union, in the details of which (I noted at the time) he appeared to take no interest at all. Although Senator Ted Kennedy, a rival, derided his 'fashionable nonsense and jellybean economics', his presidency is widely regarded as having been successful. His summit with Gorbachev in Iceland in 1986 was pivotal. I thought that when he gathered up his papers and walked away without an agreement he had held out for too much, but he had not. He played a leading part in winning the Cold War. Barack Obama said of him: 'I think Ronald Reagan changed the trajectory of America in a way that . . . Richard Nixon did not and in a way that Bill Clinton did not.' At the time of his presidency I found the force of the Reagan phenomenon difficult to convey, not to the British public but to my own editors in London.

Because American politics is conducted in a language adjacent to English, the editors tended to believe they understood it and could second-guess it. They were wrong. I spent eleven illuminating years in Washington and loved every one of them. But it was like reporting from another world – as foreign at least as Equatorial Guinea. And that was *before* the rise of Donald Trump.

The Department of Preconceived Notions surfaced again during the Bosnian War. The Muslims were the good guys and the Serbs the bad guys – right? Actually, not always so. There was no monopoly of evil in that war and no monopoly of suffering. Serbs were the victims on 3 May 1992 when the United Nations brokered an exchange: the mainly Serb garrison of a Yugoslav Army barracks in Sarajevo would be given free passage to Serb-held territory in exchange for the release of Bosnia's President Izetbegovic, who had been held hostage by the Serbs on the previous day when he flew into the airport from Lisbon. But the exchange went wrong. A short distance from the barracks, in Dobrovoljacka Street beside the river, the military convoy was stopped by government militiamen who drove across it. The door of an ambulance was wrenched open and four Yugoslav soldiers in it were shot in cold blood. At least two others were also killed. When I told the BBC about this they asked me: 'Are you sure?' Of course I was sure. I had seen the ambulance and the blood and talked to the doctors at the military hospital; the UN's account of it was entirely believable. Sometimes the truth can be so . . . bloody inconvenient.

And sometimes it can be falsified. This is one of the dark secrets of TV news, never mentioned in the glittering awards ceremonies or the networks' prolific self-promotions. The falsehoods are not endemic, but they occur too often to be entirely accidental. I suspect that this derives in some measure from the increased emphasis on *storytelling*. The story may look and sound terrific – but is it actually true? There is nothing new in this: William Howard Russell of Crimean fame accused one of his rivals of fabricating the facts to make a 'better story'.

One of the most common malpractices in TV news is the massaging of soundtracks, usually by the dubbing in of additional gunfire. A certain correspondent, still highly regarded and successful, did this in a distant war zone where his piece to camera, in its original form, was delivered against a soundtrack as quiet as Surbiton on a Sunday afternoon. When the tape editor protested at the deception, he replied that he was not going to be second-guessed by an 'oily rag' (the TV reporters' term for technicians of whom they disapprove).

The same well-known correspondent, in another war zone, had another 'oily rag' film him dashing across a peaceful road as if he was under fire. This was then edited into footage from a freelance cameraman in the thick of things who really was under fire. The deception was deliberate and became widely known.

If the reporter of a jungle war is seen addressing the camera in front of rainforest foliage, yet with the distant sound of traffic in the background, you can be sure that the footage is someone else's, and our hero has ventured no further up-country than the nearby botanical gardens. The gardens in Saigon (now Ho Chi Minh City) were widely used for this purpose.

My favourite shading of the truth, because it was harmless, was by a friend and rival from ITN who was prevented from entering Uganda at some point during the colourful regime of Idi Amin. A ceremony in the President's bunker was covered instead by an allied news agency, so all that he had to do was to voice the footage from Kenya. The report ended with a sign-off that was something like 'James Safari Suit, ITN, outside Kampala'. You bet he was outside Kampala – he was stuck on the Kenyan border! He later became a successful writer of fiction.

More serious was the case of a British correspondent who arrived late at the scene of a natural disaster, but in time to acquire the footage of an American network. The images included a dramatic sequence of a young boy being rescued from the wreckage. The footage was genuine but the script was totally fabricated, including the name of the boy and the circumstances of the rescue. And for this the correspondent was feted by his network and won one of the industry's most coveted awards. When I pointed this out to one of his editors, he said it was too long ago and they had moved on. Because the falsehood was old it did not matter. The prizes, even of the Royal Television Society, were an occasional incentive to unscrupulous and fraudulent reporting. Some of this was discussed in whispers, as among co-conspirators, but never openly. I knew a man, a good and serious reporter, who was told that it was time he won the top Royal Television Society award, Reporter of the Year. The inference was that he was expected to win it, not just for himself but for the greater glory of his network, and that how he did it was up to him.

An assignment editor told one of his reporters who was known to be a bit of a cowboy: 'We love your stuff — we don't know how you do it, but please just go on doing it.' He had *carte blanche* to carry on shading the truth. It was the damned prize system wreaking its havoc again. The accomplices in these falsehoods were invariably the videotape editors, without whom they would not have been possible, and that was how I came to know about them: the tape editors had to tell someone.

Edmund Burke once observed: 'Well is it known than ambitions can creep as well as soar.'

The networks' self-promotions tend to exalt their on-air 'talent' up to and beyond the limits of the plausible. A well-known VIP (Very Important Presenter) visited British troops in the Basra Air Station in March 2004, a year after the invasion of Iraq. He was seen, appropriately flak-jacketed, talking to the soldiers based there. The image was shown repeatedly for more than five years afterwards, to enhance his reputation as a man with war-zone credentials. Yet he appeared not to have left the Basra Air Station for the streets of the city, where the British in fact were losing their grip. A real war reporter beside him did leave the Air Station and gave a realistic account of the loss of grip and the slide into anarchy and failure, at odds with the general air of progress being communicated. The image of presenter-as-hero was later replaced by one of the same VIP getting off a helicopter in Ukraine. Again, it was a publicity exercise and had nothing to do with journalism.

The presenter as actor is an essential part of the schtick. An American VIP, reporting a hurricane in Louisiana, pretended to stumble and fall in winds that barely disturbed his slicked-back hair.

TV news offers seductions of its own. It is a quiet day in a war zone – the kind of day, to be honest, when we are more likely to be waved through the roadblock. A commander invites us to visit his trench lines. Peace of a sort has broken out. The troops are brewing up or standing to, or even fast asleep. There is not a shot to be heard, but only the birdsong. (It is a little-known feature of war zones and minefields that wildlife thrives in them, because the ground is mostly untrodden.) A soldier, seeing the camera, offers to loose off a few rounds for our benefit, and his, to ease the boredom. The same opportunity can arise on a larger scale. I once had an entire battery of 105mm howitzers to play with, if I had wished. But we are supposed to be reporting wars, not escalating them.

Another malpractice is passing off reconstructions as the real thing. I knew a highly successful reporter who was flying in a UN helicopter over Croatia when the helicopter ahead of it was hit by ground fire. He learned of it when the helicopters landed to refuel. When they took off again he had his cameraman shoot some unsteady footage to simulate the moment of impact. It made for a good story, but not a true one.

One of the tricks in Belfast was for a cameraman to rush out of the Europa Hotel (the main press hotel at the time) with the camera rolling, as if to show the effect of an explosion. It did not happen often, but it certainly did happen.

An unlabelled reconstruction is a fraud, which in one case had tragic consequences. In March 2003 an experienced Sky News correspondent, James Forlong, was embedded with the Royal Navy. One of his reports appeared to show the firing of a cruise missile from the submarine HMS *Trident* in the Persian Gulf. But it was only a drill. The submarine was docked at the time and pictures of the missile were taken from file footage. When the fraud was exposed Forlong resigned and later hanged himself. He was as much a victim of the war as if he had been shot on the road to Basra.

Less tragic but just as instructive was the downfall, at least for a while, of Brian Williams of NBC. It was a case of what is some-times known as 'borrowed courage'. You either have it or do not have it: and if you pretend to have it you will be found out. Williams was the chief anchorman of his network's *Nightly News*, the voice and face and general manager of NBC News, having succeeded Tom Brokaw in 2004. In Iraq in 2003 he was flying in a US Army Chinook helicopter when another Chinook half an hour ahead of it came under fire. As he told the story in later years, not on television but at public events, the two helicop-ters somehow became conflated into one. When he was challenged about this in 2015 in the soldiers' newspaper *Stars and*

Stripes, he had no defence. He said: 'I made a mistake in recalling the events of twelve years ago.'[2] The network suspended him without pay for six months, then reinstated him in another capacity. It was an accident waiting to happen.

The strange thing was that the American TV reporters, for all their grandeur, were more tightly controlled than the British. We envied them their logistical back-up and salaries ten times greater than ours. But we enjoyed a freedom that they did not. Their million-dollar broadcasters had to submit to a process of script approval, in which all their reports, before being broadcast, were checked by editors in New York or Atlanta for style and accuracy. At CNN it was called 'the row' – a whole row of desks where the pedants passed judgement on the practitioners. The hell with that, we thought: it was better to be underpaid and happy and work for the BBC, ITN or Sky News.

12. 'TOTALLY UNSUITED TO POLITICS . . .'

The collisions between private morality and public office were nothing new. I was aware of them when I started out in journalism at the height of the Profumo affair. John Profumo, the Conservative Secretary of State for War, had been caught up in a sex scandal and accused of lying to the House of Commons. On 15 June 1963 I reported a speech by Enoch Powell, then still a loyal Tory, to the South West Norfolk Conservatives: 'I want at the moment to say one thing, and one thing only, about this great welter of fact and fiction. But this one thing I will speak out here and now. I am convinced that from the beginning to the end of the affair, and in every aspect of it, the personal honour and integrity of the Prime Minister, Harold Macmillan, are absolutely unsullied. I look to be in my place on Monday to support him.' (Much later in his career, and mine, Profumo sent me a letter urging me to stand for re-election.)

Politics and scandal seem inseparable, maybe because the political life attracts hard-driven and high-flying characters whose principal qualification is ambition and who believe that, whatever they do, they can get away with it. Well, they would, wouldn't they?

In the 1990s Prime Minister John Major had to deal with a series of scandals involving members of his party that he, like Harold Macmillan, could well have done without. Mostly they were not about sex (although some were) but about money and influence, the use of public office for private gain: in a word, *sleaze*. I followed them from afar in early 1997, for I was making a TV documentary across three continents about Kofi Annan, the new Secretary-General of the United Nations. Without political ambitions myself, I was aware that a General Election was due in May 1997, and that one man in particular, Neil Hamilton, Conservative MP for Tatton, was under a bit of a cloud, accused of receiving cash for asking questions in Parliament, which he denied. I knew about Neil, but not about his wife Christine, who was a self-styled battle-axe. I was soon to find out.

Since Neil's majority was so great as to make him unremovable by the opposition parties, Labour and the Liberal Democrats, they came up with the original idea of standing down their own candidates and finding someone to take him on as an Independent. But who should that someone be? Various names were proposed, including Terry Waite who had roots in the constituency: he was the son of the village policeman in Styal. But he had already served one four-year term as a hostage: would he be willing to serve another? He declined. It was late in the process when they approached me, just twenty-four days before polling day. Instead of turning them down flat, which would have been the sensible thing to do, I cautiously accepted. I had fallen out of love with the BBC, and they with me – and besides, I thought, it would be good to have an insider's view. But I did not have the least idea of what I was getting into.

First I had to meet the executive committees of the two parties, Labour and Liberal Democrats, who were standing down their candidates. The Liberal Democrats were the harder to persuade, because less centrally controlled, but it helped that I knew their leader, Paddy Ashdown, from Bosnia. The Labour meeting was held in an upstairs room of the White Bear, directly opposite the Kremlinesque headquarters of the Tatton Conservatives. Someone in the pub was intrigued to know what a war reporter was doing in peaceful Knutsford. 'I suppose,' he said, 'that you are on some kind of a secret assignment?' 'Why yes,' I answered, 'actually I am.'

My helpers included my publisher Kate Jones, my battle cameraman Nigel Bateson, my daughter Melissa, my nephew Oliver Kamm, Colonel Bob Stewart, the former England cricketer Geoff Pullar and the actor David Soul, who was Hutch in *Starsky and Hutch*. One day in a pub in Wilmslow he exchanged a kiss for a vote. (There is nothing against it in the Representation of the People Act.) I also had the endorsement of the Manchester United manager Sir Alex Ferguson, which was priceless (except perhaps with Manchester City supporters) in winning over the undecided. The 'clean machine' as it was called was actually a contraption so endearingly slapdash that a visiting columnist said it had all the professionalism of a *Blue Peter* appeal.

The campaign proved to be a brutal experience both for Neil Hamilton and myself – perhaps even more for him, because he had been apparently Tatton's MP-for-life. First elected in 1983 with a majority of 13,960, he had increased it to 17,094 in 1987. In 1992 it was 15,860. In 1997, after a favourable boundary change that drew in the mainly Tory village of Alderley Edge, the notional majority was estimated to be twenty-two thousand. When the votes were counted his place was always in the winner's enclosure. He was an accomplished parliamentarian and even spoken of as a future Conservative leader. But some of the Tatton Tories had turned against him and he knew that he was facing a challenge like no other. He called me 'a nice enough man, but totally unsuited to politics'. He changed his mind about the first part, if not the second. In the thirty years of his political career, he said, it was the dirtiest campaign he had ever known, and this was by someone presenting himself as 'Mr Clean'. For my part I described him as a difficult man to admire, which is small change in the currency of political abuse.

Two days into the campaign I decided to hold a news conference on Knutsford Heath. There was no space for it in my first headquarters, the basement bar of the Longview Hotel opposite. Neil and Christine got to hear of it and decided to ambush me, amid a great tumult of cameras and reporters. They wanted to know, what exactly were the allegations that I was making against him? I replied that I did not intend to talk about him at all, but about the issue of trust; and if the voters decided they could trust him more than me, they should vote for him. I was widely held to have lost the first round on points, if not a knockout.

I wrote in my diary: 'The debacle of the Heath, entirely my fault and no one else's, has the potential of wrecking a campaign that has hardly started. Those who first invited me wish me to be more combative and confrontational. But I see no purpose being served by the daily exchange of insults.' Alastair Campbell, in his only intervention during the campaign, suggested that I should

challenge Neil Hamilton to a re-match on the Heath. Ed
Vulliamy of the *Guardian* briefed me on the libel case and the
Hamilton back story. Matthew Parris of *The Times*, whose judgement I respected, predicted that my reputation would be
completely shredded by polling day.

It was a political contest that drew a great deal of outside
attention and which John Sweeney of the *Observer*, who wrote a
book about it, described as not so much a campaign as a pub
crawl with attitude. My former friends in the press assured me
with relish that I was bound to lose – and I tended to believe
them. But something unusual happened. To my surprise, I won
with a majority of 11,007. I remember thinking that it would
have been easier to lose. Four years in Parliament lay ahead. I
promised myself that I would work at least as hard in the new
job as the old one – or even harder, since I had so much to learn.
As I collected my green and white striped Commons pass I was
still in a bit of a daze. And then in the Members' cloakroom I
found a coat-hanger with my name on it and a pink ribbon on
which to hang my sword.

It was a season of shock and awe. The awe was in entering
Parliament so unexpectedly. The shock was in what I found
when I got there. Nothing prepared me for the orchestrated
raucousness of Prime Minister's Questions (PMQs). It made the
House of Commons seem like a sort of legislative Hogwarts. I
would sit there in disbelief in my seat below the throne of the
Sergeant-at-Arms and wonder, is this really the best we can do?
It wasn't just the ritual misbehaviour – old hands said it had
been even worse before the TV cameras arrived – but the
epidemic of planted questions, usually beginning with 'Can I
congratulate my Right Honourable Friend . . . ?' There were

more plants in PMQs than in *Gardeners' Question Time*. A Cabinet minister told me that he cringed to hear some of the questions from his own side. Sometimes I sat there with my head in my hands and once, when I could bear it no longer, I just walked out. The parliamentary exchanges owed less to Gladstone and Disraeli than to Punch and Judy.

Neil Hamilton was one of my constituents. I wrote to the House of Commons authorities on his behalf and defended his right to a fair hearing on the charges against him. Simon Hoggart wrote in the *Guardian*: 'Mr Bell is so painfully fair to everyone, he is probably saying even now that we shouldn't be too hasty in condemning Richard III.'

I thought that I had entered the free parliament of a free people, but found myself trapped in what seemed a rubber stamp assembly. I have been accredited to three national assemblies. The first, as a journalist, was the US Congress, which I found to be generally democratic, though vulnerable to the purchasing power of Big Money. The second, also as a journalist, was the Volkskammer, the old East German parliament in its dying days, which was profoundly undemocratic. The third, as a Member, was the House of Commons, which was a bit of both. I wondered aloud in a newspaper column, had we won the Cold War only to adopt the values and practices of its losers?

I was helped by two great parliamentary ladies. One was Madam Speaker, Betty Boothroyd, who summoned me to see her at the outset and was most sympathetic to the lone Independent in her flock. I might have to wait four and a half hours to speak for four and a half minutes, but I nearly always 'got in', as the saying is. She sent me a letter towards the end urging me to find a way of returning to the Commons. She had become a 'Bell watcher', she said. The other great lady was Barbara Castle, by then ennobled as Lady Castle, who invited me to tea in the House of Lords. She warned me against 'those bastards', by whom she meant not the Conservatives but the architects of New Labour, especially Peter Mandelson. She was definitely Old Labour herself. Then she offered some advice from half a century of experience. 'Young man,' she said, thus winning me over completely (I was fifty-nine), 'whatever else you do, you must never be afraid to stand alone.'

Actually, I had no choice unless I defected to a political party, which was out of the question. I rather liked Alex Salmond at a personal level, but becoming the Scottish National Party MP for a Cheshire constituency would have taken a bit of explaining. Early in 1999 I received a morale-boosting letter from a schoolgirl, Kylie Donovan of Bushey Heath: 'Dear Mister Bell, my teacher says you are the only one in Parliament who has no friends and you never get to join in any parties. Never mind. We had a boy like that at school who nobody liked, but he had a super duper party with clowns and jelly and then everyone liked him and he got to lots of parties.'

For the early months I watched and waited and saw how things were done. Being totally without parliamentary experience, I needed to know the difference between an Honourable Member and a Right Honourable Member and an Honourable and Learned Member and an Honourable and Gallant Member. A Right Honourable MP was also a member of the Privy Council. To be learned it was necessary also to be a Queen's Counsel and to be gallant the MP had to have been an officer of field rank (major or above) in the armed forces. Since I had never been more than an acting sergeant in the infantry, I could not aspire to be gallant. But still I bided my time.

Then in November the story broke that the Labour Party, while in opposition, had received a donation of £1 million from Bernie Ecclestone, the Formula One impresario; while in government, it had changed its policy to allow tobacco advertising on his race tracks, thus accommodating his interests. Whatever else I had expected on entering the House, it was not a party dogfight on sleaze and corruption. Something about frying pans and fires came to mind.

On the next Prime Minister's Questions the Conservative leader William Hague was unusually off form. He was normally an accomplished performer at the despatch box, but not this time. The *Guardian*'s Simon Hoggart wrote: 'There is a film called *The Goalkeeper's Fear of the Penalty*. But it is nothing to the *Penalty Taker's Fear of the Open Goal*.'[1] Then with two minutes to spare (and back-benchers at PMQs watch the clock obsessively) Madam Speaker let me in: 'Is the Prime Minister aware that the appearance of wrong-doing can be as damaging to public trust as the wrong-doing itself? Or have we slain one dragon only to have another take its place with a red rose in its mouth?'

The question was not well received. Alastair Campbell was said to have winced. After two months the *Daily Mirror* delivered New Labour's response in the form of the headline 'How Clean is Mr Clean?' The news story revealed that the parties that had stood down their candidates, Labour and the Liberal Democrats, had also footed the bill of £9,400 for my legal expenses. These were so high because I had been facing multiple legal threats from Rupert Gray, who was Neil Hamilton's extremely able lawyer. When Hamilton had been cleared, he said, he would sue me for damages, which would not be inconsiderable. I had not known about the fees and duly paid back the money to both parties from my rather slender savings. It was the price of independence.

The following Sunday I preached a sermon (my only sermon ever) in the Unitarian Chapel in Knutsford on 'The uses of adversity'. On the same day the *Observer* carried the headline 'How the New Labour Mafia Took Revenge on Martin Bell'. The story quoted a Labour Party source whom I could easily identify: 'Bell should have been more sensible, shouldn't he? Tony Blair was in a little bit of trouble and we didn't need to hear cutting remarks from Martin Bell. It's like the Mafia isn't it? You've got to show respect.' The *Knutsford Guardian* then ran a straw poll about whether my constituents still supported me: 315 did and 50 did not. My personal mail divided into 700 for and 7 against. I was on my way to give a news conference when someone rushed across the road and said: 'Don't you dare quit!' Even the Tatton Tories came on-side, believing that I had been set upon by New Labour's puppet-masters. My most vociferous critic on the doorstep, Major Sidney Hulme MBE, wrote a heartening letter of support to the *Knutsford Guardian*. But I had received a useful warning. A friend pointed out the irony: 'Martin asks a question about Labour cosying up to a million pound donor. Then he has to pay nine grand. He had better save up before he asks another question.'

One of the disadvantages of being an MP without a party is that you have a right to a seat in the House but not on any of its committees. Then, shortly after the Bernie Ecclestone affair, my fortunes changed. William Hague offered me one of the Conservatives' seats on the Standards and Privileges Committee.

This is the panel that rules on charges of misconduct against individual MPs. Its eleven members were supposed to leave their party politics at the door of Committee Room 13 as they met and wrangled for hours on end over the difficult cases before them. I noted in my diary for 23 May 2000: 'Standards and Privileges was dreadful. MPs playing party politics. One of them [name deleted] conveyed Tea Room gossip that Elizabeth Filkin was out of control. This was in her presence. She was furious. A disgraceful whispering campaign is being waged against her, led I fear by senior MPs.' It took me a while to understand how party political was the weighting of it all. After eight meetings I wrote – to myself: I was bound by confidentiality and there was no one else to write to – 'A group of Labour MPs is blocking criticism of Peter Mandelson', who was on the brink of one of his resignations.

Elizabeth Filkin was the Parliamentary Commissioner for Standards, appointed in 1999 and let go in 2002. She dealt fully and fairly with a series of cases involving such prominent MPs as Peter Mandelson, Keith Vaz, Tony Baldry and John Reid. It soon became clear that she had no supporters on the Committee, except for Peter Bottomley and myself. When she departed, to be replaced by a more compliant figure, only forty-nine MPs signed a motion thanking her for her services. It was at about this time that I saw an MP exchange his vote for a peerage: there was no doubt of it. My stint on the Committee taught me a lesson reinforced by the later scandal of MPs' expenses: *the House of Commons is incapable of regulating itself.*

Since I was the only Independent, other MPs saw me as an oddity rather than a threat to their system, and were generous with their advice. They taught me some of the tricks of the trade and shortcuts to success. One was to intervene in debates, ask the Honourable Member whether he or she would give way, and make some remarks disguised as a question which would then be fed to the constituency newspapers, showing that their MP was busy and on-the-case. Another was to get their names and photographs in the local press *every week*, to similar effect – or, better still, to persuade the editor to give them a weekly column. A third was never to be afraid to break a promise – which after it was broken turned out not to have been a promise in the first place but only an aspiration. That was how the game was played. If an MP was on one of the phones in the House's Gothic corridors, he was either dealing with a dispute within his constituency association or phoning his local paper with a self-serving press release. If two MPs were close to coming to blows with each other, it was a sure bet that they were of the same political party.

Waiting to vote in the evenings, I spent some time watching the football in Annie's Bar (Alex Ferguson was a constituent). I was unexpectedly among the political class and reminded of what William Cobbett said in 1832: 'A man with turtle soup in his belly, and with French white wine exhilarating his brain, never yet did his duty towards the people.' It was in Annie's Bar that I saw an MP drinking himself to death. The Whips did not care so long as he followed their orders.

Since the MPs knew I had promised to serve only one term in Tatton, they gave me a masterclass in promise-breaking. They would say: 'You've got to stand at the next election – but please, not in my constituency!'

Not all MPs were so positive. I was sitting quietly in the Chamber one day and minding my own business when a New

Labour harpy came flouncing across the floor to me. She was upset by some alleged inconsistency in my voting record. 'Maybe I was inconsistent,' I said, 'and maybe I made a mistake. It can happen to anyone, you know.'

'I shall denounce you,' she hissed, and stormed off. I never heard from her again.

If you are an Independent MP and therefore your own Chief Whip, how do you decide on how to vote on issues on which you are not sufficiently informed? One of my guidelines was to follow those who did know, like Frank Field on pensions and Gwyneth Dunwoody on transport. Another was to see how the late Alan Clark voted, and go the other way. He got to hear about it and mentioned it on the one occasion when we found ourselves in the same division lobby (on a bill to ban fur farming). A mutual friend told me that Clark didn't regard me as a 'proper MP'. He was probably right, except that I had been democratically elected by an unchallengeable margin.

Another critic was David Amess (now Sir David), Conservative MP for Southend West. He said: 'The Hon. Member for Tatton is in the Chamber. His arguments for independence were totally unconvincing. Independence is a little like running with the foxes and hunting with the hounds. Both nationally and locally, it is a bit of a cop-out.'[2] And the Labour MP Siôn Simon wrote in the *Daily Telegraph*: 'Mr Bell has contributed nothing to public life. He simply stands in the middle of the melee shouting smug yah-boos at the party political compromises he despises.' Someone must have put him up to it, for he later wrote to me graciously to apologise.

My friends were mostly but not entirely of the Awkward Squad: Paul Tyler and Paddy Ashdown of the Lib Dems, the

Tory Richard Shepherd whom I seconded for the Speakership, and on the Labour benches Tam Dalyell, Andrew MacKinlay, Gwyneth Dunwoody and Paul Flynn. Flynn observed: 'So many decades have passed since Parliament had a genuine Independent MP, the system does not know how to cope with Martin Bell.'

Actually, it didn't. Even my seat in Parliament was challenged. On a day when Julian Brazier, MP for Canterbury, wished to reply to a point I had made about the NATO bombing of Belgrade, he said: 'I am particularly aware of the presence of the Honourable Member for Tatton.' The Deputy Speaker interrupted him. 'Order! The Honourable Member for Tatton is not in the Chamber, and the Honourable Gentleman should not refer to him.'

'I stand entirely rebuked, Mr Deputy Speaker,' said Mr Brazier. 'Although we can see him, I accept that he is outside the Chamber.'[3] My seat, the only one facing the Speaker, was behind the bar of the House, a grey line on the carpet, and so I was ruled to be invisible. I tried to avoid the paranoia of feeling that the whole world, or at least the whole House, was against me. The Conservatives put me under pressure to stand in a Labour held seat, Hartlepool (Peter Mandelson), Leicester East (Keith Vaz) or Coventry North West (Geoffrey Robinson). 'But no one from Coventry North West has even asked me,' I protested. 'We can easily arrange that,' replied a Very Senior Person in the party. They even floated the idea that I should stand against one of their own, Ken Livingstone, to be Mayor of London. They regarded him as a renegade.

Politicians like labels. The Conservative MP Bill Cash assured me that I was an Independent Whig. I thanked him for letting me know.

In four years as an MP I put out only one press release, and that was to advertise a penny-farthing race on Knutsford Common. My role was to start the Boneshaker Race, for early models with wooden wheels rather than tyres. It reminded me of my electioneering contraption.

My oddest Adjournment debate, at the urging of a group of like-minded MPs, was to plead for Arts Council funding for the D'Oyly Carte Opera Company. Since MPs are fortunately not allowed to sing in the House, I quoted from *Iolanthe*:

> When in that House MPs divide,
> If they've a brain and cerebellum too,
> They have to leave their brain outside
> And vote just as their leaders tell 'em to.

The Independent manifesto in just four lines!

In my last summer as an MP I bought a hanging basket, and hung it outside my cottage in Great Budworth. Its flowers were red, blue, yellow and white. When I was away it was watered by a kind neighbour who had family ties to Neil Hamilton. It was thus a cross-party hanging basket, and the symbol of a more collaborative politics. Nor did I charge it on expenses.

Visiting a primary school, as MPs do, I was invited to show off my drawing skills. I tried to sketch a scene from my father's farm in the 1950s. I did well with the wagon full of sheaves, with a stick figure of myself perched on top of it. But I failed with the horse. 'That's not a horse,' they chorused, 'that's a *dinosaur*.'

One of the kids, according to her teacher, saw me for some inscrutable reason as the sixth Spice Girl. Gratified, I asked, 'Which Spice might that be?'

'Old Spice,' she said.

And a question at another primary school: how much money did I earn, how much money did I have, and had I ever killed anyone? The answers were not a lot, enough to live on, and to the best of my knowledge no. As a soldier I had been trained to kill, but had never actually been required to do so. I did, however, receive a death threat as an MP, which the Cheshire Police took more seriously than I did.

As a politician without a party I received bundles of mail from people who felt they were the victims of a conspiracy. Much of it was in green ink and capital letters. The green ink mail rose in volume once a month at the time of a full moon. As time went by, I answered less and less of it.

I knew a loyal Labour MP who had backed his party through thick and thin during a long parliamentary career. Then one day, for the first time in his life, he rebelled. 'I am tired of voting for things I don't believe in,' he said. Behind him on the back benches was a certain Jeremy Corbyn, who rebelled against the leadership more than anyone, but no one took much notice. It never occurred to any of us that he might one day become the Party Leader.

I only ever travelled to troubled countries. In August 1998 I visited Burundi on behalf of UNICEF, together with the Labour MPs Oona King and Hilton Dawson. I had been working on and off for the Radio Four programme *From Our Own Correspondent* for more than thirty years, so I offered a report on Burundi. The editor, Tony Grant, readily accepted. On my return he phoned me with an apology. It had been turned down at a Very High Level, because I was an MP. Even an Independent MP could not be relied on, evidently, to be impartial.

And it was while I was still an MP that the BBC's Pensions Department sent me a letter to check that I was still alive. I referred them to the pages of the previous week's Hansard.

The general public were wonderful. A constituent was having a problem with the Child Support Agency at a time when I was looking at UNICEF projects in the Balkans. He wrote: 'I saw you in Kosovo and was worried that you would be kidnapped before I got to talk to you.'

Another wrote to me: 'It is such a shame you are leaving – you were so close to getting the hang of the job!'

Some of the letters came from far afield. The editor of *Penthouse* magazine asked for my endorsement for its relaunch. 'Reinventing pornography isn't easy,' he said. I politely declined: it was just not one of my causes.

Closer to home, ten-year-old Abigail wrote from Wilmslow: 'We are bored of the shops in Wilmslow. The clothes what we buy are too big or too small. We are asking you would you build a shopping mall.' I replied gently that as an MP I was not in the business of building a shopping mall; but I would never get bored of, or even with, hearing from her.

And a stranger came up to me at a petrol station. 'Don't I know you?' he asked. 'You're that TV reporter.' 'I used to be,' I answered, 'but I changed my job. I am an MP now.' 'Oh, I'm sorry to hear it,' he said, 'then you're unemployed.'

It was a sad day indeed when I left the constituency and dropped back through the letter box the key to 40 Church Street, Great Budworth, my home for four unusual years. I knew that I would miss those people and still do – and that includes those who voted against me as well as those who voted for me. No one speaks ill of a departing MP. His friends are still disposed to like him and his enemies are delighted to see the back of him. I gave a farewell lunch to Neil Hamilton's two most loyal supporters in Wilmslow, Pauline Breland and Patti Turner-Smith (described in John Sweeney's book about the campaign as his 'blonde groupies'). We left on the best of terms. I did, however, receive a letter from a constituent who threatened to haunt me for the rest of my days for letting 'that bastard Osborne' into Parliament.

And George Osborne had not even yet done anything to offend him. He was of course my anointed successor, selected by the Conservatives in 1999, when he was only twenty-seven, to inherit one of their safest seats in the country. They had fast-tracked the selection to prevent an attempted comeback by Neil Hamilton. They said that they were treating Tatton as a marginal constituency, which it never had been before or would be again. Would George still have won if I had broken my promise and stood for a second term? I think that he would. Others disagree. George himself thinks it would have been 'messy'. He was also concerned that Neil Hamilton might have emerged from the shadows and rallied his loyalists to reclaim his old seat. None of this happened. George Osborne was elected in 2001 by the usual five-figure majority. Having been secretary to the Shadow Cabinet under William Hague, and even crafted some of his sound-bites for PMQs, he probably knew the procedures of the House of Commons better when he arrived than I did when I left. After a short spell on the back benches he rose rapidly through the ranks to become a successful strategist for his party and long-serving Chancellor of the Exchequer, until the earthquake of Brexit. The Tatton Tories had always wanted a big hitter, and now they had one. You can never see yourself as others see you, but one of the traditions of a maiden speech is that the new MP pays tribute to his predecessor. George's to me was more generous than mine had been to Neil Hamilton. 'Many people come to the House as idealists and leave as cynics. I have got to know Martin Bell quite well in the last couple of years, and it strikes me that he came to the House as a cynic and left as an idealist. The man in the white suit will be missed in the corridors of the Palace of Westminster as he will be by the people on the streets of the Tatton constituency, whose interests he represented so well. I am greatly honoured to take his place in the House.'[4]

Thank you, George. But it is possible surely to be a saddened idealist.

Nineteen years after his defeat in Tatton, Neil Hamilton was elected as a UKIP Member of the Welsh Assembly. He owed his success to the democratic anomaly of the party list system, under which few voters know until it is too late whom they are actually electing. Whatever else I thought of him – and I am not a good hater – I had to admire his tenacity.

Politicians have a talent for self-deception. The Welsh Assembly was only his second choice for a comeback. The first was always the House of Commons itself. After his defeat in 1997 he convinced himself that he would win his libel action against Al Fayed, be readopted by the Tatton Conservatives and return in triumph to the House where he had so excelled in debate that he described himself as an 'ace bullshitter'. 'If they want a circus,' he said, 'they have come to the right man.'

13. NO MAN'S LAND

Martha Gellhorn, whom I was privileged to meet shortly before her death in 1998, was one of the greatest of war reporters, from the Spanish Civil War to the Normandy beaches to Vietnam. She once said: 'You can only ever love one war.' Anthony Loyd of *The Times* felt the same. The war he loved was the one in Bosnia. When I heard he was writing a book about it he was at first reluctant to tell me the title. Then I found out why. He called it *My War Gone By, I Miss It So*. He wrote: 'I cannot apologise for enjoying it so . . . I took the freedom and light that the fighting offered, feeling truly earthed with the Bosnian War once more . . . It was like falling in love again'.[1] Janine di Giovanni was another: 'I didn't like what I saw in postwar Bosnia. In a nostalgic and certainly selfish way, I preferred the spirit of the people during the siege . . . the fate of Bosnia had been decided on an American air base [Dayton] and it killed its spirit.'[2]

We shared the ordeal of the people besieged in Sarajevo, but only up to a point. As one of them put it, 'Yes, you come here and tell everyone how tough it is, but you've got a return ticket.' A graffiti slogan on the wall of the PTT building said: 'Arms are for loving, hugging and shooting one another.'

Bosnia was special for all of us, from the seasoned hack to the apprentice war tourist. Ed Vulliamy called it 'our generation's Vietnam' (his generation's but not mine: my generation's Vietnam was Vietnam). You can take the reporter out of the war zone, but you can't take the war zone out of the reporter.

I was no war junkie myself and rather wished towards the end of it to become a peace correspondent. I was even once described as a 'veteran bomb-dodger'. I had left Washington after the Berlin Wall came down on a six-month attachment supposedly to report on the emerging democracies of Eastern Europe. For most of the following six years I was covering nothing but wars, first in the Gulf, and then in the Balkans. I did not enjoy being scared out of my wits, but I did share what Winston Churchill, who had of course been one of us once, called 'the exhilaration of being shot at without result'. And at the end of the day in the Holiday Inn we would sometimes celebrate our survival with something stronger than orange juice. The war-zone whisky was Ballantine's.

Nietzsche said: 'The secret of reaping the greatest fruitfulness and the greatest enjoyment from life is to live dangerously.'

For me too Bosnia was a war zone like no other. Partly it was the beauty of the place, even the surrounding heights from which the Serbs were bombarding us. And partly it was the people, or peoples. The only ones I never warmed to were the hard-line Croats of Herzegovina. But for the rest, I would as soon take coffee with Haris Silajdzic in Sarajevo as whisky with Radovan Karadzic and Nikola Koljevic as they unrolled their maps in

Pale and harangued us on their version of Serbian history. Silajdzic, on the government side, went out of his way, at some risk to himself, to save his Serbian neighbours in Sarajevo from harassment by gangsters who were threatening them. Karadzic and Koljevic were readily accessible to us for the first two years of the war, until access was closed off in August 1994. Karadzic wrote apocalyptic poetry and Koljevic, the Shakespearean scholar, tried to broker ceasefires in its early weeks. An embittered academic, he told Janine di Giovanni: *'They never made me a full professor.'*[3] When the war ended, he did not go into hiding like Karadzic and Mladic. He took a gun to his head and shot himself.

The Bosnian conflict was uniquely hazardous in that we did not need to go out to the war every day since the war came in to us. Our first operating base was the Hotel Bosna in the suburb of Ilidza, which was held by the Serbs. The hotel and the parkland around it were repeatedly attacked with small arms and mortar fire from the government-held suburbs of Butmir and Hrasnica. In one of these attacks the Visnews cameraman Rob Celliers was badly wounded in the arm while he was filming. In the second month of the war, after Justin Webb had taken over from me, the BBC office in the hotel was damaged by mortar fire. The foreign press held a meeting in a corridor and decided to leave early next day for the safety of Split on the coast of Croatia. There was no space on the journey out even for the BBC's editing equipment, which was duly looted by the Serbs and used by them to establish their own TV service in Pale. I recovered our tapes four years later. The only TV people to stay behind were Aernout van Lynden and his team from Sky News. For the rest of the month they scooped us on a daily basis just by being there.

TV news is a competitive business, so clearly someone had to find a way back in and end Sky's monopoly. With Sarajevo under siege, the only access was across the no man's land of the airport, which had Serbian gunmen at either end of the runway and Muslim gunmen on either side. We did it at dusk and were fortunate not to be targeted. Two weeks later we risked our lives again because of an allegation of a massacre of Serbian civilians near the town of Milici. When we got there we were assured that the massacre had indeed occurred – which we found out much later was true – but the road was too dangerous to go forward. Since we did not deal in unverified atrocity stories we returned to Sarajevo empty-handed, except for an interview with a minor member of the Serbian royal family, Princess Belinda, who lived in Surrey and was visiting the troops in Lukavica Barracks. This time we were targeted. I was driving a battered old BBC Vauxhall Carlton – soft-skinned, of course – when someone ill-intentioned opened up on us with small arms. I had with me cameraman Nigel Bateson and interpreter Vladimir Marjanovic. 'Fast as you like,' said Nigel, who was South African. '*Merde!*' said Vladimir, who was multilingual. One of the bullets hit the driver's door without going through it. I wrote to Vauxhall later and thanked them for making an armoured car without knowing it.

And at that point we militarised ourselves. We pleaded for some real protection and received a four-ton beast, an armoured Land Rover, formerly the property of the Royal Ulster Constabulary. We called her Miss Piggy and loved her dearly. We were sent body armour far too heavy to be useful in a fast-moving firefight. They also gave us steel helmets. Two months later, when I was felled by mortar fire near the Marshal Tito Barracks, the steel helmet fell off because I had not fastened it properly and the flak jacket didn't save me because the shrapnel came in just below the flap where it ended. I was expertly treated by the French medical staff at the UN's field hospital in the basement of its headquarters in the PTT building. But when I recovered consciousness after the operation I realised that I had lost my money, my passport and a silver bullet that had nearly killed me two months earlier and that I kept as a lucky charm. I thus had the unusual experience of being wounded by the Serbs and robbed by the French on the same day. But it earned me a gracious letter from John Major and a bottle of whiskey from the Irish Foreign Minister.

And Morley Safer of CBS News, a veteran of the Vietnam War, wrote to me in hospital urging me to act my age and stay away from dangerous places.

We also flew the flag as a safety measure, to help establish who we were. In the summer of 1991 I bought a Union Jack in a tourist kiosk in Leicester Square and carried it to the war zones. I waved it as we walked towards an armoured column of the Yugoslav Army on the Highway of Brotherhood and Unity; we had it with us when we rescued a wounded Serbian soldier and took him to the nearest Croatian clinic, where he was well cared for. We then attached it to our vehicles in Bosnia, first the Vauxhall Carlton and then Miss Piggy. And every evening in Ilidza we held a flag-lowering ceremony, to the tune of 'Land of Hope and Glory' played from a loudspeaker on our balcony. It drew a respectful salute from a passing Serbian colonel.

By that time I had played a part in initiating an unprecedented experiment, a voluntary pooling arrangement between the TV networks and news agencies, so that there would be no exclusives, but all the coverage would be available to everyone. As the front lines settled like a noose around the city, Sarajevo became, day in and day out, the most dangerous place in the world. If the camera crews had competed with each other in the usual way, as much in the line of fire as the soldiers, the casualties would have risen inexorably. The news agencies were reluctant to cooperate at first but saw the sense of it. And so the Sarajevo Agency Pool was established, which operated successfully for three years until the summer of 1995, the time of a fierce upsurge in the fighting. A new TV news agency had come into being, APTN, which stood outside the pool and competed with it for coverage and contracts. Reuters TV backed out of the Sarajevo Agency Pool over an issue of the archive rights for its coverage. Were we really expected to risk our lives for *archive rights*? It was madness. I pleaded for a month's extension, and after that the pooling arrangement was over. It was bold and innovative and undoubtedly saved lives.

It was of course unevenly applied. It penalised some and rewarded others unfairly. One of the American networks had a Canadian correspondent, of the usual rugged good looks, who had an aversion to gunfire and spent most of his time in the basement of the Holiday Inn. His producer brought in the tapes from the other networks and the Agency Pool, where they were edited in the former nightclub. He ventured out of his hiding place once a day to address his camera – and that was all he did. He later had his contract terminated because he was unwilling to work in a war zone. This did not go down well with his network's bosses: one of them said they were looking for correspondents who would break down doors to be assigned to difficult places. The Canadian was not in that mould at all. He took his employers to the Employment Tribunal in London, where I had no hesitation in giving evidence on his behalf. Journalists should not feel obliged to risk their lives to keep their jobs. He won the case but lost on appeal. His network was owned by Disney. We called it Mickey Mouse television.

The real heroes of the Sarajevo Agency Pool were its two Bosnian cameramen, Muharem Osmanagic and Semsudin Cengic, whom we knew as Hari and Chenga. Their contribution and courage were never sufficiently acknowledged, but their coverage was transmitted all over the world and had a lasting impact. Another hero was the BBC cameraman Tihomir Tunukovic, a Croat whose armoured car was blown off the road near Jajce by Serbian gunfire in November 1992. The speech that I gave at his funeral in Zagreb was the most difficult of my life.

No medals were earned by an Associated Press reporter, a Serb who travelled from Belgrade to Sarajevo at the start of the war. Before the BBC office in Ilidza came under mortar fire, he knocked on our door and asked to see the day's coverage. Of course we agreed. He then sat down in front of the TV monitors, still wearing his dark blue steel helmet, and took copious notes. Such are the wonders of technology that he was able to send a vivid eyewitness account of the war without setting foot outside the hotel.

The Sarajevo press corps, usually not more than fifty strong, was a brotherhood and sisterhood of comrades-not-in-arms. 1992 to 1995 were our years of living dangerously. We called ourselves the Sarajevo Survivors' Club. A battle-hardened CNN producer flew into the city one day, took a look at it, and was on the first flight out the following morning. It was not for her, she said. In winter, when the freezing fog shrouded the city for days on end, we welcomed it because it blinded the snipers. We took comfort in adversity. The rooms most sought after were the ones without a view. Ellie Biles of Reuters said: 'Happiness is living in a war zone with the curtains drawn.' Ian Traynor of the *Guardian* asked: 'What is it that the Serbs have against roofs?' We discovered the nutritional value of dandelion soup. We stood our ground. We trained our cameras on the surrounding heights where the guns were trained on us. Our gurus were John Burns of the *New York Times* and Kurt Schork of Reuters. Our leading lady was Christiane Amanpour of CNN, who took the craziest risks, like reporting from the front-line zoo, and somehow survived them, although her camerawoman Margaret Moth was badly wounded. In the early weeks of the war we were all the 'international community' that there was. There were no diplomats, no European Community monitors and for a while no United Nations peacekeepers either. Sarajevo was supposedly the headquarters of the United Nations Protection Force, whose only firepower was a platoon of lightly armed Swedish infantry. UNPROFOR fled in May 1992, having been bombed out of its quarters in the Rainbow Hotel, and returned very cautiously with a battalion of French Canadian armoured infantry, the valiant 'Van Doos', in June.

In the worst of times, the summer of 1995, the UN held its briefings underground in the PTT building. As we waited for the briefers, Alex Ivanko and Gary Coward, we passed the time by rating war-zone quagmires on a scale of one to ten. Vietnam was an eight, we calculated. Bosnia was a twelve.

When we travelled to the Serbs in their mini-capital Pale, as we did regularly for the first half of the war, we called it going to the dark side. Sometimes the journeys were fruitless but always they were necessary. There was something of the Wild West about Republika Srpska. The Serbs were aggressively defensive. It was said of 'Wild Bill' Hickok that he never killed a man except in self-defence, and he spent a lot of time defending himself. So too with the Serbs.

A staff officer on the Bosnian government side asked me: 'Do we Muslims seem strange to you?'

'Not at all,' I answered, 'we are all Europeans.'

'Do you see it as a civil war?' he wondered.

'It belongs in a category all of its own: part religious, part national, part tribal. There never was a war like this before, and – God willing – there never will be again.'

The fighting was nowhere fiercer than in Mostar, which was first bombarded by the Serbs and then the scene of massive ethnic cleansing by the Croats, who drove thousands of Muslims out and blew up their homes. The outgunned Muslims retaliated by hiring the Serbian artillery, at a cost of so many Deutschmarks per shell, to bombard the Croats for them. The Serbs then fired some extra shells, as a goodwill gesture, for nothing. I wrote of the fighting: 'There is neither the will nor the means to end it. Both sides [Croats and Muslims] are using ammunition as if there were no tomorrow, which as far as Mostar is concerned seems a reasonably accurate forecast.' A Bosnian Croat soldier said: 'We fire a thousand rounds and miss everything. They fire three rounds and hit everything.' The Croats rolled barrel bombs downhill into Muslim settlements.

If a faction was losing it would plead with the UN to come and save it; if it was winning it would order the UN to get out of its way. 'If I was worried about catastrophe,' said Lieutenant Colonel Alastair Duncan, Commanding Officer of the Prince of Wales's Own Regiment of Yorkshire, 'I would have resigned five and a half months ago.' Duncan, who rose in rank to major general, was later diagnosed as suffering from acute PTSD.

We were close to our hosts in our base in Vitez, which was the home of Mato and Ruska Taraba. It was not a safe place. Mato was wounded by sniper fire while working in his field at the back. His life was saved by an army field dressing expertly applied by one of our producers. He said: 'As far as we locals are concerned it is a war of thieves.' When the town came under artillery fire Ruska said: 'That's good. It means Mr Martin will be back.' And so of course I was, complete with a heavy winter coat for Mato to wear over his threadbare HVO uniform. Ruska asked me why, unlike others, I walked rather than ran when the shooting started. 'I'm too old to run,' I told her. Besides, I could have as easily run into the shrapnel as away from it.

The British were main players, both militarily in the UN Protection Force and diplomatically in the Council of Ministers of the European Community, of which the UK held the presidency in the crucial second half of 1992. In that capacity Foreign Secretary Douglas Hurd paid a memorable visit to Sarajevo in July 1992 – memorable both for its pessimism and its brevity. He told an American reporter: 'No country, not even your country, is willing to contemplate military intervention.' President Izetbegovic clutched his arm during a brief walk-about. He wore an ill-fitting flak jacket over his diplomatic dark suit. Musicians played Albinoni's *Adagio* reproachfully on every street corner. Hurd was expected to visit the hospital, but headed straight for the airport instead. We had the impression that, like Home Secretary Reginald Maudling in Londonderry in 1970 ('What a bloody awful country!'), he could just not get out fast enough.

We should not have needed to discover the resonance of the first shot fired in anger in Sarajevo; but obviously we did. The victim was a Serb killed at a wedding in Sarajevo in March 1992. In the movie *Welcome to Sarajevo* (starring Woody Harrelson, the barman of *Cheers*, as hero) his identity was changed to make him a Croat. The falsehoods cascaded around us from the outset. Show business required the Serbs to be cast as villains not victims, although actually they were both.

I believe that the tragedy of the Bosnian War was preventable. A senior British diplomat described its prelude and accompaniment, a series of failed diplomatic initiatives, as 'a catalogue of missed opportunities'. We were walking towards a cliff and just kept going. David Rohde of the *New York Times*, one of the best and bravest reporters in the field, wrote of the Srebrenica massacre in July 1995: 'The fall of Srebrenica did not have to happen. There is no need for thousands of skeletons to be strewn across eastern Bosnia. There is no need for thousands of Muslim children to be raised on stories of their fathers, grandfathers, uncles and brothers slaughtered by the Serbs. The fall of Srebrenica could have been prevented.'[4]

The war may have happened anyway, so strong were the forces tearing the republics apart. But it happened when it did because of the fateful decision of the European Community, in December 1991, to recognise Croatia unilaterally. The timing was critical. Vukovar had fallen to the Serbs and 250 patients and staff in its hospital had been massacred. Dubrovnik, a UNESCO World Heritage Site, was under daily bombardment from the Serbs inland and across the bay. The Germans argued for immediate recognition. The British, French and Dutch opposed it.

For chapter and verse of the diplomatic exchanges I am indebted to the American diplomat Herb Okun, who died in 2011. He was a linguist and deputy to Cyrus Vance, the former US Secretary of State, in a series of Balkan peace initiatives. Before the fighting began he presciently warned Radovan Karadzic, the Bosnian Serbs' political leader, 'If you go on talking of the mortal danger to the Serbs you will end up committing war crimes.' Vance and Okun pleaded for the lives of refugees. They crossed active front lines between Serbs and Croats at great risk to themselves. Okun was an experienced crisis manager. He had translated vital Soviet cables in Moscow at the time of the Cuban missile crisis in 1962. Khrushchev called him 'the Ginger Man' because of his shock of red hair. He was appalled by the tragedy unfolding before him in Belgrade, Vukovar and Osijek. He won a measure of respect from the Serbs, but later described Slobodan Milosevic as a 'common gangster'.

Lord Carrington was the Chairman of the Hague Conference, charged with seeking peaceful solutions as Yugoslavia fell apart. He was troubled by the German campaign on Croatia's behalf. On 2 December 1991 he wrote to the European Foreign Ministers: 'An early recognition of Croatia would undoubtedly mean the break-up of the Conference... There is also a real danger, perhaps even a probability, that Bosnia Herzegovina would also ask for independence and recognition, which would be wholly unacceptable to the Serbs in that republic... This might well be the spark that sets Bosnia Herzegovina alight.' Which of course was exactly what happened.

The long-serving German Foreign Minister Hans-Dietrich Genscher replied that Lord Carrington's remarks 'were likely to encourage those forces in Yugoslavia which up to now have firmly opposed the conclusion of the peace process'. Germany was pressing for the recognition of Croatia for reasons that partly had to do with pressures within its governing coalition. Genscher was a Free Democrat and the Christian Social Union party – the Bavarian partners of Chancellor Kohl's Christian Democrats – coveted the job for one of their own. In the first major foreign policy initiative of the reunified Germany, Genscher led the campaign for recognition. He personally showed solidarity with the Croats, aligned himself with the government in Zagreb and prayed in its great cathedral. Streets and squares in Croatia are named after him.

The fateful meeting of the European Community's Council of Ministers was held in Brussels on 16 December 1991. At first the Germans had only the Danes and Belgians with them supporting their stand on Croatia. The others were opposed. Then over a lengthy meeting, and after a working dinner, the arithmetic changed. In the small hours of the morning of 17 December the Twelve agreed on the recognition. Why the change? A late night call was made by the British Foreign Secretary Douglas Hurd to Downing Street. It is hard to resist the conclusion that it had something to do with a ministerial meeting two weeks earlier, in which the Germans had been outstandingly helpful to the British on the opt-out clauses of the Maastricht Treaty, which was under negotiation. Then as now relations with Europe were the fault line of British politics. Prime Minister John Major acclaimed the Maastricht deal. In response to a question by a friendly journalist he called it 'game, set and match'. He won the General Election that followed.

Genscher said: 'The debate was very, very fierce, but the result was better than we could have expected.'

The Maastricht Treaty and the recognition of Croatia were of course separate and unrelated issues. Both John Major and Douglas Hurd have denied any link, in the form of a trade-off, between them. It was more like an unwritten exchange of favours among friends – unwritten, but not unspoken. Hurd said: 'What is true is that when we got to the crunch in Brussels on Slovenia and Croatia, the Germans did say to me "Remember we did take care of your problems three weeks ago or a fortnight ago in Maastricht, so please accept that we have a moral and political problem."'[5]

So Lord Carrington's predictions became reality; and the war began which, once started, proved unstoppable. Within four days of its outbreak it was raging on seventeen different battle-fields. President Milosevic observed: 'The Serbs are well known for making their own history.' On the slopes of Sarajevo the two armies were within hand grenade range of each other. In the first six months of the war the government side gained 100 yards in house-to-house fighting uphill and at heavy cost. As the siege tightened Karadzic said: 'We will not allow so much as a bird to fly in.' We could not count the casualties exactly, but we could see the scale of them from the death notices in the Sarajevo newspaper *Oslobodenje*, which was published from the basement of a ruin.

One of the war's features was the targeting of the innocent. The Geneva Conventions might as well not have existed for all the difference they made. Rocket-propelled aircraft bombs were fired into Sarajevo and one of its suburbs. Prisoners of war were executed. A ceasefire was just a negotiating term that lasted for only as long as it took to pick up the bodies. At various hand-over points, after local agreements, prisoners and bodies were exchanged. The dead were deemed more valuable than the living. Captain Mike Stanley (Milos Stankovic) of the Parachute Regiment coined a term for it: he called it *necrowar*. The city of Sarajevo, in which twelve thousand people were killed, was its *necropolis*.

The Geneva Conventions as drafted in 1949 included the following:

> The parties to the conflict shall at all times distinguish between the civilian population and combatants . . . The civilian population as such, as well as individual civilians, shall not be under attack . . . Indiscriminate attacks are prohibited; this includes an attack that may be expected to cause incidental loss of civilian life . . . Attacks against civilians by way of reprisal are prohibited . . . Starvation of civilians as a method of warfare is prohibited . . . All the wounded and sick, to whichever party they belong, shall be protected and respected . . . The parties to the conflict shall allow the passage of relief consignments . . . Women shall be the object of special respect and shall be protected in particular against rape, forced prostitution and any other form of indecent assault.

Not one of its High Contracting Parties' provisions for the protection of civilians was observed in the Bosnian War. The list of Geneva's prohibitions was the list of Bosnia's practices. Biljina Plavsic, one of the Serbian members of the Collective Presidency when it dissolved in 1992, told Lord Carrington's representative Colm Doyle: 'If it takes the lives of three million people to solve this conflict then let's get on with it.' The population of Bosnia at the time was four and a half million.

Sir Fitzroy Maclean, the soldier and writer who played a notable part in the making of Tito's Yugoslavia, joined us briefly in Sarajevo as it was falling apart. He struck a tragic figure in the darkened and embattled Holiday Inn and died shortly afterwards. He wrote: 'All Yugoslavs (and I use the term advisedly) have one quality in common, an utter reluctance, once aroused, to give in or compromise.'

Herb Okun memorably likened diplomacy without force to baseball without a bat – or as Thomas Hobbes put it centuries earlier in his *Leviathan*, 'Covenants, without the sword, are but words and of no strength to secure a man at all.' The first UN troops into Bosnia, the headquarters staff of the United Nations Protection Force, did not have much in the way of a bat or a sword. Their fighting strength was minimal; and when their reinforcements arrived, in October 1992, they were without heavy weapons and with an unworkable mandate. They could escort aid convoys to Sarajevo but open fire only in self-defence. It was like handing aid supplies in through the window while the murderer stood at the door, so the victims would not be starving when they were shot. UNPROFOR's heavy weapons, including the field artillery of the Rapid Reaction Force, arrived only towards the end in mid-1995. But the RRF was conceived not only as a means of forcing the Serbs to the conference table, but also as an extraction force in case the UN had to cut and run for a second time. For most of its deployment UNPROFOR was peacekeeping in a war where there was no peace to keep. 'We have to defend a policy,' said the UN spokesman Alex Ivanko, 'which no one can coherently explain to us.' The French General Philippe Morillon called it 'a mandate of *angélisme*' – just equip a soldier with a blue helmet and suppose that all will be well.

In March 1995 I recorded an exchange between a British United Nations officer and a BiH (Bosnian) soldier at a roadblock in the Lasva Valley.

'I am from the United Nations. I wish to go through your roadblock.'

'I have orders to turn you back.'

'But the UN has freedom of movement. I *have* to go through.'

'You may not. I have orders to turn you back.'

'Are you sure about that?'

'Quite sure.'

'All right then – have a nice day!'

In May 1995 I wrote in my diary: 'Sniper fire crackles past the Holiday Inn, now almost deserted. There have been no flights for five weeks, and whatever moves on the mountain road is targeted. The war tourists, visiting delegations and international well-wishers have left, and will not return. The patient is dying and its friends are no longer at the bedside. The UN is inert – just *parked*.' This was the desertion of mission and principle that led to the Srebrenica massacre two months later.

The United Nations were specialists in gesture peacekeeping. One of the gestures in 1993, after the failure of the Vance-Owen plan, was the establishment of the International Criminal Tribunal in The Hague. Another was the announcement of the six so-called 'safe areas' – Srebrenica being one of them – implying their protection but without the will to protect them. It was all smoke and mirrors. UNPROFOR was a mixed and variable force: one of its contingents came to Bosnia unarmed and without winter clothing; others were of such poor quality that they might as well not have been there; the Ukrainians traded shamelessly on the black market. At the time of the war's worst atrocity, the Srebrenica massacre, there were more than thirty thousand UN troops in Bosnia who could have prevented it. They stood aside and protected themselves instead. The senior officers in Zagreb and Sarajevo were of different nationalities and too often at odds with each other. Napoleon said: 'Nothing is so important in war as an undivided command.'

I was reminded of the arrival of the UN observers on the Suez Canal after the Yom Kippur War of 1973. However many were deployed they would not be enough. The United Nations had long and hard experience of being stationed on Israel's borders, both in Lebanon and Gaza. It was sometimes tedious and sometimes dangerous duty. I wrote: 'I'm told they have their own private codename for the job they're being asked to do. They call it Operation Sitting Duck.'

It took a combination of facts and forces to bring an end to Operation Sitting Duck in Bosnia. One of these was the Srebrenica massacre; another was the second market-place bomb in Sarajevo of 28 August 1995; a third was the advance of main force Croatian armoured units into Bosnia and the progressive collapse of the Serbs' front lines. The Serbs sued for peace when their real capital, Banja Luka, was within artillery range of the Croats. But still their weakness was rewarded and they got a better deal than they would have done under the Vance-Owen plan. It was the worst solution, but the only solution available at the time.

Herb Okun's explanation of the Dayton Agreement was that the Serbs were finally bombed into accepting their own peace plan. Although they had to give up their districts of Ilidza and Grbavica in Sarajevo, they were left with almost forty-nine per cent of the national territory and their own mini-state, the

Republika Srpska, in which they ran their own affairs unimpeded by outside authority, and regularly threatened to secede. They had originally bargained for sixty-four per cent, on the grounds that they were a people who needed space, while Bosnia's Muslims, concentrated in the cities, were used to living on top of each other.

The General Framework Agreement for Peace in Bosnia and Herzegovina, also known as the Dayton Agreement, brought peace that was only an absence of fighting and peace that was bought at a price. It established a dysfunctional state on the basis of the most expensive and unworkable constitution that the world has ever known, with two separate 'entities', fourteen governments and no fewer than 230 ministers. The story was told of a man who walked into a coffee shop and said: 'Good morning, minister.' Everyone there answered him. They were all ministers of one sort or another.

I imagined what it must be like to be a young Bosnian who had fought in the war and been lucky enough to survive. 'What do I do with the rest of my years, now the war is ending? And how do I do it, in a broken republic where there is no economy, no properly functioning government even, where so many of the young, the better educated and the resourceful have fled, leaving a country of the old and the dispossessed, a shell of the old Bosnia?'

More than twenty years after the end of the war the Bosniaks (Bosnian Muslims), Croats and Serbs mostly live apart from each other. Even the schools are segregated – a legacy of the side war between Muslims and Croats in 1993 and 1994. This is the phenomenon of two schools under one roof, mostly in mixed communities in central Bosnia. Either the children study in different shifts, the Croats in the morning and the Muslims in the afternoon or vice versa; or else the Croats stay in one part of the building and the Muslims in another. A wire fence runs down the corridor between them. The children use separate entrances and playgrounds. They have different curricula, including different versions of their history. They are separated for life, from childhood onwards. They are as unreconciled in peace as they were in war.

In a civil war, wrote Antoine de Saint-Exupéry, the firing line passes through the hearts of men.

'We have no friends but God,' said Radovan Karadzic. And the deputy commander of the Bosnian Army's 7th Glorious Muslim Brigade countered: 'You know on which side God is, and whom he helps.' Amid the war that victimised them all, I wondered what made them so sure.

When the war was over a mini-industry sprang up, in the academic world, fine-combing our coverage of it and wondering, usually from a pro-Serb perspective, if we were not part of some great conspiracy to favour one faction against another. Even at the time of the NATO bombardment, in September 1995, an academic wrote to me asking for my thoughts on the 'inferred frameworks' and 'informing models' of war reporting. Next time I run the trench lines, I thought, I must take with me his precious frameworks and models and see how well they stand up to machine gun fire.

The only growth industry, except for academic speculation, was the building of places of worship. The Serbs erected a great new Orthodox cathedral in open country on the Romanija plain; it became a place of political as well as religious pilgrimage: images of Karadzic and Mladic were sold like icons outside it on holy days. The Serbs then started building a church in Potocari, on a plot of land beside the burial ground of the Muslims killed in the Srebrenica massacre. Sarajevo has more mosques than it needs, many of them paid for by Saudi and Malaysian benefactors. The Croats raised one of the tallest church towers in the world to mark their ownership of the west bank of the Neretva River in Mostar. After all that had happened between them, the peoples of Bosnia built mosques and churches as if they were the holiest people in the world.

And none of it had to happen: the broken cities, the ethnic cleansing, the toppled minarets, the uncleared minefields, the eighteen- and nineteen-year-olds laid to rest in heroes' cemeteries. The war could have been forestalled, or at least foreshortened, by a timely intervention by the western democracies. But the western democracies had no appetite for it. They retreated into language like Douglas Hurd's 'ancient hatreds' and warnings like David Owen's 'don't dream dreams'. A Foreign Office Minister, Douglas Hogg, wrote: 'Armed intervention cannot force people to live together and to refrain from persecuting each other once hatreds are revived.' The result was a war that not only shamed us all but gave a mighty boost to the cause of the Islamic warriors and the jihadism now afflicting the whole of Europe. Two of the 9/11 hijackers, in their 'martyrdom videos', gave the war in Bosnia as their reason for volunteering. Its aftershocks are still with us. It was the most *consequential* war of the late twentieth century.

So why was it right to intervene in Bosnia in 1992 but wrong in Iraq in 2003? Because on an issue of armed intervention to prevent or end a war, every case is different. There are certain tests to be met. First, it must be legal under the Charter of the

United Nations or an authorising resolution of the Security Council. Second, it must be proportionate and within the Geneva Conventions' rules of war. Third, it must be sufficiently supported by public opinion at home: there is no lonelier soul on the planet than a soldier in an unsupported war. Fourth, it must be *doable*. Bosnia passed all these tests. Iraq failed them. Afghanistan failed on the test of *doability*.

Either we intervene or steer clear. There can be no half-measures or middle way. On 19 April 1999 I made a speech in the House of Commons on the bombing of Kosovo and Belgrade.

I shared a television studio with the Minister for the Armed Forces [Dr John Reid] last week, and I was interested to hear him remark that the Government were doing more than some had urged them to do and less than others had urged. It is as if the Government were piloting a great ship through a large waterway with a channel on either side and a great rock in the middle. They will not take the left-hand channel because of the voices urging them to take the right-hand channel and vice versa, so they head straight for the rock . . . I assure the House that genocide requires not only the brutality and hatred that make it happen but the indifference that lets it happen. Let not that indifference be ours.[6]

When the war in Sarajevo was at its worst, I met an old man, well dressed for those times, with a bunch of wild flowers for sale. I paid him an inflated amount for them, because he must have risked his life to pick them, and he had an air of luminous goodness about him, like the ghost of a saint. He murmured his thanks, and said that something extraordinary was going to happen to me, even more extraordinary than had happened already. Looking back on the politics of 1997, I suppose that he was right.

Three more stories of Bosnia stayed in the mind. One was of a reporter who wished to interview a sniper in Sarajevo. Both sides had them, each as indiscriminate in their targeting as the other's. So he fixed it up with the man's commander. At the appointed time he visited the sniper, who was peering out between the breeze blocks of his forward defences. The journalist asked the sniper: 'What do you see?' The sniper answered: 'I see two people walking in the street. Which of them do you want me to shoot?' It was at this point that the journalist realised that he had made a dreadful mistake. He pleaded with the sniper to shoot neither. As he turned and left, he heard two shots in rapid fire behind him. 'That was a pity,' said the sniper, 'you could have saved one of their lives.'

The second story concerned Radovan Karadzic's daughter Sonja, who ran the International Press Centre in Pale, the mini-capital of the Bosnian Serbs' mini-state. We found her deeply unattractive at every level. For an accreditation fee of twenty Deutschmarks a day she would tell us where we were not allowed to go and whom we were not allowed to interview. To get our revenge we invented the golden fish story, which went like this. One day when the international negotiators were trying to get her father to agree to their map of a postwar Bosnia, he stormed out of the session and went fishing, taking the map with him. On the river bank, he caught a golden fish with magical properties. 'If you put me back in the river,' said the fish, 'I can grant you any wish you want.' 'Very well,' said Karadzic, 'then make this map acceptable to my people.' The fish rubbed its fins in embarrassment. 'I'm very sorry,' it said, 'I should have told you that I don't do maps. Is there anything else I can do for you?' 'Yes,' said Karadzic, 'you can make my daughter the prettiest girl in Bosnia.' Then the fish said: 'I think I'll take another look at that map.'

The third story was told by Karadzic himself, who was not a humourless fanatic (not humourless anyway), as Bosnia's Collective Presidency fell apart in February 1992. It was about two prisoners in one of Tito's jails.

One asked the other: 'How long is your sentence?'

'Ten years,' he replied.

'What did you do?'

'I did nothing.'

'That can't be true, you must have done something. The most you get for doing nothing is eight years.'

14. TERRORISM AND JIHAD

The late 1960s and 1970s were years of what we called terror-ism. We were much obsessed by terrorism back then, usually in the context of Israel/Palestine, however well or ill we understood it. Terrorists hijacked the Munich Olympics in 1972. They hijacked aircraft, including an Air France flight to Entebbe, in 1976. They hijacked a meeting of OPEC oil ministers in Vienna in 1975, and demanded an aircraft to fly them – hijackers and ministers together – to Algeria, or they would kill a hostage every fifteen minutes. The Austrian government of Chancellor Kreisky complied and broadcast the hijackers' demands at regu-lar intervals as they made their successful and well-publicised getaway. This was the exploit that made Carlos the Jackal, the Venezuelan Ilich Ramirez Sanchez, the most wanted man in the world. Not only the Palestinians and their sympathisers but also the Irish were active in hostage-taking. I felt that I had been unofficially appointed the BBC's terrorism correspondent. One month I would be staking out a house in Monasterevin, Ireland, where an IRA gunman had kidnapped an innocent Dutch businessman, Tiede Herrema. The next month I would be chasing after the aircraft hijackers, always an airport behind them. Or I would be in the Middle East, reporting on the Israelis' counter-terrorism. (It was their word for it: after Munich, they had vowed to fight terrorism with counter-terrorism.)

In January 1968 I reported from the Gaza Strip: 'The Arabs themselves are feeling the effects of terrorism. A hand grenade was thrown from one of these houses at a passing army jeep. The area was cordoned off but the culprit escaped. And the Israelis responded by blowing up four of the houses. The Arabs of course were cleared from the area first, and given the opportunity to take their belongings with them. Afterwards they were allowed back in to pick up some of the pieces. Israelis insist that action of this kind, stern and swift, is the only way to tackle terrorism.'

Another note was of a Palestinian attack on Beit She'an in northern Israel in 1974. The Arabs had stormed an apartment block. Eighteen Israelis were injured jumping out of windows, before the three Palestinians were killed in the counter-attack. 'The crowd demanded that the bodies [of the attackers] be thrown down to them. There was a feeling gripping them of tribal anger . . . Here again was a case where Israel's tighter border security had failed. The final scene was a gruesome one. Two of the bodies were thrown down and burned. Later, women and children spat on the ashes.'

Nearly thirty years before 9/11, I wrote in my notebook: 'Any aircraft is a bomb, an aircraft controlled by a maniac is a bomb, not necessarily to drop milk churns, as the IRA ineptly attempted.' This was a reference to a failed plan to drop a bomb in a milk churn on the police station in Strabane, Northern Ireland. One of the conspirators was an English woman, Rose Dugdale, whose partner had kidnapped the unfortunate Dutch businessman in Monasterevin. Everything seemed to connect. The Dutchman survived and is now an honorary citizen of the Irish Republic.

Terrorism is not only the province of revolutionary groups and non-state actors. There can be terrorist states as well. An obvious example is revolutionary France under its reign of terror in 1793 and 1794. Stalin's Soviet Union fitted the description, as did Idi Amin's Uganda – and, in our time, so does Kim Jong-un's North Korea and the ISIS mini-state in parts of Iraq and Syria. The Iran hostage crisis of 1979–81, in which fifty-three Americans, mostly diplomats, were held prisoner by the Iranians, was an act of state terrorism that (my notebooks of the time remind me) denied President Jimmy Carter his second term. If Operation Eagle Claw, the attempt to rescue the hostages in April 1980, had succeeded, he believed that he would have been re-elected. But it ended in death in the desert when two of the helicopters collided. The hostages were released on the day when Ronald Reagan rode in triumph to the White House.

And a *counter-terrorist* state? That surely has to be Israel. One of my many assignments during those years was the trial of six Mossad agents in the Norwegian ski resort of Lillehammer in 1973. They had been assigned there, with at least nine others, as part of Operation Wrath of God to assassinate Ali Hassan Salameh, one of the leaders of Black September, which had carried out the Munich massacre of Israeli athletes. They got the wrong man, and instead killed Ahmed Bouchiki, an innocent Moroccan waiter. I wrote: 'Lillehammer was not exactly the murder capital of the frozen north. No murder had been committed there since 1936, and the Norwegian police did not have to work forensic miracles to deduce that there must have been an extraordinary motive.

There was. Bouchiki was tracked and hunted by a murder squad assigned by the Israeli intelligence service Mossad. The group had the name of a contact, Ben Haman, who they believed would lead them to Salameh.' Instead the hunted Black September leader had managed to deceive the Israelis by spreading false information about his whereabouts and the innocent Moroccan paid the price. Most of the Mossad gang got away. Of the lesser figures who were arrested, one was acquitted and the others received prison sentences of one year to five and a half years for complicity in the killing. They were prosecuted under a law dealing with hostile actions on Norwegian soil in a conflict in which Norway was a neutral. The prosecutor said: 'It is not difficult to understand why Israel fights a kind of terrorism the world abhors; but in Norwegian law we cannot accept such an act.'

Israel has also regularly deployed what is surely the ultimate terrorist weapon, yet is not in the armoury of any non-state terrorist organisations: it is the cluster bomb, which is essentially a system for scattering anti-personnel mines across a target zone. Cluster munitions were first used by the Germans in the Second World War. They then became an area denial weapon dropped principally on enemy airfields. In recent conflicts the casualties inflicted by them have been ninety per cent civilian. They were used in southern Lebanon by the Israelis from 1982 onwards. In the summer of 2006 more than a million bomblets were fired into areas from which Israel had been attacked by rocket fire. An eyewitness wrote: 'There is no possible justification for the continued manufacture and use of these vile weapons. I currently live in Lebanon and see their impact all around me on a daily basis in the hordes of mutilated and incapacitated men and boys who have no other option but to beg in the street.'

Sometimes the bombers will get through, as they did in our skies in the Second World War. We have defeated aggression before and can do so again. Our values are stronger than our enemy's and will prevail. It rests on consent and the settled will of the people to choose or change their government. As Vaclav Havel said of Czechoslovakia's Velvet Revolution: 'The acquiescent, humiliated and sceptical Czech people managed to find the enormous strength in the space of a few weeks to shake off the totalitarian system in a completely decent and peaceful way.'

The path to our present predicament led through Bosnia. The Mujahedin had brought down the Soviets in Afghanistan – quite literally, with their American supplied Stinger shoulder-held missiles. Some of them and their allies were looking for their next battlefield. They found it in Bosnia. Foreign fighters made their way there in early 1993 under some kind of humanitarian cover. More than a battalion strong, they soldiered in the centre of the country as part of the Mujahed Brigade, alongside but not under the command of the BiH (Bosnian) Army. They fought not only the Serbs but the Croats. The HVO (Croatian Defence Force) showed us their identity cards after a suicidal early morning attack on the town of Vitez. The dead included Iranians, Saudis and Yemenis (always in the forefront of Islamic fighters).

The images that we beamed across the Islamic world, of Muslim victims and ruined mosques, were hugely influential in recruiting volunteers in the jihadists' cause. And yet the western democracies hesitated to take the actions that could have ended it all. Malcolm Rifkind, when he succeeded Douglas Hurd as Foreign Secretary, quoted Lord Palmerston with approval: 'The furtherance of British interests should be the only object of a British Foreign Secretary.' But look back on it now: our failure to intervene when we could have intervened in Bosnia ran contrary to both our interests and principles. We sowed the wind and reaped the whirlwind. We are reaping it still.

And now the time of jihad is upon us. Wherever we are and wherever we travel we are threatened by the enemy without (the foreign jihadis) and the enemy within (the home-grown variety). By bombing and beheading they wish to murder their way to the establishment of a worldwide caliphate. They are not open to compromise or negotiation. It looks unending – a war that we must not lose but may not win, but will just have to adapt to and go on fighting. It calls for patience, resilience and the maintenance of the best intelligence agencies in the world.

We have to deal with suicide bombers, and even with *child* suicide bombers. Suicide attacks are a twenty-first-century innovation. They were not used by the Mujahedin against the Russians in Afghanistan. In all the violent history of that country they were never used until the Taliban took on ISAF (the International Security Assistance Force), especially after its surge into Kandahar and Helmand in 2005 and 2006. Suicide attacks are brutal, indiscriminate and difficult to defend against. It will be a long haul.

We tend to think of jihadism and terrorism Euro-centrically, as if we were the principal victims. We are not. The reign of terror is worldwide. In Orlando, Florida the principal victims are Americans. In Nigeria they are Nigerians. In Mali they are Malians. In the Democratic Republic of Congo they are Congolese. In South Sudan they are South Sudanese. In West Equatoria, its most remote province, I came upon an eleven-year-old boy who had been forced by the Lord's Resistance Army to club his own father to death. It was an inexpressible horror. As Elie Wiesel said of an earlier genocide, 'There are things I cannot say; I cannot say them.'

To draw support from the jihadist 'enemy within' the British government embarked on a number of initiatives. One of these was 'Remembering Srebrenica', a series of commemorative events that would in effect give the Muslims their own 'Holocaust Day'. I introduced the first at Lancaster House in July 2013 and then led a multi-faith delegation to Srebrenica and Sarajevo. The difficulty was that other Bosnian atrocities – with fewer victims but of the same character – were not marked in this way; and in some of these the Serbs were not perpetrators but victims. So the doubt arose: were we engaging in dialogue at home in ways that actually impeded it abroad? The Bosnian War continues to cast long shadows.

It is also important that we in our vulnerable western democracies do not damage our open societies by our manner of defending them – for instance, by doubling or trebling the length of time for which a terrorist suspect can be held without charge. In that case the bomber will have won twice over, the first time by the original loss of life and then by a panic-driven response to it. In 2011 the Conservative MP David Davis quixotically resigned his seat in south Yorkshire and called a by-election on the issue of civil liberties. His co-speakers on the hustings were not mainstream politicians but Bob Geldof, Shami Chakrabarti of Liberty and myself. His fellow Conservatives thought it a bit of a nuisance. He was easily re-elected.

In the town hall in Hull, and apparently off the back of an envelope, Bob Geldof gave an oration about civil liberties that impressed all who heard it and was by no means a conventional stump speech at election time.

> This time uniquely you are being asked to decide about what kind of people we are and what kind of country we wish to live in. This is a fight about the legal boundaries of the state and how much the state can and should remove our liberties before it fundamentally changes the nature of who and what we are. I was told that David Davis was out on a limb on this one. Shamefully that is true. But it is the right limb to be out on. This is about justice. It is about liberty, it is about your rights, it is about Magna Carta and what Britain was, is and must continue to be. It is against the whole flabby, conforming, brainwashed, gullible crap of it all.

There is no escape from the jihadist perils ahead of us. The only way to survive a typhoon, said Joseph Conrad, is always to face it.

15. IRAQ – THE RECKONING

In April 2000 I gave my one and only concert performance, at the Bridgewater Hall in Manchester. The BBC Philharmonic provided the music, and I (who have a tin ear) the narration for Aaron Copland's *Lincoln Portrait*, in which Copland's music underscores some of the greatest of Abraham Lincoln's speeches. Before the performance, the orchestra sent me a tape of Margaret Thatcher's rendition of the same piece, which was characteristically dramatic, and I would even say over-the-top. Mine was quieter. One speech struck me in particular as appropriate to our time. It was delivered at the height of the American Civil War. Lincoln said: 'As our case is new, we must think anew and act anew. We must disenthrall ourselves.'

One of the beliefs from which we must disenthrall ourselves in our own time is that there can be military solutions to political problems. I experienced this as a young soldier in Cyprus. I met it again as an MP forty years later.

Tony Blair's first military adventure as Prime Minister was Operation Desert Fox, a four-day campaign of bombing Iraq from 16 to 19 December 1998. It was conducted alongside the Americans, with the British as usual the junior partners. Critics described it at the time as 'recreational bombing'. The *casus belli* was Saddam Hussein's alleged defiance of a UN Security Council resolution and his denial of access to weapons inspectors. The targets were the sites where he was believed to be developing his weapons of mass destruction (WMD), his command and control centres and even one of his palaces. The operation was as usual claimed to have been a success, although there were growing doubts about the accuracy of the bombing; and the WMD, of course, were never found.

The short campaign foreshadowed the Great Mistake of Blair's prime ministership. Regime change was already on his agenda. He warned of 'the risks if we do not halt Saddam's programme of developing chemical and biological WMDs'. He told us in the Commons that he was seeking ways of 'improving the possibility of removing Saddam Hussein altogether'.

I was in the House at the time, on my cross-bench seat, and found myself making common cause with the Awkward Squad. On matters of armed intervention a Prime Minister must make a convincing case. In December 1998, as in March 2003, he failed to do so. I wrote in a newspaper column: 'As an Independent MP I have voted with this government more than against it, and will probably continue to do so [Actually, as time went by, I did not], but I cannot support this enterprise.'

Operation Desert Fox was the overture. The main event was the invasion of Iraq, which followed five years later in 2003. The origins of the Great Mistake are well enough known by now and the facts are beyond challenge. The intention to go to war was concealed, and even denied, until shortly before its outbreak.

The intelligence was framed to fit the policy, rather than the policy to fit the intelligence. The vital decisions were taken without due process by the Prime Minister and his inner circle. The Cabinet was sidelined and not adequately consulted. Even the Cabinet Secretary was excluded. Proximity and partnership with the Americans were everything. The ambassador in Washington, Christopher Meyer, was inelegantly instructed to get up the arse of the Bush Administration and stay there. Tony Blair told his intimates: 'It's worse than you think: I actually believe in this.'

The military were by no means of one mind. On the eve of the war Admiral Sir Michael Boyce, Chief of the Defence Staff, threatened to resign unless the Attorney General, Peter Goldsmith, gave an unequivocal judgment – or, 'better view' – that it was legal. He too had been kept out of the loop. He changed his mind and followed the beat of the war drums. So thin was the intelligence and so high were the stakes that there should even then have been a resignation at Chief of Staff level. If General Sir Rupert Smith had been one of them (which he very nearly was), I believe that there would have been. Senior army officers on the ground were worried that the war lacked sufficient public support. One described his front-line soldiers as 'down in the mouth'. Acts of indiscipline damaged the Army's reputation. General Sir Michael Rose, a former Adjutant General, believed that Tony Blair should have been impeached for embarking on a war on such flimsy grounds.

I visited Basra for UNICEF in April 2003, a month after the invasion. It was a thieves' paradise. The Ali Babas, as they called themselves, were stripping the copper wiring from schools and government buildings. They were looting the fixtures and fittings of the Sheraton Hotel. They were tearing down UN outposts on the border with Kuwait. It seemed that the only plan for Day Two was occasional and ineffectual baton charges. Brigadier (later Major General) Graham Binns concluded that 'the best way to stop looting was just to get to the point where there was nothing left to loot'.

It was left to a brave individual to hold Tony Blair to account. Reg Keys was a quiet and unassuming paramedic from Solihull, approaching retirement. His son Tom was a soldier who had served in the Parachute Regiment in Sierra Leone, then transferred to the Royal Military Police on his father's advice. Reg feared for his son's life and thought that the RMP would be safer. In June 2003 Tom Keys was on duty with six other RMPs in the town of Majar al-Kabir near Basra when they were isolated in a police station and surrounded by an angry mob. Their radios failed them and they were hacked to death.

Reg then became a founder member of Military Families Against the War, a group of parents whose children had been killed in Iraq. With no political background himself he decided to stand against the Prime Minister in his Sedgefield constituency in June 2005. It was Tony Blair's last campaign and Reg's first. I was asked to support him and had no hesitation in doing so. So did a number of others including Brian Eno on the left and Freddie Forsyth on the right. Standing in the rain outside the war memorial to the Durham Light Infantry, Freddie delivered a stirring speech about our debt to our soldiers. I drove up to Sedgefield and knocked on doors with Reg for the next three weeks. He had originally planned to stand against the Defence Secretary Geoff Hoon in Ashfield; but then he reasoned, why go for the monkey when he could take on the organ-grinder? It was the first time in the long history of British warfare that the politicians had been obliged to deal with a militant campaign by the families of the fallen.

We knew that he would not win the seat but that he would do well. His 4,252 votes were, for an Independent, an extremely strong performance. In this expectation I had drafted an election-night speech for him. He improved on it immeasurably on delivery. The speech was note-perfect and the undisputed highlight of election night. The Prime Minister had to stand there and take it.

Reg Keys said:

Fighting this campaign has not been an easy task for me. But I had to do it for my son Thomas Keys, killed in Iraq four days short of his twenty-first birthday. He went to war under controversial circumstances – *extremely* controversial circumstances. [Applause.] If this war had been justified by international law I would have grieved but not campaigned. If weapons of mass destruction had been found in Iraq I would have grieved but not campaigned. Tonight there are lessons to be learned. I hope in my heart that one day the Prime Minister will say 'sorry'.

After the war there were two limited inquiries into certain aspects of it. One was by a judge, Lord Hutton, into the circumstances surrounding the death of the MOD scientist David Kelly: it exonerated the government and excoriated the BBC. The other was by Lord Butler, the former Cabinet Secretary, into the uses of intelligence about Iraq's weapons of mass destruction (the WMD that were never found): he concluded, with understatement, that the government had placed more weight on the evidence than it would bear.

It took regime change at home before there could be the full investigation that the circumstances required. In June 2009, two years after Gordon Brown had become Prime Minister, he announced the setting up of the Chilcot Inquiry. Its terms of reference were to establish what had happened and to identify the lessons learned, so that the country might be better placed to deal with similar emergencies in the future. Its chairman was Sir John Chilcot, a former diplomat who had also served on the Butler Inquiry. The other members were two historians, Sir Lawrence Freedman and Sir Martin Gilbert; Sir Roderic Lyne, a former ambassador to Moscow; and Baroness Prashar from the cross-benches of the House of Lords. Critics noted that it lacked anyone with legal or military experience, although General Sir Roger Wheeler was one of its advisers; that Sir Lawrence Freedman had provided the original draft of Tony Blair's notorious Chicago speech; and that the Churchill scholar Sir Martin Gilbert had been an outspoken supporter of the war, writing in 2004 that President George W. Bush and Tony Blair might one day 'join the ranks of Franklin D. Roosevelt and Winston Churchill'.

The Inquiry began its work on 30 July 2009. Between November 2009 and February 2011, 190 witnesses were called in three rounds of public hearings. They included all the main decision-makers: politicians, diplomats and senior military officers. Tony Blair appeared twice and was typically impenitent: 'In the end there was a decision that had to be made: on the basis of the information available, to decide whether to join the US coalition and remove Saddam; or to stay out. I decided we should be in.'[1] At the end of his first day's evidence he was asked if there was anything further that he wished to say, which was an open opportunity to express regret to the families of the 179 British soldiers, marines and airmen killed in the war. He chose not to take it.

The Inquiry was supposed to have completed its work by the end of 2010. Instead it dragged on . . . and on . . . and on for another six years. It began with five members and ended with four, following the death of Sir Martin Gilbert in 2015. Its report was postponed first until after the General Election in 2015 and then until after the European Referendum in 2016. The long delay in its publication was ascribed to the process of Maxwellisation, which was the late Robert Maxwell's legacy to the English language. He was a former newspaper publisher, Labour MP and generally shady character who borrowed from his newspaper's pension fund and drowned in mysterious circumstances in 1991. The Department of Trade and Industry, in an inquiry into his affairs that ran between 1971 and 1973, concluded that he was not a fit person to hold the stewardship of a public company. He then took the DTI to court, and the judge ruled broadly in his favour. From that point on, official inquiries were required to give the right of reply to those who might be criticised.

The report was finally published in July 2016. It ran to eleven volumes and more than two million words and was emphatically not a whitewash, but a devastating analysis of 'an intervention which went badly wrong, with consequences to this day'. It included a revealing note from Prime Minister Blair to President Bush nine months before the invasion: 'I will be with you, whatever.' It found that the invasion was not a last resort and that military action had been chosen 'before peaceful options had been exhausted'; that Saddam Hussein posed 'no imminent threat' at the time; that policy on Iraq was made on the basis of 'flawed intelligence and assessments'; that an intelligence report 'may have lifted a key claim about Iraq's chemical weapons capability from a Hollywood film *The Rock*'; that planning for the aftermath had been 'woefully inadequate' and that no hindsight was required to have identified the risks of regional instability.

This was the basis on which the men and women of the armed forces had been sent to war, some of them ill-protected and with shoddy equipment, and so many of them had been killed. The blame was shared by the deceived majority of Labour and Conservative MPs who had voted for the war: some of them described it to me later as the worst mistake of their careers.

As with Nuremberg, so with Chilcot: the force of the process lay not only in its verdicts but in the accumulated mass of the evidence on which they were grounded.

And Reg Keys concluded: 'Thank you, Sir John, you have done the families proud.'

16. OBSERVATIONS

Forget about fiction. The events that I lived through were so extraordinary and *unimaginable* that it seemed a waste of time to try to turn them into make-believe. In the quieter moments of a war, I would sometimes look around me at the details of the wreckage both human and physical, the lost childhoods and broken lives and blitzed buildings, and recall the dark humour and strange liaisons and the singular smell of death, and wonder how some future movie-maker could *begin* to reconstruct it all. The answer was that he (and it was always a he) could not. From *Apocalypse Now* to *Salvador* to *Welcome to Sarajevo* I walked out of all the movies of the wars that I had been in. For all of the multi-millions spent on them, none of them even got close.

As the man said in the *Daily Mail*, you couldn't make it up.

In Alexandra Palace, the home of BBC TV News until 1970, the bar was twice the size of the studio. Some of the cameramen were originally taxi drivers: whatever the quality of their news film, they knew their way around the back-doubles, drunk or sober. Their lockers contained expenses claims, dopesheets, shot-lists, cans of unexposed film and bottles of booze. They worked in two shifts, the drunk shift and the not-so-drunk shift. Their travelling essentials included changing bags for the film and corkscrews for the bottles. One of them with a taste for Irish whiskey hung a sign in his room in the Grand Central Hotel in Belfast: 'Emergency Powers'.

The cameramen worked extensively abroad but were neither linguistically gifted nor internationally minded. They referred to all foreign currencies as 'grotniks'. Their expenses claims, which were marvels of creativity, financed girlfriends, swim-ming pools and conservatories.

The technical foul-ups were not only regular but popular. The sequences of film were threaded onto a machine called a tele-cine – and then, when a news story was dropped on transmission, the system could not cope. Michael Aspel was so brilliant at deal-ing with these mishaps that the audience looked forward to them and were disappointed when things went smoothly. In 1966 BBC Two experimented with two newsreaders, a double act, the Morecambe and Wise of TV news. There was a telephone on their desk. When it rang, one of them handed it to the other. 'It's for you,' he said. The opening of BBC Two coincided with a power cut and was introduced by candlelight.

Before electronic graphics there were cardboard graphics, complete with a children's lettering set. Then there was a techni-cal innovation, the magnetic board on which symbols and figures, like those for the trade deficit, were moved by the presenter. (The trade deficit was a constant staple of TV news back then.) One night the board demagnetised and Michael Aspel had to pick up the pieces.

On another well-remembered night, on a news summary on BBC Two, the newsreader stumbled and fell over the trade deficit. The numbers defeated him. He said it was 'awfully large'. Fleet Street took an interest. The incident was explained by the BBC press office as a reaction to medication. The medication had been taken in the bar.

The reporters' room in the Television Centre was a fiercely competitive environment, in which two of its rougher characters came to blows. Michael Buerk drily recalled his first meeting with Kathryn Adie in the early days of BBC Radio Bristol: 'I don't know what became of Kate, but she must have made her mark.' The relationship between Kate and John Simpson was like a global skirmish ranging across the world from Beijing to Bucharest, although she never saw him as a rival. The reporters' room was an all male environment until the welcome arrival of Kate and Angela Rippon, who did their best to civilise it.

In 1966 the Chinese forced the government of Macao, still then a Portuguese colony, into a humiliating climb-down. After eight weeks of negotiation, the Governor was forced to read out a public apology for the use of force against a demonstration. The Chinese achieved this peacefully by the original means of closing their restaurants to the Portuguese.

My mission was to try to report the Cultural Revolution – not from mainland China, which was closed to us, but from Macao, Hong Kong and Taiwan. No lens was long enough. My insight into the Chinese mind was provided principally by taking tea (at the price of malt whisky) with an attractive lady called Elizabeth in a nightclub in Taipei.

So much of television in the early days was, in fact, radio. In July 1970 a Dan-Air aircraft crashed in Spain killing 116 people.

The cameraman was arrested and the camera was impounded at Barcelona Airport. All that was left was the telephone. 'The bodies were brought down from the mountainside in four covered wagons, and buried by a team of four British doctors and five assistants, working by the light of a hurricane lamp. A trail of blood led up the cemetery steps. Beyond that the scene was simply too appalling to describe.'

Although we were supposed to be broadcasters, we travelled without any means of communication whatsoever. Radio reports were shouted down landlines and TV reports were airfreighted to Heathrow, where the BBC and ITN had their own shipping offices. All we took with us on our overseas missions was a file of old newspaper cuttings provided by News Information. Everything else we had to find out for ourselves. Before the age of electronic newsgathering we either had the story or we did not: we could not 'fold in' other people's footage as if it were our own.

The war-zone hotels were special. They were not necessarily the best hotels in the city, but the ones where we gathered and traded gossip and kept an eye on each other. They included the Continental Palace in Saigon, the Commodore in Beirut, the Camino Real in El Salvador and the Holiday Inn in Sarajevo, which was the greatest of them all because of its shell-shattered exterior and its proximity to the front line. Sometimes the press corps divided. In Zagreb the newspaper reporters ('pencils') used the Excelsior and the TV people the InterContinental. In Saigon the American networks took over the Caravelle, where the prostitutes were charged on their credit cards as room service, which we supposed in a sense they were.

The balcony bar of the Continental Palace, once frequented by Graham Greene, was known as the Continental Shelf. It was the *Exchange and Mart* of news and rumour. Graham Greene being absent, I made do with the company of John Pilger.

The most unusual war-zone injury I heard of was that of a correspondent who broke his foot while getting into the hotel Jacuzzi. I thought that the exploit deserved an ode.

> Never himself a soldier, he did well,
> He knew his stuff, Kalashnikov and Uzi,
> Tactics and troops were all grist to his mill;
> He covered wars successfully until
> One day in one of them he slipped and fell
> While getting into the hotel Jacuzzi.
> He limped on painfully, since war is hell,
> And then, being wounded, he sued the hotel.

In a war zone you welcome oncoming traffic: it means that the road ahead is not yet closed. If you come upon a village with no people in it *and no chickens either*, it means you are in no man's land and should beat a hasty retreat.

In the 1973 Yom Kippur War the great conductor Zubin Mehta asked if he could hitch a ride with us to the Golan Heights. He was a strong supporter of Israel and wished to see the war for himself. I reluctantly turned him down on the trivial grounds that he had no accreditation. I have regretted it ever since.

Like all reporters, but war reporters especially, I hated being 'spiked'. On 5 November 1972 a report from Vietnam about a firefight on the highway north of Saigon was dropped to make space for a story about twelve dead swans on the Upper Thames. The name of the editor who did it was Derek Maude. He wore a black eye-patch, sometimes on the left eye and sometimes on the right. I admired him but never forgave him.

In those days the news was compressed, rather than expanded, to fill the space available. Derek Maude instructed us in the virtues of brevity. He said: 'The greatest story in the world was told in two words, "Jesus wept".'

The next worst thing to being spiked was being 'ooved'. 'Oov' stood for out of vision. What this meant was that a report was scrapped except for a few of its pictures, which were narrated by the newsreader in the studio. In March 1992 I was covering a Turkish earthquake during a British election campaign – an unequal contest. Before I went I sought an assurance from head-quarters that there would still be an appetite for 'real news'. There was not. My diary noted:

Awoke to find that my previous day's report, an account of the suffering of Turks in outlying communities, has been 'ooved' – victim of election overkill. Only nine minutes of real news out of forty. Consider strike action. Resolve to soldier on . . . Dash back with the story. Road blocked by avalanche. Avalanche cleared. Power failure. Can't edit. Power restored. Edit rushed and completed. Feed point locked. Frantic calls to Ankara. Feed point unlocked. It finally works. Does anyone care?

Three weeks later the war in Bosnia broke out – and then, for a while, they did care.

When there was no room at the inn, in 1968, I stayed in the Bar Flores, a windowless brothel in Equatorial Guinea, which was a staging post for aid for stricken Biafra. Who else but a war reporter would know the whereabouts of brothels in Equatorial

Guinea? Or that the prostitutes in the Federal Palace Hotel in Lagos wished to be known as seamstresses?

As a general rule the size of a country is in inverse proportion to the splendour of its airport VIP lounge, or lounges. The principal airport in Malawi has three of them. There is a VIP lounge for ministers coming and going, a VVIP lounge for visiting heads of state, and a VVVIP lounge for the President himself.

In 1970 the Europa in Belfast had the distinction of being the most bombed hotel in the world. ('In such surroundings,' said the hotel brochure, 'you instinctively relax.') The bombs were usually planted in the lift shaft and blew up the water supply. On one occasion the general manager, Harper Brown, provided us with half a bottle of champagne each to brush our teeth with. The bar was renamed Harper's Bar in his honour.

In Londonderry we stayed in the Melville Hotel, which was like a war-zone Fawlty Towers. One morning the cameraman scanned the menu and asked for bacon and egg without the bacon. 'Bacon is compulsory, sir,' said the waiter.

When the United Kingdom joined the European Community I reported the farmers' frustration: 'Someone's trying to take your Christmas turkey and wrap it up in six pages of Common Market regulations.' We nearly did not get into the Common Market because of a row over New Zealand's dairy exports in 1971. I described the haggling, which seemed interminable, as a 'running crunch'. The camerawork on the historic conclusion was somewhat shaky, because it was three o'clock in the morning and the cameraman was blind drunk.

And when the protracted process to move from imperial to metric weights and measures began, I started a report on the evening news in February 1966 with the words 'Consider the common screw . . .'

In Cabanha Maior, a remote village in northern Portugal in 1974, an army officer, Captain Freitas d'Oliveira, was trying to persuade the people of the virtues of revolutionary democracy. He said he had to break the myth that the Communists ate babies for breakfast. All the parties were democratic and the Christian Democrats were no more democratic than anyone else. But it was a hard sell. The revolution had bypassed Cabanha Maior.

Sir Mark Tully, the BBC's majestic Voice of India, was banned from the country by Prime Minister Indira Gandhi from 1975 to 1977. A post was found for him in the London newsroom. Some broadcasters are just not studio animals. He was one. (I am another.) The unhappiest newsreader I ever saw was Tully Sahib.

Somewhere along the line I met the reporter who, in the Congo, asked the notorious question 'Anyone here been raped and speaks English?' He started at the *Mirror* and moved to the BBC, which was then recruiting from the heavy end of Fleet Street. Edward Behr of *Newsweek* used it as the title of his memoirs. Years later, on Bloody Sunday, the reporter made an ignominious escape from Londonderry, when the cameraman Cyril Cave smuggled him out in the boot of his car.

Even the name was contentious. The rule was that we called it Londonderry (Protestant) at the start of the report, but could use Derry (Catholic) for the rest. A local comedian, Gerry Anderson, found the perfect compromise: he called it Stroke City.

Slogans at the Organisation of African Unity Summit in Uganda in 1975 were notable for their propaganda on behalf of the head of state, who could rival the TV networks in self-promotion. The slogans included 'Field Marshal Amin's brilliant operation' and

'We are happy under the care of Field Marshal Amin'. A Ugandan beauty queen became Miss OAU, which was not surprising, since the other contestants were all from Uganda too.

To western journalists seeking to work in Uganda, one of three things could happen. You could be thrown out and kept out; you could be imprisoned; or you could be let in and treated as an honoured guest. It was as an honoured guest that I was shown the brewery at the source of the Nile. It was formerly under Asian, and then African, ownership. The beer that they brewed there was called 'Economic War'.

If you are assigned to a country that has a Ministry of Information, it is probably a dictatorship. If you are assigned to a country in which the Director of Information is also the Director of Security, it is certainly a dictatorship.

The highest level of debate in a democratic contest was surely achieved in the Independence Referendum in Quebec in 1980, with the federalist Pierre Trudeau on one side and the separatist René Lévesque on the other. And they did it in two languages. Even the insults were special: Trudeau described Robert Bourassa, the independent-minded provincial premier, as '*un mangeur de hot dogs*'. Justin Trudeau, the current Prime Minister of Canada, has inherited his father's way with words.

Royal reporting is an art form all on its own. In 1983 I had the temerity, on a nature reserve in the Cayman Islands, to ask the Duke of Edinburgh why he was in favour of preserving wildlife abroad while shooting it at home. His look said it all. If he had been a Plantagenet, I would have been consigned immediately to the Tower of London.

Prince Charles and Princess Diana, on their 'honeymoon tour' of Canada, did not leave a visitor's book unsigned or a commemorative tree unplanted. It was so repetitive that by the time they reached Prince Edward Island I sent my final report in iambic pentameters and rhyming couplets – *and no one even noticed*.

At a time of BBC cut-backs one of our senior executives resigned his position because he could no longer smoke in his office and he could not stand seeing grown men cry in front of him.

After the meltdown in the Three Mile Island nuclear power station in March 1979, the people of Harrisburg, Pennsylvania fled for their safety. Having chartered a light aircraft and flown into the unknown, I quoted the Chairman of the Nuclear Regulatory Commission describing himself and the Governor Richard Thornburgh as being 'like a couple of blind men staggering about and making decisions'.

In 1978 Independence Day in St Lucia did not go according to plan. A petrol strike crippled the transport system. The visiting Royal Navy frigate rammed the pier head. The airport was closed by an accident. The prisoners rioted and burned down the jail. The opposition leader George Odlum, who boycotted the ceremonies, was unimpressed by the street decorations that had formerly hung in Regent Street. He said that they made the capital, Castries, 'look like the whore of Babylon'. When I took note of these things a Labour peer, Lord Segal, objected in the House of Lords to what he called 'a half-baked and slanted report'; and on the island itself a calypso group, the True Tones, accused me of taking bribes to blacken the good name of the island: 'The BBC should be ashamed,' they sang, 'to associate itself with Martin Bell's name'. The calypso, which proved very popular, was called 'Foreign Journalists'.

Prime Minister Margaret Thatcher visited Ronald Reagan's White House at least once a year for the eight years of his presidency. It was said of their talks in the Oval Office that first she told him what she thought and then what he thought. Now *there* was a special relationship. He said later that they got on so well because he was more frightened of her than she was of him. She held the Foreign Office in low esteem. 'I know nothing about diplomacy,' she said, 'and so far I've managed to do very well without it.'

For Mrs Thatcher's TV interviews when she travelled overseas there were two conditions to be met. She needed a bowl of flowers and a make-up artist. At a summit meeting in Cancun, Mexico one was easier to find than the other. Bonnie Anderson, ace war reporter of NBC News (and later portrayed in the movie *Salvador*), did me a favour by pretending to be the make-up lady.

History might have taken a different course if the SAS had gone ahead with its plan to infiltrate Iraq and kill Saddam Hussein after his forces had invaded Kuwait. The military believed that it was doable. Margaret Thatcher vetoed it on the grounds that the United Kingdom did not do targeted assassinations.

It is impossible to report from the United States, as I did for eleven years, without being tempted from time to time by the craziness of the place and the category of news that we call *Americana*. In Beaver, Oklahoma I witnessed a cow chip throwing contest. A cow chip is American for a cow pat. As it hardens under the Oklahoma sun it takes on the aerodynamic quality of a frisbee. On the day of the contest there was a big crowd and a sudden gust of wind. The chip hit the fan.

Next – a chicken flying contest in Rio Grande, Ohio. 'It is no trivial matter, this contest. It is run by the International Chicken

Flying Association. It has a weigh in, and classification by weight, and the strictest rules and procedures. It's distance from take-off to touchdown that counts. In chicken flying, as in other sports, there are competitors lacking the big match temperament, and embittered coaches complaining of fowl play.'

In 1981 I reported a baseball strike – and, in the minor leagues, a game between the Rochester Red Wings and Pawtucket Red Sox that was the longest in baseball history. It never ended, but was adjourned after forty-eight hours. *And they thought that cricket was boring.* Compared to this, I noted, a wet weekend at Old Trafford was a frenzy of wild excitement. CBS liked the story and ran it.

In 1975 I attended the fiftieth birthday party of Anastasio Somoza, the dictator of Nicaragua. *'Feliz Navidad'*, sang his friends and supporters. Outside the Presidential Palace his National Guard were cutting the long grass down to the roots, so the Sandinista rebels could not sneak up on them unseen. Four years later he fled to Paraguay, where the Sandinistas assassinated him.

In thirty-five years I had one expenses claim queried by my masters. It was for a taxi in New Delhi driven by an Indian who, being illiterate, was unable to give me a receipt. The Accounts Department sent a stern memo to the foreign editor: 'Tell MB there may be no unreceipted expenses.'

Our first armoured Land Rover, Miss Piggy, was notoriously hard to drive on the icy roads of a Bosnian winter. To one of my most eminent colleagues, whom I shall not be so ungallant as to identify, there befell three road accidents in the space of just one morning. At that point the interpreter threatened to resign and the cameraman confiscated the ignition keys.

The phone rang in the BBC office in Sarajevo, the one with sandbags over the windows. It was the foreign duty editor. 'Martin, what's your report about today?' he asked. I answered: 'About a minute and forty-two seconds.'

Before the outbreak of the war in Bosnia, the Vice President of the Bosnian Serb mini-state, Nikola Koljevic, had been a Shakespearean scholar in the University of Sarajevo. I asked him which of Shakespeare's plays the war in Bosnia most reminded him of. He said *Timon of Athens*, because of the extent of the bloodshed.

It is one of the constants of warfare that the approach of a ceasefire causes a fierce upsurge in the fighting. This happened from Vietnam in 1972 to Bosnia in 1995. History does not repeat itself but it rhymes.

In a refugee camp in Yemen I met a nine-year-old girl who had been bombed out of her home by a Saudi Arabian warplane. She was so shell-shocked that she did not know who she was or where she was. The difference between PTSD in a child and PTSD in an adult is that with the child it lasts longer.

Towards the end of the first year of the Bosnian War, in March 1993, I was invited to address the Army Staff College at Camberley. While the Cheshire Regiment was engulfed in the new world disorder in Bosnia, the home-based officers were still playing old war games on a sand table, the Red side against the Blue, as if the Soviet Union was still in business. Soldiers hold on to their traditions. They tend to fight the next war like the last. The end of the Cold War was a bonfire of the certainties.

Belgrade in November 1993 was a city of destitute million-aires. They were fed at soup kitchens paid for by the philanthropist George Soros. Inflation was running at one per cent per hour. I kept and framed a 500 billion dinar note. It was enough to pay for lunch.

In May 1999, before he became a politician, Boris Johnson interviewed the Serbian warlord Arkan (Zeljko Raznatovic) for the *Daily Telegraph* in the tea room of the Grand Hyatt Hotel in Belgrade. Arkan was wearing a white suit. He told Boris: 'I would like to be like Martin Bell. I consider him a friend of mine.' But he had enemies too. He was assassinated eight months later.

Shipwrecks can be useful. When nuclear scientists need pure steel, uncontaminated by the minute amounts of radiation in the atmosphere, they can find it in the German warships scuttled in Scapa Flow in 1919.

There is a pecking order among TV journalists. It goes from reporter to correspondent to special correspondent to editor. A correspondent is a reporter who has lunch. A foreign correspondent can work his or her patch for years awaiting the big news story – and then, when it happens, have it hijacked by one of the network's mega-stars. This process is known as 'big footing'. It is of no discernible benefit except to the self-esteem of the 'big foot'. The mega-stars seldom speak well of each other – and if they do, they usually don't mean it.

When I joined the BBC in London they presented me with a wristwatch that was also a stopwatch, previously the property of a political correspondent who became the Conservative Party's Director of Communications. The watch was necessary because we were forever timing scripts against footage: 100 feet of 16mm news film lasted for two minutes and forty seconds. When I left to go into politics I gave them back my credit cards, my mobile phone, my flak jacket – and the stopwatch. The BBC is the only organisation in which, when you retire, they don't give you a timepiece, but take one away.

They then forget you as though you had never been. When I was an MP a former POW of the Japanese sent me a letter that reached me at the second attempt. He sent it first to BBC News, who returned it with the words 'Not known at this address'.

In January 2001 Peter Mandelson resigned from the government, for a second time. The Strangers' Bar ran out of champagne. It was all drunk by Labour MPs. 'Just drowning our sorrows,' said one of them.

Halfway through my time in Parliament, the *Guardian* ran a feature about who might be the next MP for Tatton. George Osborne, then twenty-seven, had just been chosen as the Conservative candidate. A lady in Knutsford remarked: 'I don't think, quite honestly, that this area will ever vote Labour. It's a fairly law-abiding town.' The local weekly, the *Knutsford Guardian*, had news values of its own. One day it ran a story about a motorist who drove into a swarm of bees. The headline was 'Driver Nearly Crashes'.

In 2004 I stood as an Independent for election to the European Parliament in the Eastern Region. A would-be constituent wrote to me later and said she had not realised that I was a candidate until she saw my name on the ballot paper. And then, assuming I was an impostor, she voted for someone else.

When I testified in The Hague against Radovan Karadzic, former President of the Bosnian Serbs, the session ended with an unexpected question. One of the four judges, who was British, asked: 'Is that the tie of the Royal Suffolk Regiment?' 'Yes,' I said, 'but we were never royal.' The Norfolks were, but we were not. The court then adjourned.

It is a general rule of TV news that the important people are behind the camera and the self-important people are in front of it. Beware especially those who affect a false modesty. They do it because if they don't put themselves down there are plenty of others who will.

17. GOLDEN RULES OF TV NEWS

Question authority. Especially in politics, information received at second hand will come to you with a spin on it, imparted for the benefit of the spinner. Your job is to unspin it. As Jeremy Paxman put it, 'My interviewing technique rests on one question: why is this lying bastard lying to me?'

The best approach for a TV interviewer is to be attentive, courteous and curious. Don't sit there with a list of questions on a clipboard, or anywhere else except in your head. You are an explorer not an inquisitor. Listen to the answers and follow them up. If a question is dodged you are entitled to ask it again (twelve times in Jeremy's famous encounter with Michael Howard). Think of the analogy of a tennis match: the critical shot is the return of serve. If the interviewee is a politician, you may be sure that there will be an abundance of spin on it.

Never use fake cutaways, shots of the interviewer filmed afterwards apparently listening and nodding and asking the questions all over again, to be edited back into the interview. They are sometimes called 'noddies' or 're-asks'. The eye line is always wrong, unless there is a second camera rolling on the interview. They are a trivial fraud, but a fraud nonetheless, and already a step along the primrose path. No self-respecting network should ever use them.

Be wary also of the CSO (Colour Separation Overlay), also known as the Green Screen. This is a device that projects an image onto a screen behind you. You appear to be outside the White House. You are actually in a TV studio on the corner of 20th Street and M a mile away. It saves time, but is mildly fraudulent. On BBC One on Sunday mornings Andrew Marr appears to be overlooking London. He is actually in the depths of Broadcasting House.

Truth and trust are your only currency. If you devalue one you lose the other. Therefore report only what you know with reasonable confidence. Do not give airtime to unsourced and unverifiable video, even with health warnings. Do not speculate. Do not guess. Assume nothing. Trust no one. Check everything. It is better to be delayed and truthful than first and fastest and falsest with the news. You can take years to build up a reputation for reliability and screw it up in just a couple of minutes.

Keep your notes in case you are challenged. If you are a foreign correspondent, you are as certain to be challenged at some time, or many times, as to be arrested and deported. People will often complain about what they think you said rather than what you actually did say. The Middle East especially is teeming with potential complainants. So is Golders Green. When in doubt, *check legal*. News executives have a reasonable aversion to lawsuits and scandals. Your notebook can protect you. A Croatian general, Slobodan Praljak, wanted me as a defence witness at his trial in The Hague because he claimed he had been meeting me in Prozor (central Bosnia) on the day when, according to the charge sheet, the famous bridge in Mostar had been blown up:

the alibi might have worked for him, except that my notebook told me the timing was one day out.

Master your communications or you will fail. The technologies change. Baron Paul Julius von Reuter, founder of the news agency that bears his name, was obsessed by pigeons. In due course pigeons were superseded by the wireless telegraph. There was never a *Daily Pigeon*, but there still is a *Daily Telegraph*. The admired war correspondent William Howard Russell was scooped in the Franco-Prussian War because he did not understand the new technology and his leisurely style of writing was not suited to it. His manager urged him to use the telegraph and added: 'The *Daily News* has beaten us hollow and continues to do so.' However eminent you are, if you don't get the story you will get the call-back.

As late as the 1960s the old Africa hands were still filing their reports in telegraphese. Since the cable companies charged by the word, the art was to compress many words into a few – the original joined-up thinking. The *Daily Mail* man in Nairobi, John Bierman, wished to tell his news editor that a rival's report had been denied at the highest level of government. He did it in just three words: EXPRESSTORY PISTON EXGREATHEIGHT.

Study – and even take with you – Evelyn Waugh's *Scoop*, written about the war in Abyssinia and published in 1938; it is the most timeless and truthful account of journalism ever written. It includes the essential ingredients of skulduggery and romance, the cut-throat rivalries, the ignorant proprietor, the frantic messages of reproach and 'herograms' of congratulation, the inevitable up-country expedition and moving pictures – not television yet but a cinema newsreel. It even has a Max Hastings figure, Sir Jocelyn Hitchcock, the original war-zone grandee.

Keep an eye on your competitors and treat them with caution.

In their desire to shaft you they may be completely unscrupulous. Shared aircraft charters and satellite feeds can easily end in tears. And remember that the fiercest rivalries are not between networks but within them. (The same applies to politicians and political parties.)

Stay humble. However familiar your face you are not a celebrity. You will be remembered tomorrow and forgotten the day after. Avoid appearances on *Strictly Come Dancing* and *I'm a Celebrity Get Me Out of Here*. Keep out of network politics. Never envy anyone or intrigue against a rival. Just get on with whatever the assignment may be, however unrewarding. You have to believe in the scoop-of-a-lifetime that surely awaits you tomorrow.

Beware the insidious prize system of BAFTAs and Royal Television Society awards. The only prize worth having is a reputation for accuracy and the good opinion of those who work with you, and even more of those who work against you. If you don't have that, then, instead of journalism, you should have done something useful, like growing apples or keeping bees.

If you went into journalism to make your fortune, you took a wrong turning.

Avoid unnecessary arguments with head office. You may indeed possess an outstanding talent, but you will never be forgiven for throwing a tantrum. Your assignments will deservedly dry up.

Treat your camera crews with respect. I knew a TV reporter who was somewhat cross-eyed and made the mistake of falling out with his cameraman. The cameraman retaliated by filming him in close-up.

Find yourself a role model. Mine was Charles Wheeler, the greatest of BBC correspondents, who deserves to be remembered for much more than being Boris Johnson's father-in-law. He did not just narrate, he also explained – as he did, memorably, with the riots in Los Angeles in 1965. He was constantly asking, 'How do I know this?' Then as time goes by you can develop a style that suits you and is unique without being flashy. One of the BBC's younger generation of reporters, James Reynolds, has done this to great effect.

'Going live' is different *in kind* to being recorded. Don't get into a sentence without having some idea of how to get out of it. If you are in some remote location and being interviewed by the all-knowing presenter in London, prepare yourself by thinking of two things to say. Then, if you forget one, you can always fall back on the other. You cannot afford to 'corpse'. Sadly, you will be remembered more for your disasters than your triumphs. Learn from your mistakes: as Senator Ernest Hollings of South Carolina once said, 'There is no education in the second kick of a mule.'

In a two-way interview, avoid using the phrase 'I have to say . . .' Unless someone is holding a gun to your head, you say what you choose to say not what you have to say.

You do not have to be a journalist to be able to read convincingly from an autocue. But you do have to be a journalist to find out something worth putting on the autocue in the first place. It is possible to be a gifted journalist but a useless broadcaster. And vice versa: such people are called presenters.

If on assignment to the 'sharp end', travel light, with half the clothes and twice the money that you think you are going to need. The cash should be in euros or dollars, and kept in a money belt that does not look like one. Pack whisky and cigarettes for trading at roadblocks and negotiating with warlords. Slivovitz must be downed in a single gulp. Take a Maglite torch with extra batteries. The torch unscrews to become an electric candle for whenever the power supply fails, which it certainly will. So will the water supply, so the first thing to do when arriving in your hotel room is to fill the bath. Keep everything within easy reach, for you may have to exfiltrate in a hurry. And remember the old army maxim that a fool and his equipment are easily separated.

If you find yourself in a dangerous place, don't be afraid of being afraid. Fear helps to keep you alert and alive. Panic can be what kills you. And cultivate the quality of *bouncebackability*. I knew an extremely gifted reporter who was badly beaten on a war story and whose confidence never recovered; and another, much less talented, who had an uncanny ability to be in the right place at the right time. He was often out-performed and out-written, but never scooped.

Be especially careful with casualty figures. When they are not yet known but can only be estimated, there is a natural tendency to go for the high end estimate, which makes a 'better story'. For years we put the death toll of the Bosnian War at two hundred thousand. The true figure, established by the International Commission on Missing Persons, was about ninety-eight thousand. Conversely, I first estimated the numbers killed in the Srebrenica massacre as fifteen hundred. The true figure was more than eight thousand. Calculation is one thing: guesswork is another.

In reporting disasters – whether natural or man-made, a tsunami or a bomb blast – the tone of voice is important. It should be low key, measured and respectful to the victims. Economise with the words and leave the pictures to tell the story. Write even more silence than usual. And never ask the question 'How do you feel?'

Beware the health and safety wallahs, for they can actually endanger your health and safety. If they require you to wear one of the cumbersome old-style flak jackets weighing 50 pounds, do so only occasionally and on camera, to appease them. For the rest of the time take it off and set it aside, for what you lose in protection is more than made up by what you gain in speed. Never wear it either among civilians who may be themselves in the line of fire. It is discourteous to them to advertise that you are safer than they are. This is not only my opinion: it is shared by Christiane Amanpour, the warrior queen of TV news, whom I seldom saw in a flak jacket.

Never go trouble-shooting at night. Your first mistake can also be your last. The camera's red light can make it a target for an enterprising sniper. You can assess the risks much better in the daylight. And if land mines are suspected, walk only on a metalled surface or in someone else's footsteps. There are at least a dozen countries in the world where the most important subject to study is land mine recognition.

If you don't speak the language, choose your interpreter with the greatest care. I know of a reporter who, stopped by a militia-man at a roadblock, delivered a great speech on the freedom of the press and the importance of his network and demanded to be let through immediately, upon pain of unspecified consequences. The interpreter translated this as a tribute to the historic friend-ship between the British and Serbian peoples. The roadblock was lifted. 'There,' the reporter said, 'just as I told you, it is the only language they understand!'

Take some official-looking paperwork with you to establish your credentials. It needs to be of substantial size, stamped and laminated, and with an impressive signature on it. Wherever we went, at home or abroad, we carried our Scotland Yard press pass, signed by the Commissioner of the Metropolitan Police. It was seldom of much use in London, but brilliant at getting us through war-zone checkpoints or into the Presidential Palace in Tegucigalpa.

Never carry a weapon, however dangerous the war zone. I have known journalists who did in Vietnam, in Rhodesia/ Zimbabwe and in Iraq. It is against the Geneva Conventions and identifies you as a combatant. I broke the rule once, on the insistence of an Israeli escort officer, while reporting on the reopening of the railway line between Gaza City and the Suez Canal in June 1967. I was properly chastised by the BBC and never did it again.

Avoid press buses. They are usually organised by the Ministry of Information. They are closely escorted, time-limited and full of unhappy and quarrelsome journalists. No good ever comes of them. Also avoid Ministries of Information.

Beware governments offering hospitality: they can entertain you lavishly one day and expel you cheerfully the next. In Angola we fell for a bus ride to an exotic game reserve, just to get us out of the way while a high level delegation from East Germany was visiting the capital. The East Germans were the Soviet Bloc's specialists on internal security (i.e. repression).

Be meticulous with your expenses. The days of freeloading, also known as 'recip' (reciprocal hospitality), are long gone. The BBC had a correspondent based in a foreign capital who was well regarded and thought to be destined for great things, until he put in a claim for the purchase of a lawnmower. The problem was that he lived in a block of high rise flats. He was immediately let go *pour encourager les autres*.

Unless you are a woman (in which case the choice is yours), avoid make-up. Real TV reporters don't wear lip gloss or face powder. A certain ruggedness is very much in order. Avoid clothes that are inappropriate or distracting. An American network reporter who was a total anglophile reported from Israel in the Six-Day War dressed like an English country gentleman. A smart tweed suit and tie seemed somehow out of place on the Golan Heights. I was equally at fault in East Germany after the fall of the Berlin Wall. I protected myself with a black leather overcoat against the icy winds blowing in from the Caucasus. This drew an instant telex from Chris Cramer, the Head of Newsgathering: he said that he did not wish his correspondents to look like U-boat captains, not then and not ever. The overcoat was given to a refugee.

Good looks are optional. Sandy Gall of ITN and I were once described by a TV critic as having faces like the relief maps of the countries we were covering – in his case Afghanistan and in my case Bosnia, neither of which is blessed with regular features.

Never talk about yourself. You are the messenger not the message. The viewers will not be interested in how many times you have been to Ruritania or how difficult was your journey. They just might be interested in what you found when you got there.

Words matter – and the fewer the better. Use them sparingly and sometimes not at all. Prefer short words to long ones and the active to the passive. Let your script unfold in simple declarative sentences. Avoid acronyms (except only the UN and NATO) and jargon. Never write wall-to-wall – which is to say, start talking at the beginning of a piece and never stop till the end, hardly pausing to draw breath. Journalists who have moved successfully from print to broadcasting, like the BBC's Andrew Marr, have had to reinvent their style of writing. (Andrew was given three months in which to do so.) First you drop the adjectives and adverbs. Sometimes you may find that the verbs are redundant too. The images will do all the describing for you. And you never repeat the obvious, the visual information that the viewers have on the screens in front of them. You caress the images with words that complement them. You never pause for breath when you run out of it but at a natural point in the narrative. You pay attention to the rhythms and cadences of the English language. Don't feel obliged to be seen on camera, just because your network has paid for your air fare. And never, ever, read a script off a computer screen. The emphasis will be on all the wrong words. Better to work it out in your head and then just *speak* it. The human voice is not a machine but an instrument; and the written word is not a help but a hindrance to good broadcasting.

Remember that the English language is a unique and magical resource. A colleague from German television, matching one of my scripts against his, remarked that to have said the same in German would have taken half as many words again. Always minimise. Never elaborate. Write in the silences. Someone who practised this to perfection was the BBC's Allan Little.

A short report, like a short speech, requires more time to write than a long one.

Pay attention to *The Television News Handbook: An Insider's Guide to Being a Great Broadcast Journalist* by Vin Ray, my former field producer and a consummate TV newsman. It is full of sound advice. One of his chapter headings is about avoiding hackneyed phrases: 'Dawn revealed the full extent of the cliché'.

If you are working with or alongside the British Army, remember that it is run principally not by its officers but by its senior NCOs. Because they have not had media training (also known as 'sound-bite school') they will make better interviewees. They will also probably be better informed. The backbone of the Army, said Rudyard Kipling, is the non-commissioned man.

18. THE DEATH OF NEWS

The technology advances, but the journalism retreats.
It has been a long and gradual drawing down of blinds.
As far back as 1983, after the great leap forward from film to
videotape, I was complaining in one of my pocket-sized *vade
mecum* notebooks about the business I was in, that it was technically liberated but editorially crippled. BBC News was in one of
its phases of obsession with the Royal Family. A story about them
had appeared on the front page of the *Daily Mirror*. I was
instructed to charter a jet from Washington DC and fly to the
small town of Industry, Illinois. Once there, I tracked down an
obscure and very minor royal whose father was alleged to have
fought for the Nazis in the Second World War. (Since he was
Austrian it would have been surprising if he had not.) She was
protected from my questions on her doorstep by her elderly
husband who was dying of cancer. The 'story', such as it was, was
fed from the NBC bureau in Chicago. It was the only time I had
ever hoped for a satellite feed to fail. Sadly, it did not. The news
agenda ebbs and flows, and this was its low tide.

It is in the nature of journalism that our commanding officers, the editors of TV news, from time to time and usually on taking office, will produce cheerleading messages to the troops, urging them on to further triumphs and magnifying the opportunities and minimising the challenges that they face. It is like a president's inaugural address. Such a document was produced by Alan Protheroe, the incoming head of BBC TV News, in December 1977 and classified 'confidential'. (Protheroe was also a colonel in the Territorial Army.) The *Nine O'Clock News* on BBC One was his flagship offering, and he proposed to shake it up. 'The Bulletin is dead,' he announced, 'the *Nine O'Clock News* is a *programme*.' He called for a quantum leap forward in our operations and for changes of pace and better storytelling. 'Let's finally abandon – as a deliberate act – the idea that we have to mention everything, even the unimportant... let's stop approaching the *Nine* like a man with fifteen six-inch nails and a sledgehammer and slam fifteen stories into the forehead of the viewer... Let us recover our sense of wonder. Let us stop being so bleak.' He set us a target of ten million viewers a night for his revamped news.

Occasionally we achieved it and usually we did not. But the audiences were larger anyway, more than three times what they are today. We were operating in a stable media environment in which news was what we said it was, we faced no competition except from the formidable ITN (then in its well-funded heyday), there was still no internet or Facebook or Twitter to distract us, and the switch from film to videotape, long overdue, was the only foreseeable change on the horizon.

Nearly forty years on all the old certainties have gone. The media landscape is aquiver with new technologies. The question

'What is news?' is harder to answer. BBC News is having to cope with deep cost-cutting, splintering audiences and a crowd of noisy new rivals, some with national and political agendas, a Tower of Babel with a multitude of transmitters. Clouds of unknowing are gathering above us.

It was against this background of ever-accelerating change that, in January 2016, the BBC's Director of News and Current Affairs James Harding produced his own manifesto, *Future of News*. In it he argued blithely that news in the age of the internet has changed infinitely for the better, that we are living in the most exciting time for journalism since the advent of television, and that in the hustle and bustle of web-driven journalism the need for news – accurate and fair, insightful and independent – is greater than ever.

He also addressed the downside, which he called 'the disruption'. He distinguished between *news* and *noise*. In a world where millions of citizen journalists and bloggers see themselves as purveyors of unique truths, the noise is increasingly drowning out the news. Harding wrote: 'The internet has ripped a hole in the business model of many great news organisations. And, as a result, vast swathes of modern life are increasingly unreported or under-reported.' How the news could have improved infinitely while neglecting so much of the real world was left unexplained. Nor did his analysis take account of the *celebrification* of the news agenda. Even the staid old *Telegraph* has a celebrity section online. The *Mail* has little else. If *Strictly* and *Big Brother* are essential to the news, and the overhyped comings and goings of the Kardashian family, then what is optional – the war in Yemen or the attempted coup in Burundi? Probably both. We will know nothing of them. They cannot compete with Kim Kardashian being robbed at gunpoint in Paris.

There are actually websites with the appearance of being regular news providers but which exist to make mischief (and money) by propagating falsehoods and fabrications. Their lies are no longer lies but 'alternative truths'.

It is a strange time indeed for journalism to turn its back on swathes of modern life. We stand precariously at the most dangerous juncture in world affairs since the Cuban missile crisis of 1962. Some of the dangers are old and others new: nuclear proliferation, rogue states, border disputes, catastrophic climate change, wars for oil and wars for water, the plague of jihadism, the great tides of refugees flooding out of the Middle East and Africa into Europe, the wild-card presidency of Donald Trump and 'black swan' events of one sort or another.

It is surely no time for soft news, the fluff and froth of a journalism crafted to entertain rather than to inform. Yet that is the trend. It started at home, with the evisceration of the local weekly newspapers. And the internet, the engine of the new journalism, was at least partly responsible for it. When I was an MP my constituency was well served by two newspapers, the *Knutsford Guardian* and the *Wilmslow Express Advertiser*, each with a visible presence in the community. If you had a story to tell or a case to make to the editor, you could knock on her door. No matter that one of the papers, though not the other, was in my view intimidated by then MP Neil Hamilton, and printed a great tract on his behalf. They were real newspapers. They employed reporters who actually found things out and printed them. They ran editorials (even criticising his successor, which was their right). But even then they were haemorrhaging advertising to the free sheets of the hand-out press and the new phenomenon of the web. By the time I left, the *Knutsford Guardian* was charging 35p for thirty-two pages – 'more than a penny a page', said its editor mournfully. Both of their offices are now closed, and their titles are edited – or assembled from press releases – from media hubs elsewhere. Advertisements for houses and cars in Cheshire are compiled in distant Mumbai. Readers with a news story to tell are invited to leave a note in a drop box at the local supermarket. And that was just the start of a long decline. Some titles closed completely. Others are shadows of what they used to be.

More ominous still has been the retreat of the media from news of countries whose instability threatens our daily lives. Here again the internet is partly to blame. News executives cannot see from their newspapers which pages are turned and which are left unread; but they can see from their online editions which stories attract more 'hits' than others. Foreign news is not usually a ratings winner. It is both more expensive to gather and less popular with the readership than home news, especially the 'soft' and lifestyle features that are an expanding part of the package. The same applies on both sides of the Atlantic. Between 2003 and 2010 the number of international reporters working for US newspapers fell by nearly a quarter. The amount of airtime that the original 'big three' of American networks – CBS, NBC and ABC – devoted to foreign news is less than half what it was in the 1980s. As far as the viewers were concerned whole regions disappeared from the map and ceased to exist – unless they received the benediction of a presidential visit. Switch on one of the once respected news programmes and you may find a celebrity profile or a five-part medical series (the audience is predominantly elderly): there will be nothing from Africa and little from Europe.

The myopia would be dangerous at any time. It is especially so in a world as turbulent and interdependent as ours is. One of the lessons of history, it seems, is that we don't learn the lessons of history. We may not be interested in war, said Trotsky, but war can be interested in us.

The swathes of modern life that are left unreported include the humanitarian emergencies in the failed and failing states of Africa. My first foreign assignment, in 1966, was the overthrow in a military coup of President Kwame Nkrumah of Ghana, the founding father of African nationalism. It was more violent than we knew at the time. Ghana's new rulers accused him of trying to subvert the governments of friendly states like Tanzania: they found a Chinese training manual showing how to hide a hand grenade in a coconut. When the soldiers held their victory parade through the streets of Accra, chanting slogans against their former Commander-in-Chief, it seemed that all of Fleet Street was there. It was recognisably still the world of Evelyn Waugh's *Scoop*. Even the tabloids and mid-market papers took Africa seriously, but with imaginative reporting. The news was never knowingly understated. John Monks of the *Express* and Peter Younghusband of the *Mail*, friends as well as rivals, competed with each other in dodging bullets and crossing crocodile-infested rivers in pursuit of improbable stories. Donald Wise, the David Niven look-alike who was the *Mirror*'s 'man-on-the-spot', began a despatch from Luanda with a line about how a dead Angolan fell into his beer. One of the old Africa hands even travelled to an obscure town in Zaire (now the Democratic Republic of Congo) so that he could file a story with the dateline 'Banana, Sunday'. Another *Mirror* man seldom left the bar of the Federal Palace Hotel in Lagos, where he plied his thirsty competitors with drinks in exchange for information and regularly filed their stories before they did. One of his rivals wrote for a Scottish newspaper: 'I have just seen the faces of the stick-thin children of Biafra. I have seen the horror of starvation and homelessness with my own eyes.' Like the man from the *Mirror* he had never left the hotel. 'I'm in Nigeria,' he said, 'it's all the same place, innit?'[1]

Mostly we left francophone Africa to the French. They had their Emperor Bokassa of the Central African Republic to report on. We had our Field Marshal Idi Amin Dada of Uganda VC DSO MC CBE and President for Life (all his medals were self-awarded and the CBE was 'Conqueror of the British Empire'). He was a former sergeant in the King's African Rifles, a buffoon and a killer and one of the most dangerous men on the continent. I waited a week for the interview. The phone rang and I was rewarded. He sat in his bunker on a throne so ornate and enormous that I found it impossible to interview him except on my knees, which pleased him. The room then filled up with visitors including Yasser Arafat, and more than twenty children by earlier marriages, for his wedding to Lady Sarah of the Mechanised Suicide Squad of the Ugandan Army. It was not to the credit of the Organisation of African Unity that he was actually its chairman for more than a year. The finale of the OAU's Kampala Summit in 1975 was a staged attack by the Ugandan armed forces on a simulated 'Cape Town', actually an island in Lake Victoria. The bombs all missed and fell into the lake.

The 'Field Marshal' in his prime was so powerful and such good copy that I regret that we courted him so much, as he did us. I wrote: 'Good relations with Britain mean more to Uganda, and Idi Amin in particular, than those with any other country.' The fever abated when he had the foreign press, including Sandy Gall and Donald Wise, imprisoned and then deported.

Idi Amin was overthrown in 1979 and disappeared into exile in Saudi Arabia. Lady Sarah was next heard of in West Ham. The journalists moved on and out, except for a few resident correspondents in Kenya and South Africa. One of these was the BBC's Michael Buerk in Johannesburg. In 1984, with the help of the incomparable Mohammed Amin of Visnews (now Reuters Television), he produced a report on the famine in Ethiopia that was one of the most memorable ever broadcast and had a world-wide impact. Michael noted the irony of being wined and dined at various media awards ceremonies for a report about a *famine*. Astonishingly, it was only the third item that night on the BBC's *Nine O'Clock News*, which led to a bitter and long-running dispute inside the newsroom. Interest in Africa revived for a while, then declined and finally vanished almost to the point of invisibility.

My later assignments in Africa were not for the BBC but for UNICEF. Since the time of Danny Kaye and Audrey Hepburn they have recruited 'celebrities' (I use the term loosely) to draw attention to their work and help to raise funds for it. Time and tastes change. Now they have David Beckham, Robbie Williams and a number of others, including me since 2001. The idea is to travel where the journalists don't and file what appear to be news reports but in fact are promotions for the work of UNICEF. Mine would appear on the BBC's *Newsnight* or on Channel 5 News, and even on what used to be ITN. I would also file a two thousand word newspaper report, usually for the *Mail on Sunday*.

In this role, part journalist and part advocate, I visited Malawi, Darfur, South Sudan, the Democratic Republic of Congo and Somalia. (Also Iraq, Afghanistan and Yemen.) On the way into

Somalia, at Nairobi Airport, I met the Mayor of Mogadishu who invited me to visit his city. It was perfectly safe, he assured me. Later that week it was attacked by a force of three thousand Al-Shabaab fighters who seized a third of it and set about training young Somalis in the techniques of 'holy war'. If the Taliban in Afghanistan were seen as a threat to our security, then so were Al-Shabaab in Somalia. Yet we covered Afghanistan extensively and Somalia hardly at all.

I had been out of Africa for thirty years. That was the first thing that struck me on my return: it was even more violent, anarchic and turbulent than in the immediate post-colonial years. The eastern Congo was ungoverned and perhaps ungovernable. A United Nations force of seventeen thousand men was waging the UN's first war since Korea in the 1950s. The enemy was a rebel force based partly in a national park. Tens of thousands of refugees from the fighting settled in Goma under the shadow of Mount Nyiragongo, the most active volcano in Africa. Every country had its own special mix of natural and man-made disasters. Three million people had been killed in Africa's Great War in the Democratic Republic of Congo (formerly Zaire). As I flew over it in 2005 I reflected that it was the only war zone I had ever known where the worse things got the more they were ignored.

And this was the second thing I noticed. With the exception of Peter Greste of the BBC (and later Al Jazeera) whom I met in Somalia, the journalists appeared to have fled. I had noted the same phenomenon in Central America in 1980: 'The war in El Salvador is not much heard of now, not because the guerrillas have gone away, but because the journalists have.' There are fashions in war reporting; and foreign correspondents tend to perch like starlings on a wire: either everyone is there, or no one is.

Everything changed after 9/11. This was when free-ranging and independent journalism lost its foothold. Up till that time, the chief danger that we faced in a war zone was to be caught in the cross-fire. After that time, we were at risk of being targeted, kidnapped, ransomed and executed. And the forces threatening us were not only Islamic fighters.

Terry Lloyd, an experienced war reporter unwisely assigned by ITN in March 2003 to report the Iraq War unilaterally (unembedded), was blown away by US Marines on the road to Basra. Two of his team, one of them a close friend, were also killed. The Marines were applying their doctrine of force protection. Either you were for them or against them. It admitted no neutrals. Only the Belgian cameraman survived, by sheltering behind the engine block of the car. I worked with him later in Yemen. He still believed that risking his life unilaterally was the right thing to have done.

Another casualty of the new world disorder was the veteran war reporter Marie Colvin of the *Sunday Times*. She was killed by the Syrians in 2012 in the rebel-held city of Homs. She was not caught in the cross-fire but targeted. The Syrians knew she was there, since she had appeared on CNN the day before in a report in which she pleaded for outside intervention to help the wounded children. She was inside the rebels' press centre. The Syrians knew where it was, and where she was, and they bombed it.

Western journalists were not the only targets. The Arab satellite channel Al Arabiya lost eleven of its staff, killed by both sides, before it was closed down by the Baghdad authorities in the fourth year of the war in Iraq. The casualties included a woman, its chief correspondent, Atwar Bahjat, assassinated near Kirkuk in February 2006. The Saudi-owned channel had been set up supposedly 'to cure Arab television of its penchant for radical politics and violence'. That was a dig at Al Jazeera, whose offices were bombed by the Americans in both the wars in Iraq and Afghanistan. The use of a satellite uplink was seen by the Pentagon as evidence of 'hostile activity'. The wars of the twenty-first century offer no immunity to anyone not carrying a gun. Anthony Loyd of *The Times* was lucky to survive after being shot in the ankle by his minder-turned-kidnapper in Syria.

Over a period of a century and a half, war reporting as a more-or-less honourable profession has come and gone and been book-ended by reporters for *The Times*: William Howard Russell at the beginning and Anthony Loyd at the end.

Since journalists were an endangered species, they retreated to green zones and fortified compounds, venturing out occasionally and under close escort for no more than twenty minutes at a time, if at all. Or else they withdrew even further and reported from the safety of a distant hotel rooftop. This wasn't the beginning of rooftop journalism but its evolution into standard practice. It actually began, according to my notebooks, in San Salvador on 29 April 1982. Elections had been held in the middle of a civil war, in an attempt to move from military rule and establish El Salvador as a fledgling parliamentary democracy. The results were inconclusive, but the technology was available to report them live to America. The US networks therefore set up their cameras and satellite dishes on the roof of the Camino Real Hotel. The crisply dressed TV anchor people were duly installed on canvas chairs with umbrellas to protect them from such grievous hazards as the glare of the sun. I noted:

There was a strange scene this morning, on the roof of the Camino Real Hotel as the network talk shows beamed the results back home. Barely a mile away a firefight was raging on the north side of the city, but the shows went on undisturbed. Their cast of characters included all the main politicians except President Duarte . . . Major D'Aubuisson [hard-line right-wing politician] was taking a soft line with the American public. And all the time the fighting was going on.

From that point on rooftop reporting became routine. I once came upon the great Peter Arnett, formerly with the Associated Press in Saigon, and later with CNN. He was reaching into what looked like a handbag and applying his make-up on the roof of the TV station in Sarajevo, before being interviewed live from Atlanta. He wished to return to ground level and find things out for himself, as he had in Vietnam, and report them for CNN. Instead he was a prisoner of the dish. I realised at that point that TV journalism was no longer a reporting but a performing art. Its surface was attractive, its graphics were glittering, but you could wade in its depths without getting your feet wet.

And it reverted to formulaic even-handedness. The BBC in its coverage of the EU referendum campaign in 2016 returned to the old curse of on-the-one-hand-this-on-the-other-hand-that journalism. There was neither insight nor assessment, but only *balance*, timed by the stopwatch. Truth and falsehood, those who knew what they were talking about and those who did not, were given equal time. The broadcasts were therefore meaningless. The result was a feast of unreason and an outcome deeply damaging to the national interest. The pound plummeted, hate crime soared, the economy trembled, and the next thing we knew even our supplies of Marmite were under threat.

I already had a sense of foreboding in September 1992 when, after a hard stint in Bosnia, I was invited to address the RTNDA (Radio-Television News Directors Association) in New Orleans, a world away from Sarajevo. One of the sessions was entitled 'My anchor can't read, my reporter can't write'. Another was on how to 'increase resonance, polish articulation and keep your voice healthy'. One of the news directors complained: 'The cult of personality isn't delivering any more.' The news agenda was already in free fall. One of the networks was offering its O&Os (owned and operated stations) a ratings-friendly report on *keeping bats as pets*. The wars of the world, one of which was keeping me awake, did not begin to figure.

And I remembered what I was told by Ike Seamans, a veteran correspondent of NBC News, who worked alongside me from the Sinai to El Salvador and thought that I was in need of some career-enhancing advice. 'Marty,' he said, 'in TV news all you need is sincerity, and if you can fake that you've got it made!' Ike became disillusioned by the networks' hype and hysteria. 'The star system is broke,' he wrote after the Brian Williams affair, 'and it needs to be fixed.'

The age of the arm-wavers was upon us. Scripts were not just spoken but semaphored. The BBC even employed a style coach from Iowa to teach its performers how to walk and talk and wave their arms at the same time. A senior correspondent, who used to stand there in the old-fashioned way and deliver his words plainly, was told by the style coach that it was time he acquired a new set of hand signals. The emphasis was not on accuracy but style, not on reporting but storytelling.

The war photographer Robert Capa said: 'If your pictures aren't good enough, you aren't close enough.'

The new journalism (or 'churnalism' or 'newsak') lacked authenticity, the sense of being where the news was. I came upon it next in December 1995 at the gates of the airfield in Tuzla in northern Bosnia. The Dayton Agreement had been signed and we were awaiting the arrival of the American troops who were supposed to be playing a part in enforcing it. I expressed my feelings, which were not at all neutral, in a book about Bosnia published in the following year.

The networks threw money at the story of the Americans' arrival as if it were the Second Coming, the Super Bowl and the New Hampshire Primary all rolled into one. They threw money at it long before it happened. Bosnia had no other reality for them ... They built stages and platforms and commentary booths at the entrance to the air base, so that their million dollar performers could report, live and continuously, about ... Well, about the fog and the floods principally, which had delayed the troops, and the dozen who had arrived had gone into hiding. I was fascinated. Everything that I most dislike about the business I was in was camped in one shouting, seething, self-regarding compost at the entrance to the air base – the hype and hysteria, the tyranny of rolling news, the deference to a distant newsroom, the live-shot lunacy, the inane exchanges with an anchorman called Mort ... The electronic circus that came to town was reputed to have cost six million dollars. It left me wondering, what else might Tuzla – poor, sulphurous, war-battered Tuzla – have done with that six million dollars?[2]

The networks' telephones in Tuzla had a 212 (New York) area code, and at one point were receiving misdirected calls from a mental hospital in the Bronx. I wondered if anyone noticed.

Journalism subsequently retreated even further from reality, to the point where it faced an existential crisis, identified by President Obama towards the end of his presidency when he spoke of the pressure 'to fill the void and feed the beast with instant commentary and Twitter rumours, and celebrity gossip, and softer stories. And then we fail to understand our world or understand one another as well as we should.'[3] This was at a time when the frenzy of the twenty-four-hour news cycle boosted the fortunes of the ultimate celebrity candidate, Donald Trump, the property magnate and reality TV star, whom Obama had previously dismissed as a 'carnival barker'. The Trump phenomenon was train crash politics reported by train crash television. Untruths went unchallenged, a principal interviewer failed to do his homework and with the complicity of the news channels the showman hijacked priceless hours of airtime. The frenzy drove the media coverage and the media promoted the improbable Trump. The result was a mudslide, and the 'carnival barker' won his party's nomination. Even his gaffes and falsehoods, which were frequent, resulted in ever higher poll numbers. He upset the predictions to win the presidency in the most ominous election since that of Herbert Hoover in 1928. Like Hoover – and unlike Ronald Reagan – Trump was a Republican with no experience of elective office before entering the White House. Neither did he appear to have any sense of history besides that which he intended to make for himself as a Chosen One. When he looked in the mirror he thought that he saw the smartest man he knew.

It has happened on both sides of the Atlantic. A single word can speak volumes: the Oxford Dictionaries' word of the year in 2016 was *post-truth*. If lies go unchallenged, and prevail by the sheer force of repetition, then democracy withers and journalism with it.

Goebbels said: 'It is not the task of propaganda to be intelligent: its task is to lead to success.' Born before his time, he had only the press, radio and cinema to manipulate. Imagine what he might have achieved in the age of fake news, 'clickbait' and the wide open sluice gates of the internet.

News makes money. News also costs money. The relationship will always be a troubled one. If nothing in journalism matters but money – and the circulation and ratings that are its measurements in print and broadcasting – then news is only what you say it is. It is whatever sells newspapers or pulls in viewers. It gives space and airtime to endless conspiracy theories about Diana and Madeleine, and to Trumpery and red carpets and low necklines. It is the strategy you adopt to defend your prime-time slot in the schedule. If that means foreign news only on Tuesdays and Thursdays (an ITN project for a while) – or in the end no foreign news at all – then so be it. The news is dead. Long live the infotainment.

'If you are on a sinking ship,' wrote George Orwell, 'all that you think of is the sinking ship.'

The technology is extraordinary and should contribute to a better understanding of the world. But like all instruments it is morally neutral and depends for its impact on who is using it, whether it be for good or ill, for news or infotainment. Ted Koppel, the experienced and renowned anchorman of ABC News, understood this exactly. He said: 'The capacity to go live creates its own terrible dynamic. Putting someone on air while an event is unfolding is clearly a technological tour de force, but it is an impediment, not an aid, to good journalism.'

And Don Hewitt, the creator of the CBS news magazine programme *60 Minutes*, sounded the alarm as far back as October 1997: 'The floodgates were opened when the three networks [CBS, NBC and ABC], which used to have something called "standards and practices", allowed their owned-and-operated stations to dig down in the mud and come up with reality-based syndicated talk shows that are little more than cesspools over-flowing into America's living rooms.'[4] When television is bad, nothing is worse.

Those of us who hold to certain standards of steadiness and truthfulness are dismissed by the defenders of the 24/7 news frenzy as '*so* twentieth century'. But our principles are just as valid in the twenty-first.

We are ingenious people. We have the best communications in the history of the planet. We should be better informed than ever before. We *need* to be better informed than ever before. We can reach out to each other in an instant by satellite, on the internet and through social media. We can circle the world with our iClouds. We can 'friend' or 'unfriend' each other in an instant. But the technology has run ahead of us: it is not our servant but our master. The lie is halfway round the world before truth has got its boots on. More speed means less truth and more truth means less speed. We know increasingly less about more, and more about less. We are entering a new Dark Age – and doing so, like Kipling's deserters, blindfolded and alone. News as we have hitherto known it has died and been laid to rest.

ENDNOTES

2. GEUNYELI

1 Bower to Alan Lennox-Boyd, 5 August 1958, CO926/906

2 CO 926/906

3 CO 926/906

4 FCO 141/3849

5 Internal memo of the Royal Horse Guards, reporting back to Regimental HQ in Windsor (Cavalry Regiment Museum)

6 FCO 141/3849

3. UNDERTONES OF WAR

1 Edmund Blunden, *Undertones of War* (London: Penguin, 2010), p. 79

2 Blunden, p. 10

3 Blunden, p. 69

4 Blunden, p. 20

5 Letter to Edward Marsh, late December 1915

6 Tom Bower, *Broken Vows* (London: Faber & Faber, 2016), p. 62

7 Rupert Smith, *The Utility of Force: The Art of War in the Modern World* (London: Allen Lane, 2005), p. 1

8 *Iraq: the Futility of War*, Channel Four, 13 January 2006

4. LESSONS OF VIETNAM

1 Robert S. McNamara, *In Retrospect: The Tragedy and Lessons of Vietnam* (New York: Times Books, 1995), pp. 321–3

2 McNamara

3 *From Our Own Correspondent*, April 1968

4 Henry Kissinger, *White House Years* (Boston: Little, Brown), 1979

5 *From Our Own Correspondent*, November 1972

5. VICTOR'S JUSTICE

1 Niklas Frank, *In the Shadow of the Reich* (New York: Alfred A. Knopf, 1991), p. 21

2 Hansard, 3 April 2001, column 257

6. THE SOMETHING MUST BE DONE CLUB

1 *50 Years of BBC Television News* (BBC, 2004), p. 5

2 Martin Bell, *In Harm's Way* (London: Hamish Hamilton, 1995; revised edition published by Icon Books, 2012), p. 215

3 *Panorama*, BBC One, 8 February 1993

4 John Simpson, *Strange Places, Questionable People* (London: Pan, 2008; first published by Macmillan, 1998), p. 159

5 Speaking on 'Lies, Misreporting, and Catastrophe in the Middle East', at the First Congregational Church of Berkeley, 22 September 2010

6 Speech on press freedom, New York, 22 November 2016

7. THE VIOLENT SCREEN

1 *Radio Times*, 2 December 1971

2 *The Spectator*, 30 August 1969

3 *The Listener*, 5 June 1972

4 Hansard, 3 June 1974, column 888

5 Eds. Peter F. Mahoney et al., *Ballistic Trauma: A Practical Guide* (London: Springer, 2005, 2nd edition), p. vi

8. NEVER WRONG FOR LONG

1 Interview with Steven Livingston, Houston, 13 May 1996, quoted in S. Livingston, 'Clarifying the CNN Effect: An Examination of Media Effects According to Type of Military Intervention' (June 1997)

2 James A. Baker III, *The Politics of Diplomacy* (New York: G.P. Putnam's Sons, 1995)

9. THE AGE OF THE EMBED

1 John Laurence, *The Cat from Hué: A Vietnam War Story* (New York: PublicAffairs, 2002), p. 147

2 Brian Hanrahan writing in *50 Years of BBC Television News* (BBC, 2004), p. 42

3 https://www.theguardian.com/world/2003/apr/28/gender.uk. Accessed 30 November 2016

10. THE LANGUAGE OF WAR

1 Evidence to the Chilcot Inquiry, 15 January 2010

11. 'TRUST ME . . . I'M A JOURNALIST'

1 Nicholas Rankin, *Telegram from Guernica* (London: Faber & Faber, 2003), p. 132

2 *Stars and Stripes*, 4 February 2015

12. 'TOTALLY UNSUITED TO POLITICS . . .'

1 The *Guardian*, 13 November 1997

2 Hansard, 16 December 1998, column 917

3 Hansard, 17 December 1998, column 1158

4 Hansard, 3 July 2001, column 184

13. NO MAN'S LAND

1 Anthony Loyd, *My War Gone By, I Miss It So* (London: Doubleday, 1999)

2 Janine di Giovanni, *Madness Visible: A Memoir of War* (New York: Alfred A. Knopf, 2003)

3 Di Giovanni

4 David Rohde, *A Safe Area* (London: Pocket Books, 1997), p. 353

5 *Evening Standard*, 29 October 1997

6 Hansard, 19 April 1999, columns 606–7

15. IRAQ – THE RECKONING

1 Chilcot Inquiry, 14 January 2011

18. THE DEATH OF NEWS

1 Tom Mangold, *Splashed!* (London: Biteback Publishing, 2016), p. 167

2 Bell, p. 291

3 Remarks by President Obama at the 2016 Toner Prize Ceremony, Washington DC, 28 March 2016

4 Institute for Public Relations, Annual Distinguished Lecture, New York, 9 October 1997

INDEX